JOURNALISM IN THE GREY ZONE

This book is dedicated to our children:
Elma, Serin and Adam
Ella and Petter Kristian

JOURNALISM IN THE GREY ZONE

Pluralism and Media Capture in Lebanon and Tunisia

Kjetil Selvik and Jacob Høigilt

IN MEMORIAM
Kjetil Selvik 1973-2024
My friend and co-author Kjetil passed away just before the paperback edition of our book was published. His kindness and remarkable depth and breadth of knowledge will be missed by many.

With gratitude,
Jacob

EDINBURGH
University Press

Edinburgh University Press is one of the leading university presses in the UK. We publish academic books and journals in our selected subject areas across the humanities and social sciences, combining cutting-edge scholarship with high editorial and production values to produce academic works of lasting importance. For more information visit our website: edinburghuniversitypress.com

© Kjetil Selvik and Jacob Høigilt, 2023, 2024

Edinburgh University Press Ltd
13 Infirmary Street
Edinburgh EH1 1LT

First published in hardback by Edinburgh University Press 2023

Typeset in 11/15 Adobe Garamond by
IDSUK (DataConnection) Ltd

A CIP record for this book is available from the British Library

ISBN 978 1 3995 1581 8 (hardback)
ISBN 978 1 3995 1582 5 (paperback)
ISBN 978 1 3995 1583 2 (webready PDF)
ISBN 978 1 3995 1584 9 (epub)

The right of Kjetil Selvik and Jacob Høigilt to be identified as authors of this work has been asserted in accordance with the Copyright, Designs and Patents Act 1988 and the Copyright and Related Rights Regulations 2003 (SI No. 2498).

CONTENTS

Acknowledgements vii
A Note on Transliteration ix

1 Introduction 1
2 Hybrid Politics and Media Instrumentalisation 24
3 Being a Journalist in the Grey Zone 44
4 Finding a Role: Tunisian Journalism after the Revolution 67
5 Navigating a Field of Tensions: Journalism and Politics in Lebanon 91
6 National Security and Free Speech in Tunisia 112
7 Elections and Media Capture 134
8 Protests and Disruptive Journalism 155
9 Conclusion 179

Appendix 1 – Interviews: Lebanon 189
Appendix 2 – Interviews: Tunisia 191
Bibliography 193
Index 218

ACKNOWLEDGEMENTS

This book is the outcome of a four-year research project funded by the Research Council of Norway (grant number 250794). Writing it has been a very stimulating and rewarding process, not least thanks to the efforts and generosity of many good friends and colleagues who helped us bring it to fruition. We owe a special thanks to Professor Katrin Voltmer, who participated in the project from the start and contributed to the conception of the research idea. She guided our orientation to media and communication studies, which was a new terrain for us when we started. Her lucid thoughts and openhanded sharing of knowledge have been a constant source of inspiration. We are also deeply indebted to Sara Merabti Elgvin and Khaled Zaza, who assisted us with the research. Thanks to their groundwork on the Tunisian and Lebanese media scenes, the empirical tasks became much easier to handle. Sara reached out to journalists and facilitated the media content analysis, which is an important and labour-intensive ingredient in the book. Khaled provided precious fieldwork support, especially when the 2019–20 uprising in Lebanon happened. Both impressed us with their enthusiasm and competence. We thank Soumaya Hedhili for translating and transcribing the recordings of two roundtable discussions with Tunisian journalist. Cherine Randi Sellami helped us collect data for the case study on journalists' reactions to the Bardo National Museum attack in 2015. Muslema Shahal analysed media coverage of the 2015 prisoner swap between the Nusra Front and the Lebanese army. Faten Ghosn provided advice on the same topic. A big thanks goes to Robin Blanton who proofread the manuscript and sharpened many of our formulations. We are grateful to Barakat Khalil for tidying up the Arabic language references in the book. Needless to say, we are responsible for any remaining shortcomings and blemishes.

We learned a lot from the scholars and journalists who collaborated with us during conferences and meetings in the course of the research project, beginning with Fatima El Issawi, whose expertise we have been lucky to draw on. Walid al-Saqaf, Kristin Skare Orgeret and Helge Rønning were members of the project advisory board and all provided valuable inputs at various stages of the research. Hege Moe Eriksen accompanied us to Tunis to take part in roundtable discussions with journalists. Carola Richter, Claudia Mellado and Marc Owen Jones were stimulating discussion partners at conferences where we presented our project, and we thank Sadok Hammami for fruitful academic exchanges in Tunisia.

Most of all, we would like to express our heartfelt thanks to the journalists, activists and analysts who met with us in Lebanon and Tunisia and patiently answered our many questions. Without their generous welcome and sharing of experiences and perspectives there would have been no book. They took time off to meet us during very trying times for the media in both countries. Lebanese and Tunisian journalists deserve our deep respect for continuing to pursue their vocation despite all the hurdles they face.

A NOTE ON TRANSLITERATION

This is not a philological or linguistic work, so we have kept transliteration to a minimum to enhance readability, using the transliteration standard of the *International Journal of Middle East Studies*. Most Tunisian and some Lebanese journalists and newspapers habitually employ transliteration based on the French Orientalist standard when they write their names with Latin script, and this makes for some complications. Several of these creators are referred to in English and French publications, and readers may want to look them up on the web or elsewhere. Since some names and titles are well known and almost invariably transliterated the French way in English and French language media, we do not insist on the IJMES standard in those cases. Thus, when referring to the Tunisian president, we write 'Kais Saied' instead of 'Qays al-Sa'id'. However, we write 'Maya al-Qusuri' when referring to the Tunisian public figure, not 'Maya Ksouri'.

Rather than transliterating titles of books, television shows, newspapers and websites, we refer to the Arabic original title, supplying an English translation in the bibliography.

1

INTRODUCTION

In the aftermath of the Arab Spring, Tunisia and Lebanon enjoyed a position as the freest Arab countries, with a degree of media pluralism seldom witnessed in the region. Aided by a sense of freedom of speech and the possibilities of digital technologies, journalists pushed the boundaries of the media's role vis-à-vis the elites. National media stood at the centre of political dramas that culminated in nationwide protests in Lebanon in 2019 and a suspension of democracy in Tunisia in 2020.

In Lebanon, public anger against nepotistic and incompetent political elites exploded after the government tried to ameliorate an economic crisis by levying new taxes on gasoline, tobacco and WhatsApp calls. The taxes hit ordinary people hardest, leaving the super-rich kleptocracy at the top of Lebanon's political system untouched. As the demonstrations raged, a conspicuous divide appeared between Lebanon's biggest television channels. Traditionally, they had aligned with the businessmen and politicians that funded them, in competition with other elites. Now, too, many television channels loyally made their reporting and commentary conform to the positions of their respective sponsors. Three of the most important channels, however, lent support to the protest movement, roundly condemning the entire Lebanese political establishment. Dedicated journalists played important roles in the confrontation between the people and the elite.

In the same year in Tunisia, the little-known jurist Kais Saied was elected president, defeating the flamboyant businessman and media owner Nabil Karoui. Both men nurtured populist images as political outsiders, but their relations to the media were radically different. Karoui used his television channel Nisma, one of Tunisia's top three channels, to showcase his philanthropism and present his political platform. Saied, on the other hand, shunned privately owned media altogether. Two days before the election, the Tunisian public broadcaster televised a live debate between Saied and Karoui: a historic first in the Arab region. The debate was widely viewed and notable for its fair and equal treatment of the candidates. Less than a year later, Saied suspended the elected parliament and made himself the centre of political decision-making. Tunisia's unique level of press freedom plummeted. Sensing the risk that their newfound liberty would wither away, journalists fought hard to prevent a return to autocracy.

In a region marked by pervasive authoritarianism, Tunisia and Lebanon stood out in the second half of the 2010s. After overthrowing the dictator Zinedine Ben Ali in 2011, Tunisians embarked on a process towards democratisation. One of its most visible results was the introduction of freedom of speech and a pluralist media landscape. This made Tunisia something of a laboratory for experiments in politics–media relations. Lebanon, for its part, has historically been the politically freest Arab country. It has been called the 'cradle of Arab journalism' (Dajani 2019: 18), having sustained the publication of popular newspapers for more than 150 years. In both countries, the public sphere functioned as a real arena for the exchange of opinions, rather than as authoritarian window-dressing.

However, pluralism is not the same as democracy. In a trendsetting article from 2002, Thomas Carothers argues that a growing number of countries worldwide are located in a political grey zone. By this, he means that despite possessing some attributes of democracy, including liberal constitutions, regular elections, and space for opposition parties and civil society organisations, they suffer from serious democratic deficits. Among the typical signs of this grey zone are poor representation of citizens' interests, low levels of public confidence in state institutions and persistently poor institutional performance by the state (Carothers 2002: 9). Media instrumentalisation is another characteristic of the political grey zone. In Lebanon and Tunisia, political elites seeking to maintain their grip on power have found ways of mitigating the challenges to their domination in the public sphere. In Tunisia, there are often-obscure connections between media owners, businessmen and political figures, and recurring, fierce conflicts about the regulation of the media (El Issawi 2021). Political television programmes are sometimes accused of being tendentious. In Lebanon, the most important media serve as the extended arm of the strongmen and the political organisations that have been the self-styled representatives of the country's many religious communities since the end of the civil war in 1990 (El-Richani 2016). Although competition between these elite actors ensures a pluralist media sphere, it has also resulted in extensive manipulation of media and journalism.

'Trumpets' and their Discontents

The tension between free and manipulated media is felt on a daily basis by media workers. Tunisian and Lebanese journalists have an ambiguous position in society and face a peculiar mix of opportunities and constraints in their work. They are free to speak their minds but also frequently pressured or incentivised to say certain things. They must weigh any impulse to criticise the powers that be against the wishes of their employers. Some run the errands of decision-makers while others raise questions and agendas they find troublesome. Journalists are torn between professional ideals and political and economic constraints.

The problem of journalism-for-hire is explicitly acknowledged in plain language, albeit to different degrees in the two countries. It has a name in Arabic: a journalist or media person who serves as the mouthpiece for a party, interest group, politician or other strongman is pejoratively described as a 'trumpet' (*buq*). The analogy is to a medieval herald who blows a horn to announce his master's message. To be a 'trumpet' for a person or group is to be their propagandist. Pleasing journalists may thus be dismissed as 'trumpets for the politicians' (*abwaq al-siyasiyin*).

Such labelling tells us that the practice is considered a break with journalistic professional norms. The manipulation of journalism may be common, but it is not necessarily accepted. In fact, the word 'trumpet' is often used as the antonym of 'journalist' (*sahafi*). It conveys that a person lacks the transparency and integrity one expects from a 'true' journalist. Arab journalists themselves often draw attention to these tensions.

For example, the Lebanese journalist Sami Kulayb wrote a public Facebook post in 2015 entitled 'Journalists, not trumpets' in which he defended his right and responsibility as a journalist to present a balanced account of the Syrian war:

> Some blame me for criticising their party. Others want me to define my political position firmly. My followers reproach me for taking 'middle' or 'grey' positions. My trick in answering this is nothing but saying: 'I would rather be a journalist ruled by consciousness than a trumpet glorifying this and praising that.' (Kulayb 2015)

Kulayb went on to explain that a journalist should be committed to informing people rather than misleading them by serving up propaganda. His lofty defence of critical journalism was somewhat marred by the fact that he worked for a TV channel, al-Mayadin, which consistently refused to disclose who its owners were, identifying them only as anonymous Arab businessmen. The channel was strongly supportive of the Asad regime and Hizbullah. In any case, this statement and its controversial source speak volumes about the conditions of journalism in Lebanon, and Tunisian journalists would also immediately recognise the problem. Kulayb precisely describes a polarised society where journalists are expected to take sides and have become spokespersons for 'politicians, parties, groups, regimes, rulers, presidents, kings and princes'. It is equally clear that this reality clashes with the professional principles and standards journalists are supposed to live by.[1] Kulayb formulates a professional dilemma that most journalists in Tunisia and Lebanon would recognise, and one that is relevant to a growing number of countries in which media-politics connections are suspect. It is also at the heart of the question we address in this book:

Where does the mix of pluralism and manipulation leave Arab journalism as a political force?

Arab Media, Democracy and Journalism

News media have played an important role in Arab politics since the first newspapers appeared in Lebanon and Egypt at the turn of the twentieth

---

[1] As Kai Hafez documents in his comparison of journalism ethic codes from Europe and the Islamic world, there is a 'broad intercultural consensus that standards of truth and objectivity should be central values of the journalism' (Hafez 2002: 225; 2008).

century. Beyond informing readers of current affairs, they served as arenas in which to debate questions of national independence and political ideology, and they contributed to mobilising people in the struggle against colonialism. In the post-colonial system of states, newspapers, radio and later television were of immense importance, despite the absence of democracy in the Arab countries. William Rugh captured the political role played by Arab media with his typology dividing national media systems into mobilising, loyalist, 'diverse' and transitional (Rugh 2004). Following an international trend in political communication, the topic of Arab media systems has received fresh attention recently, with studies of national contexts as well as the regional picture (El-Richani 2016; Richter and Kozman 2021).

Besides Tunisia and Lebanon, Iraq and Kuwait are prominent examples of Arab states that have introduced media pluralism. This has not been accompanied by a deepening of democracy; in many ways, the opposite has occurred. Iraq experienced a sudden surge of freedom after the ousting of Saddam Hussein in 2003, leading to a plethora of new media outlets (Isakhan 2008). This newfound media freedom was, however, soon compromised by the political elites' stoking of sectarian conflict and their authoritarian politics, as well as foreign meddling in the media by Iran, Saudi Arabia and the United States. Competing religio-political organisations set a direction for and censored several media outlets, and a weak advertising market left Iraqi media at the mercy of these powerful owners (Amos 2010; Kim and Hama-Saeed 2008).

Kuwait liberalised its press and publication law in 2006, easing restrictions on the issuance of licenses for private newspapers, radio and television stations. Three years later, ten new Arabic-language newspapers had been created and the number of private television stations increased from five to eighteen (Selvik 2011b). Under the veil of this new pluralism, members of the Al Sabah ruling family and affiliated businessmen fought each other through proxies in the public sphere (Selvik 2011a). The result was a state of perpetual political crisis (Alnajjar and Selvik 2015).

The advent of satellite television and the Internet precipitated a surge of studies investigating the media as a controversial driver for change. Qatar's soft-diplomacy deployment of the thrillingly critical and pluralist al-Jazeera channel led the development towards a transnational 'new Arab public', in which voices of ordinary citizens across the Arab region mingled with those of the elites who had been accustomed to setting the parameters of public debate (Lynch 2006). The new satellite channels, several of which were controlled by private investors rather than a government, raised the question of whether the increased media complexity entailed a redistribution of power in the region (Sakr 2007: 14). However, despite the hopes of many, the new transnational Arab media did not necessarily have a democratising effect. Instead, scholars have often viewed them as tools of influence and persuasion in the hands of powerful actors, whether states, political movements such as Hizbullah, or well-connected 'media moguls' whose interests merged with those of one or more states in the region (Fandy 2007; Hroub 2012; Khalil and Kraidy 2010; Sakr et al. 2015). A telling example is al-Jazeera. Its editors and journalists revolutionised the Arab media scene by crossing all the red lines set by the autocrats in the region, reporting on diplomatic affairs, corruption and social conditions with a frankness unmatched elsewhere. However, the channel refrains from critical coverage of Qatar. Its reporting is often prone to biases that coincide with Qatari foreign policy positions, and it is considered a tool for Qatar's soft power diplomacy (El-nawawy et al. 2002; Figenschou 2013; Miles 2010; Zayani and Sahraoui 2017). Other countries have created their own satellites in this regional contest for influence: Saudi Arabia funds and steers al-Arabiya, Turkey has TRT Arabi and Iran broadcasts al-Alam and al-Kawthar in Arabic. Lynch (2006) argues that the pan-Arab media have increased the extent of identity politics and populism across the region as much as they have contributed to a more pluralist public sphere.

Technology and media structures are also at the core of the wave of studies dealing with Internet-based political communication since the Arab uprisings in 2010–11. The Internet boosted satellite television's promise of a more pluralist public sphere in the region. Digital media, such as blogs, nurtured citizen journalism in several Arab countries. An early study of the Egyptian revolution found that new types of media 'supported the capabilities of democratic activists by allowing forums for free speech and political networking opportunities; providing a virtual space for assembly; and supporting the capability of the protestors to plan, organise, and execute peaceful protests' (Khamis and Vaughn 2011: 1). Optimistic analyses suggest that social media and satellite television worked in symbiosis to strengthen the protest movements across the Middle East (Howard and Hussain 2013:

119). Others have drawn attention to the unprecedented potential for state manipulation presented by media such as Twitter, Facebook and YouTube and the polarising effect of suddenly free media in a time of great turmoil (Lynch 2015). While the new public arenas of Facebook and Twitter enable new and dissenting voices to come to the fore, powerful Arab state agencies can use the same applications to spread disinformation on a massive scale and monitor opposition, as a recent study of Bahrain lays out in detail (Jones 2020: 273–8). Whatever the case may be, a strong argument has been made, based on the Arab Spring, that for all the disruptive potential of social media, they remain tools in the hands of social agents, and it is the latter that are crucial. Digital media accompany political events and processes rather than causing them (Tucker et al. 2017; Wolfsfeld et al. 2013).

In this rich literature, the role of journalism and journalists has received relatively little attention. With the partial exception of Egypt (Elmasry 2012; Elmasry et al. 2014; El-Nawawy and Khamis 2016; Hamdy 2009; Ramaprasad and Hamdy 2006; Sakr 2005, 2013), the scholarship on Arab journalism as a political force is sparse. This is despite the fact that journalists are the people who actually populate the media and produce both news and comment. As such, understanding journalism is vital to make sense of the dynamics between the media and politics in Arab countries. Among the previous studies in the field, a few research monographs stand out. Mellor (2007) introduced modern Arab journalism, identifying central areas of investigation, including globalisation and the dichotomy of the public/private spheres. She also critically discussed the relevance of the idealistic view of journalism in the region as a beacon for democracy. The book complemented a related study on Arab news media (Mellor 2005) and provides a valuable conceptual overview. In a follow-up article based on the reading of memoirs of journalists in primarily Egypt, Lebanon and Syria, Mellor (2009) argued that Arab journalists were able to negotiate partial autonomy by acting as eyewitnesses and authoritative historians under repressive regimes (Mellor 2009: 318). Pintak (2011) has presented a more empirically oriented view of Arab journalism based on survey material, interviews and personal experience of reporting from the Middle East. The survey material revealed that journalists perceived their role as driving political and social reform and self-identified as 'democrats' (Pintak and Ginges 2008). At the same time, they considered the independence of Arab media organisations to be 'poor', the level of professionalism low and the practice of taking money from sources widespread (Pintak and Ginges 2008; Pintak 2011: 155–88). The Arab uprisings inspired further in-depth studies of journalism in the region. The first, tentative accounts were optimistic, hailing a new professional culture and improved organisation among journalists in Egypt (Sakr 2013). However, optimism was soon replaced by bleaker analyses. Exploring the work conditions for Egyptian, Libyan and Tunisian journalists after the 2011 uprisings, El Issawi (2016) has discussed Arab national media's contribution to the hoped-for democratic transitions. In the crucial case of Egypt, she found that the sudden media freedom made possible a critical, interventionist journalism for a limited time. However, powerful political pressures and weak professional structures soon led journalists to fall back into clientelist obedience to their political masters (Issawi 2020).

Whether we look at the literature on the 'new Arab media' or studies on Arab journalism, both tend to be preoccupied with processes of change and the elusive goal of democratisation. At the same time, nearly all the reviewed works conclude that political manipulation distorts the pluralism of the media environment that has emerged since the 1990s. Since the political developments in the region are not necessarily heading for democracy, it is arguably just as useful to connect the ambiguities of Arab media, journalism and democracy to conditions in the present that contribute to prolonging a political life in the twilight zone between autocracy and democracy. The Arab region is not at all unique in this respect. In a global perspective, the 'capture' or instrumentalisation of purportedly democratic media is a growing cause of concern. Media *instrumentalisation* denotes 'the process whereby outlets' owners and sponsors use the media under their control to advance their particularistic interests' (Roudakova 2008: 43). In this book, we direct our attention to the professional and political tensions that accompany journalism under such conditions.

Journalism under Media Instrumentalisation

Media instrumentalisation is a manifestation of the wider concept of *clientelism*: 'a pattern of social organization in which access to social resources is controlled by patrons and delivered to clients in exchange for deference and various kinds of support' (Hallin and Mancini 2004: 58). Its consequences are felt across the world. Media instrumentalisation occurs across political and cultural contexts. While the formal guarantee of freedom of expression is a necessary condition for democracy, it does not automatically translate into an informed and inclusive public debate. In the West, disinformation and polarisation are growing causes of concern. In aspiring democracies, soft control and pressure often continue to impede media and journalistic freedom after authoritarian rule is lifted (Guerrero 2014; Schiffrin 2017). Media instrumentalisation can be exercised directly, through ownership of a media organisation, or indirectly, through advertising or applying pressure or conferring favours on editors. Situations where 'governments or vested interests networked with politics control the media' are also known as *media capture* (Schiffrin 2018: 1).

The ways in which businessmen, politicians and interest groups use media outlets to maintain their hold on power is a favourite theme in media and communication studies. World-famous examples such as the influence of Rupert Murdoch and the career of Silvio Berlusconi have paved the way (Arsenault and Castells 2008; D'Arma 2015). Scholars have traced media ownership structures and owners' political agendas (Baker 2006; McKnight 2010). They have analysed how such agendas influence media coverage and why targeted political communication yields political results (Entman 2007; McCombs 2018). The global surge in populism is tied to transformations in the media domain (Bracciale and Martella 2017; Engesser et al. 2017; Krämer 2014; Mazzoleni 2014). The rise of world leaders who publicly favour some media and demonise others puts the viability of the free and critical media at risk. The former US President Donald Trump made it his trademark to claim that the news was 'fake' (Kellner 2016; Wahl-Jorgensen 2018).

Because of these realities, the political role of news media and journalism is increasingly in question: are they really a fourth estate – a source of critical, informed opinion – or just instruments of manipulation? What does media capture do to the profession of journalism, and how do journalists react to it?

Journalism under media instrumentalisation is an understudied topic. Compared to our sophisticated understanding of the media strategies of politicians, owners and lobbies, nuanced accounts of how media professionals deal with instrumentalisation are in short supply. We address this research gap through close empirical investigation of political journalism in Tunisia and Lebanon. Both provide windows to observe and discuss the implications of the journalistic navigations, compromises and struggles that co-constitute an instrumentalised media sphere. Building on eighty face-to-face interviews with journalists, we bring personal motivations and interpretations into the analysis. Being a political journalist is a challenging job in the best of times, and in the context of instrumentalisation the challenges become even more severe. Yet many people still choose to become journalists. Moreover, they are often idealistic and passionate about their work, even when it is a constant uphill struggle against difficult working conditions and powerful elites. In this book, we focus on how journalists act under instrumentalisation and what the political results of this process might be.

The scholarly interest in media instrumentalisation is on the rise in large part thanks to developments in the former Eastern bloc countries. The fall of Communism led business tycoons to buy up media outlets and impose new forms of control and constraints on journalists (Stetka 2012; Zielonka 2015). Media corruption became a serious impediment to the deepening of democracy (Mungiu-Pippidi 2012). The use of media outlets to smear opponents or glorify oneself or one's political allies is especially widespread in Hungary, Bulgaria, Ukraine and Romania (Örnebring 2012: 506–9; Herrero et al. 2017: 4810; Ryabinska 2014). Similarly, there are close connections between business, politics and the media in the Czech Republic that have resulted in compromised editorial freedom (Stetka 2010: 880). Perhaps the most dramatic example of instrumentalisation and its deleterious effects on journalism is the Russian one. Roudakova describes how powerful elites on the regional and national levels gained control over media outlets and journalistic content post-1990. The result was that journalists felt compelled to jettison their professional integrity, leading to a de-professionalisation of Russian journalism. Consequently, the media lost credibility with the public, and the social value of truth and truth-telling was severely degraded (Roudakova 2017).

Increasingly, the scholarship on media and journalism in the Global South is also concerned with the causes and consequences of political instrumentalisation. Studies of Latin America have pointed to a culture of political clientelism as an underlying cause, amplified by market liberalism

(Fox and Waisbord 2009; Guerrero and Márquez-Ramírez 2014; Hallin and Papathanassopoulos 2002; Hughes and Lawson 2005). Relatedly, scholars of sub-Saharan Africa argue that material deprivation makes the continent's media susceptible to political and economic pressures (Mabweazara et al. 2020). Turkey diversified its media environment as early as the late 1980s and early 1990s, introducing private broadcasting and expanding the media infrastructure. However, the media's tight connections and subservience to the principal political forces in the country stayed the same (Kaya and Çakmur 2010). Under Recep Tayyip Erdoğan, media freedoms have been dramatically reduced although a semblance of pluralism remains (Tansel 2018; Yıldırım et al. 2020). By creating a loyal private media, imposing financial sanctions on unruly contenders and intimidating and criminalising journalists, Erdoğan and his party have built the communication foundations of authoritarian rule (Coşkun 2020). In Myanmar, media instrumentalisation put a brake on democratic reforms and helped preserve the interests of the self-deposed military junta. Long before the 2021 coup, military elites and their business cronies took control of the most central communication channels to protect themselves against independent journalism (Brooten et al. 2019; McElhone 2017).

But we can cast the empirical and theoretical net even wider. Several of the characteristic problems that we will describe and analyse in this book appear as extreme versions of challenges faced today by many Western democracies. Aeron Davis's *Political Communication: A New Introduction for Crisis Times* starts with a long list of challenges in the West, including a breakdown of faith in political institutions and elites, ideologically fragmented parties, identity politics replacing the left–right divide, hollowed-out legacy news organisations outmanoeuvred by social media networks, polarised and fragmented public spheres, and a growing divide between visible politics and the opaque processes of actual policy-making that are hammered out behind the scenes (Davis 2019: 7–9). For Davis, democracy has reached a tipping point. At the same time, the news media are buckling under external and internal pressures. Ownership structures, intimidation by populist politicians and pressure exerted through advertising combine to produce journalism that serves the interests of the mighty and powerful. The news media organisations' own business model contributes to the problem, inasmuch as they are expected to produce a steady stream of consequential, well-researched news stories with an aura of expertise and detachment, while in reality they have too little time and too few resources to do this. The result is a decline in investigative reporting: 'Real investigations of policy, finance and banking, climate change, poverty and energy issues, all of great importance to citizens, have become all too absent' (Davis 2019: 83). Davis posits a 'fourth age of political communication' in which democracies themselves are in crisis partly because of the way political communication has evolved.

Political communication scholars have been studying the link between media and democracy for some time (e.g., McChesney 1999), and the debate has also found its way into journalism studies (Zelizer 2013). Contributors to a recent volume (Peters and Broersma 2017) question the modernist paradigm of journalism, according to which journalists provide a crucial service to democracy. A broken business model, challenged by the digital transformation of the media scene, prompts journalists to become entrepreneurs catering to customers rather than to the public (Singer 2017). The very idea of what constitutes journalistic practice has come into dispute with the emergence of satirical news, Twitter activism and blogging (Wahl-Jorgensen 2017). Various digital media feed on legacy media and generate a bewildering surplus of information. Peters and Broersma argue for a reconsideration of the Western conception of journalism, which is premised on the idea that journalism provides information to the public and is therefore fundamental to democracy. They claim that the 'unrelenting emphasis on democracy' prevents us from understanding the actual role and relevance of journalism in a new media environment (Peters and Broersma 2017: 5, 15). As an alternative to the teleological view of journalists as agents of democratisation, we propose framing the study of journalism under instrumentalisation in terms of three notions: hybrid politics, media hybridity and the latent conflict between grassroots and elites.

Hybrid Politics

There is a tendency to simply assume or take as a premise that Arab journalists strive for freedom and struggle against repressive systems. In reality, this assumption does not always hold. As we alluded to above and shall provide ample evidence of throughout this book, the picture is more complex. True, Arab journalism has its share of 'change agents' who defend democratic values and the civil society's struggles in their countries. However, there is also no shortage of those who curry favour with the incumbents. To capture this complexity and make sense of the relationship between Arab media and politics, we draw on the notion of *hybridity*. The term has found purchase in both political science and media studies. As Carothers argues, pluralism can be reconciled with autocratic rule. Three decades after the end of the Cold War, the new global political landscape appears as an ambiguous and volatile array of regimes that seem to mix and match elements of supposedly irreconcilable principles: democracy and authoritarianism, liberalisation and oppression, pluralism and hegemony. Contrary to widespread assumptions, the breakdown of dictatorships did not result in the global spread of Western-style democracy, but in the rise of a multitude of political regimes that, despite having introduced periodic popular elections, lack many or most of the key ingredients of liberal democracy.

Scholars have struggled to classify these regimes that escape clear-cut categories, arguing over terms such as semi-democratic, semi-authoritarian, electoral authoritarian, competitive authoritarian and liberalised authoritarian, to name a few. The notion of 'hybrid regimes' has emerged as an umbrella term for political systems in which democratic institutions coexist with autocratic practices (Diamond 2002; Levitsky and Way 2010; Morlino 2009). Hybrid regimes have adopted the main elements of democratic rule but still lack other essential features such as the rule of law, effective checks and balances and civil rights protections (Collier and Levitsky 1997; Diamond and Plattner 2001; Jakli et al. 2019; Merkel 2004). Stubborn elites resist further deepening of democracy and find ways to perpetuate their control over political decisions.

Defining the cut-off point between democracy and hybrid regimes (as a sub-category of authoritarian rule) is often difficult in practice. Different scholars use different criteria, and some countries are labelled differently depending upon the classification scheme.[2] In this book, we shift the emphasis

---

[2] For example, in 2018 Lebanon was regarded as a 'democracy' in Polity IV and a 'hybrid regime' in the Democracy Index, while Freedom House labelled it 'partly free'. Tunisia was also named a 'democracy' in Polity IV, but the Democracy Index counted it as a 'flawed democracy' and Freedom House labelled it 'free'. Overall, Tunisia fared significantly better than Lebanon in terms of democratic development.

from structures to processes and actors. We use the term *hybrid politics* about political practices that blur the distinction between autocracy and democracy: practices where democratic and authoritarian elements combine. Media instrumentalisation is such a practice. Despite variation in the extent to which they affect a given political system, hybrid practices may be compared across the democracy/autocracy divide. To take our cases as examples, Tunisia had arguably tilted into democracy in 2019, whereas Lebanon remained on the autocratic side. Nonetheless, there was a family resemblance in the way the political game was played in the two countries. True, Tunisia had a democratic constitution and a sound institutional set-up, but important decisions were still made via informal backroom deals, and the state continued to act in heavy-handed ways; extensive patronage networks coexisted with formally democratic power structures and were responsible for endemic corruption. In February 2018, as protestors denounced corruption and deteriorating living conditions, some 900 people were thrown in jail. So too was the business mogul Nabil Karoui when he announced his candidacy in the 2019 presidential election. He remained incarcerated for most of the election campaign period, before negotiating his release.

Media Hybridity

The same reorientation – focusing on hybridity instead of clear-cut categories and on processes rather than systems or models – is also useful when it comes to media and journalism (Farmanfarmaian 2021). Writing about Eastern Europe, Voltmer (2015: 218) notes that media systems become hybrid by, on the one hand, adopting Western ideals of journalism, and, on the other, 'incorporating structural and behavioural elements of the previous regime into the newly established institutions and processes'. More specifically, private media are no bulwark against media manipulation. Often, markets are too small to support a diverse media, and so privatisation does not lead to increased pluralism but instead to 'partisan watchdogism', wherein specific elite actors use the media to attack other parts of the elite. The result is a 'hybrid form of private, but dependent media' (Voltmer 2015: 226). As will become clear in this book, the exact same points may be made about Tunisia and Lebanon.

Hybridity in the media encompasses more than political pressure. In an influential book on communication technology and the media, Chadwick

(2017) argues that traditional and digital media converge into a largely overlapping sphere of meaning construction, in which messages are produced and controlled by a growing number of both professional and non-professional gatekeepers. As a result, the emerging hybrid media system presents an assemblage of different media logics. This challenge to elite-controlled mass communication as the predominant mode of public communication suggests a wide-ranging redistribution of informational uncertainty, as more players gain the ability to promote alternative narratives through a multitude of channels (Voltmer et al. 2021).

Finally, hybridity seems to be a defining feature of contemporary journalism. Despite, or perhaps rather thanks to, recent large-scale attempts to define clear-cut 'cultures' and 'role orientations' among journalists in different countries across the globe (e.g., Hanitzsch et al. 2011; Hanusch and Hanitzsch 2017), scholars have realised that such national or regional distinctions easily become too coarse-grained and static. Instead, we can speak of 'multilayered hybridisation' in journalism, where journalistic role orientations and practices are 'contingent upon the changing nature of local sociopolitical conditions' (Mellado et al. 2017: 961; see also Mellado 2020; Hallin et al. 2021). In the Arab news media, scholars have seen signs of such hybridisation for decades (Mellor 2005; Sakr 2005).

The shifting landscapes that are implied in these studies on media hybridity suggest that a focus on practices and processes will serve us well in our investigation of journalism under instrumentalisation. Ever since the seminal work of Hallin and Mancini (2004) on media-politics connections, there has been a steady stream of important scholarship about media systems around the globe, and the concept of media instrumentalisation is part of that literature. This structural approach to instrumentalisation may tell us something about the power relations between political or business actors and journalists. However, it is of limited use in explaining how and why journalists make the choices they do, and, not least, how journalists themselves make sense of those choices (Roudakova 2008). In short, the structural approach tells us little about the meaning of instrumentalisation. This question is even more pressing in contexts of change and instability – as in Tunisia and Lebanon – because there, media–politics relations are being remade. Orienting to process rather than system allows us to investigate how journalists try to reconcile different ideals of their mission and role with the political realities they face, their need to earn an income and their personal political convictions. Through this approach we can aim to better explain how media instrumentalisation works and shapes political outcomes outside the West.

The Latent Tension of Media Instrumentalisation

To analyse how journalists respond to media instrumentalisation and play into the political process, we conceptualise their navigational space as a field defined by both horizontal and vertical conflicts. The horizontal refers to competition between politicians or other elites, while the vertical denotes opposition between the elites and ordinary citizens. On the face of it, the impact of media capture is straightforward: it reduces journalism's autonomy and thereby its ability to serve as a check on the powers that be. Media instrumentalisation implies an unequal power relation between the journalists and their patrons who deploy them as tools to promote their own narrow aims. Under these conditions, the liberal ideal of journalism as a counterweight, charged with overseeing the proper functioning of the legislative, executive and judicial authorities (Siebert et al. 1956), becomes more difficult to accomplish. In countries marked by political clientelism, where oligarchs, industrialists, parties or the state control the news media, journalists have little room to manoeuvre outside the will of their masters (Hallin and Papathanassopoulos 2002).

The literature has shown that journalists working under media instrumentalisation may be reduced to 'attack dogs' on behalf of the elites (Hanitzsch 2007; Waisbord 2009). The objects of attack are typically political or business rivals. Mancini (2018) demonstrates how the logic of instrumentalisation plays out in the coverage of corruption in Eastern and Central Europe, for example. Asking why national newspapers write more critically about domestic corruption than their Western European counterparts, he argues that the actual level of corruption is only half the explanation. The exposure of a corruption scandal is also a golden opportunity for newspaper owners to 'attack or destroy the reputation of competitors' (Mancini 2018: 3081). Zielonka (2015: 24) has coined the phrase 'business parallelism' to describe how business tycoons instrumentalise media outlets to smear opponents or glorify themselves or their political allies.

The implication of these practices is that journalists become part of what we call *horizontal conflict*. They work for elites against opposing elites. They produce media content to undermine the legitimation claims of adversaries or repel attacks from other camps. However, media instrumentalisation has also a latent effect, of which the literature has taken little heed: it is a source of *vertical conflict*. In countries where the diffusion of clientelist ties is widespread, an opposition between elites and the grassroots is unavoidable. Large swathes of the population feel disenfranchised, if not oppressed, and bear a grudge against the politically powerful. Through the manipulation of the media, political regimes may protect themselves against the destabilisation risk that accompanies this sentiment. But media instrumentalisation is also a source of frustration among journalists.

While rival politicians certainly compete for power and harness the media for that purpose, a gulf of mistrust and disillusion also divides those elites and the citizens who must live with the consequences of the politicians' wheeling and dealing. For journalists, there is a danger of tarnishing one's reputation by being too close to a politician. Many of the ordinary citizens are also journalists, and this is an important point: the relationship between political groups and the media can be observed along the vertical conflict axis, where journalists have negative views of the elites. In critical situations, the built-in tension within the media may explode.

Tunisia and Lebanon allow for an interesting comparison of journalist responses to media instrumentalisation. Both countries have recent experiences with large-scale popular unrest and political upheaval. However, those episodes occurred against very different historical backdrops. In 2011, ordinary Tunisians succeeded in overthrowing a dictatorship and sought to make a clean break with the past, profoundly changing the media scene. But ghosts from the Ben Ali era remained, and new forms of media instrumentalisation kept slipping in through the back door. Journalists had to navigate this new reality, oscillating between democratic progress and setbacks. In Lebanon, by contrast, both pluralism and media capture were long-standing features of the system. Lebanese journalists knew their place in the system, but many were deeply frustrated with the situation. In the massive demonstrations against the political establishment in 2019, leading journalists launched virulent attacks against the entire political class.

The latent tension within media instrumentalisation can be observed through these processes. Media instrumentalisation nurtures a contradictory effect: political manipulation weakens journalism's potential to become a counterpower, but also generates grassroots resentment of a potentially explosive character. In other words, media instrumentalisation places a lid on vertical conflict – up to a certain point. However, it is also an additional source of frustration and may therefore backfire on the political elites.

Method and Data

Our research process was guided by three questions:

1. Why has media instrumentalisation accompanied press freedom in Tunisia and Lebanon?
2. How do journalists deal with media instrumentalisation and react when key democratic assets are at stake?
3. What are the political implications of the media instrumentalisation and the journalists' responses to it?

To answer these questions, we have relied on a combination of semi-structured interviews, media content analysis and harvesting of Twitter feeds. The interviews are the backbone of our contextual understanding. Through the analysis of news content and Twitter feeds we dive into specific events and take a deeper look at journalism's political role in them.

The interviews were conducted during field trips to Lebanon and Tunisia between 2016 and 2020. We collected 42 face-to-face interviews with journalists in Lebanon and 38 in Tunisia, supplemented by interviews with two focus groups. In addition, we interviewed 5 civil society activists in Lebanon and 11 civil society activists and politicians in Tunisia. We recruited interviewees through snowballing but took care to cover as many different news outlets as possible, including television, radio, newspapers and digital news sites across the political and ideological spectrum (for details of the sample, see the Appendixes). With a few exceptions, the journalists were based in Beirut and Tunis, mirroring the heavy centralisation of Lebanese and Tunisian media. The interviews were conducted in Arabic and lasted 30–60 minutes on average. We relied on an interview guide foregrounding the conditions of journalism and the relationship between media and politics. The interviews were transcribed into English and anonymised and are on file with the authors. The inductive coding of the interviews resulted in a detailed picture of the everyday challenges journalists face in a hybrid, instrumentalised context.

The content analysis adds empirical depth to our picture of the everyday life of journalists and their contributions to the public debate. It focuses on critical issues where democracy is at stake in different ways. We singled out three such issues: (1) the tension between national security and civil rights; (2) elections; and (3) popular protests. For each, we studied the positions of journalists as displayed in newspaper opinion pieces, TV debates and electronic media. Our observations from this content analysis were triangulated with the interview data. The critical issues can be read as case studies where the latent conflict of media instrumentalisation is activated. In situations where democracy is in question, the contrasting impulses of journalism under hybrid politics come into play.

Finally, even as we were working on the October 2019 protests, Lebanese journalists started tweeting intensely, discussing the protests and the media's role in them. We harvested tweets by some of the most influential media figures in Lebanon, adding a third empirical layer to our reading of journalists' contributions to the pivotal 2019–20 period of unrest. One week into the protests, we started to collect large-N Twitter data through an application developed by information technicians at the University of Oslo. We analysed the content of these tweets based on a keyword search and how many retweets they generated.

Scope and Limitations

Our empirical investigation focuses on the years 2015–20. While we were finishing our manuscript, Kais Saied suspended the Tunisian parliament and started ruling by decree. The long-term consequences for Tunisia's transition to democracy – and the freedom of the media – are unclear. During the period we have focused on, Tunisia had the freest media in the Middle East and North Africa. However, the media was a constant source of political friction and popular frustration with the political process. Kais Saied capitalised on that popular discontent during his election campaign in 2019 and again when he seized power on 25 July 2021. Hence, our analysis of journalism and media-politics relations in 2015–20 helps understand why Saied enjoyed sufficient popular support to seize the reins of power.

This book focuses on national media and journalism in Tunisia and Lebanon. It is not about the role of the regional and international media, although, as explained, political instrumentalisation is a relevant topic in these arenas as well. Most Arab news outlets are not pan-Arab, but, historically, censorship has been more inhibiting for national than pan-Arab media. When the Arab satellite channels emerged in the 1990s, their attraction was their ability to bypass state authorities and present new narratives and ways of reporting on events. International media had the same comparative advantage. However, the national media are closer to audience concerns and take precedence when freedom of speech exists. After the 2011 Arab uprisings, for example, public interest in national media outlets soared in Tunisia, Egypt and Libya (El Issawi 2012; Webb 2014; Wollenberg and Pack 2013). Put simply, the question that piqued our curiosity and led to this research is what Arab journalism looks like without state censorship. Accordingly, we decided to concentrate on the two freest countries in the region.

Structure of the Book

We start our investigation by discussing why media instrumentalisation has accompanied press freedom and pluralism in Tunisia and Lebanon. Chapter 2 introduces the countries' political and media contexts, situating hybrid politics at the intersection of formal and informal institutions. We explain why fragile institutions, a culture of informality, and social volatility make countries that have recently democratised or that oscillate between democracy and autocracy especially vulnerable to media capture. The chapter compares the trajectories of Tunisian and Lebanese journalism, which many of our interviewees describe as contrasting stories of rise and decline. Their different political situations are reflected in how media instrumentalisation manifests itself in the two cases. Lebanon is the hardest hit and the problem is openly addressed among journalists there. Their Tunisian counterparts are also exposed to political influences but shyer to acknowledge it. In Chapter 3, we look in detail at the conditions of journalism in Lebanon and Tunisia, building on our interviews with journalists from a variety of media and occupying a range of positions in both countries. We show that legacies of the past and political divides have contributed to a fragmented professional environment, preventing journalists from realising their full potential power. Several factors – the working environment, pressures from editors and owners and limitations on the freedom of expression – contribute to a skewed playing field where the media often sing the power holders' tune. At the same time, there is a simmering frustration with political instrumentalisation among many journalists.

The tensions that instrumentalisation produces in journalism come to the fore in Tunisia. In Chapter 4, we ask what kind of journalism emerged in Tunisia following Ben Ali's ouster, and what aims and ambitions journalists hold. There is a divide between activists who cherish an interventionist ideal and proponents of disinterested journalism. The ideal of professional autonomy is robust in Tunisia but collides with politicians and businessmen who use their power to instrumentalise the media. The result is disagreements and disgruntlement among journalists. The chapter focuses on the divide between rank-and-file journalists and the journalist-commentators known as *chroniqueurs*. Leading *chroniqueurs* are celebrities and entrepreneurs and accused of being on politicians' payrolls. By contrast, other journalists refuse to ride the wave of instrumentalisation. They are supported by an institutional framework – a professional syndicate and a national audiovisual regulator – that is defunct in Lebanon. As we show in Chapter 5, Lebanon's media organisations and political forces are closely aligned, a situation known as 'political parallelism'. Combined with widespread political clientelism, this results in contrasting journalisms. We investigate how journalists navigate the media–politics terrain of horizontal and vertical conflicts when largely left to fend for themselves in a highly fragmented and privatised media system. Some journalists play leading roles in settling scores between decision-makers, while others devote themselves to struggles between the grassroots and the elites. We argue that despite the difficult professional environment in Lebanon, journalists turn contradictions in the political system to their advantage to carve out a professional space. As a bridge to the rest of the book, we demonstrate their navigation strategies with two recent examples: the coverage of a prisoner swap between jihadists and the Lebanese army and coverage of the You Stink anti-government protests in 2015.

Chapters 6–8 interrogate how journalists react when critical features of democracy are at stake. Chapter 6 discusses the balancing of national security and civil liberties in Tunisia. Both Tunisia and Lebanon face real and home-grown problems of violent extremism, but security is also invoked to justify infringements of civil rights. We investigate how Tunisian journalists handled the tension between a heightened sense of insecurity and the country's frail democratic opening in the wake of the 2015 terrorist attack at the Bardo Museum in downtown Tunis. We argue that commentators fell back on interpretive schema from the Ben Ali era when they tried to make sense of the terrorist attack, thus facilitating the authoritarian drift of the Tunisian government at the time. Civil society activists and critical journalists later paid the price for that. Chapter 7 considers the role of media and journalists in elections, focusing on the 2018 general election in Lebanon and the 2019 presidential election in Tunisia. In Lebanon, several journalists ran as candidates, either for established political parties or for civil society lists. We analyse the significance of their political engagement and their platforms. In Tunisia, media owner and election frontrunner Nabil Karoui was imprisoned during the election campaign, and his television channel Nisma was shut down for a time at the behest of the High Independent Authority of Audiovisual Communication (HAICA). Both incidents generated much public controversy, and journalists took different stances in the debate. The other main candidate in the presidential elections, Kais Saied, made his own controversial decision to boycott the media in his campaign – and went on to win the election. In such unusual circumstances, how did Tunisian journalists themselves make sense of the media's political role? Chapter 8 moves on from elections to contentious forms of politics: protests and uprisings. The chapter focuses on the popular revolt in Lebanon in 2019–20. Following the media trajectory of some influential media professionals during this period, we study the conflicting media narratives about the self-proclaimed 'revolution' and how their use of social media contributed to the political dynamics. The chapter concludes that media and journalists contributed to the protests in significant ways, illustrating how journalists were able to disrupt the political communication of the elite.

The final chapter, Chapter 9, compares the process of instrumentalisation in Lebanon and Tunisia and discusses lessons for Middle Eastern studies, media and communication and comparative politics. We think media instrumentalisation in hybrid contexts is a double-edged sword. Political manipulation weakens journalism's potential to become a counterpower, but it also generates grassroots resentment that can backfire on the elites. By directing journalists to focus on elite-level, horizontal conflicts, media instrumentalisation puts a lid on vertical conflict between elites and ordinary citizens, up to a point. However, at critical junctures, the undemocratic practices that go hand in hand with media instrumentalisation become a trigger for popular discontent, dramatically illustrated by the media's role in the Lebanese protests in 2019–20. Our findings from two Arab countries contribute to the sobering accounts of the media's role in democratisation that are increasingly replacing upbeat, teleological ideas of the connection between press freedom and a healthy public sphere. Yet, we also question the idea that the media are merely a tool for elites to use for their own purposes in hybrid contexts, in the Middle East as elsewhere. The combination of press freedom and media instrumentalisation does not make for political stability in the long run; it is combustible and creates uncertainty for the political elites.

2

HYBRID POLITICS AND MEDIA INSTRUMENTALISATION

The media ecology in Lebanon and Tunisia is vibrant and pluralistic. A wide variety of voices can be heard across multiple platforms, ranging from traditional newspapers to activist electronic media. Still, most Lebanese and Tunisian journalists would agree with the Lebanese journalist Nidal, who said that the news media 'rely on political funding', a business model that is 'an impediment to freedom and independence and keeps the journalist on a leash held by the funder' (L38, 6 March 2019). As stated in the previous chapter, press freedom and pluralism are marred by widespread media capture, or instrumentalisation of the media. Why is this, and how does it happen?

Countries that have recently democratised or that oscillate between democracy and autocracy are especially vulnerable to media instrumentalisation (Voltmer 2013). While they are liberated from direct state control over information flows, the institutions, norms and economic arrangements that protect citizens' interests and free journalism in stable democracies are often underdeveloped. The quality of the media depends on the level of political progress. Discussing Eastern Europe after Communism, Zielonka (2015) gives several reasons why political interference in the media in young democracies is rife. We shall emphasise three of them in this chapter. First, the political institutions in young democracies are fragile, in the sense that the democratic structures have weak roots and continue to suffer from deficiencies. The state itself is often frail, and institutional instability harms the media's development. Second, a culture of informality reigns, because institutional shortcomings incentivise actors to seek influence and solutions outside formal political channels. Both politicians and journalists have acquired habits in the past that are hard to break. On Eastern Europe, Zielonka's (2015: 18) judgment is candid:

> The lack of respect for law, institutionalized evasion of rules, distrust of authorities, double standards of talk and conduct [. . .] lead to lax and non-transparent 'Potemkin institutions', 'economies of favour', hidden advertising (also known as 'pens for hire'), the practice of 'compromat', i.e. smearing political and business competitors, and ordinary corruption in some cases.

Third, the politics of aspiring democracies are volatile. Institutional fragility combines with simmering tensions in society to generate political unrest. Poverty and polarisation fuel social and political turbulence. Typically, the economies of emerging democracies are in a brittle state where popular expectations exceed the capacity to deliver. Unemployment rates are high and salaries low due to transnational economic competition. Making matters worse, the old authoritarian regimes have often put a lid on social conflicts or exacerbated them through divide-and-rule tactics. Acute polarisation may therefore be the result when restrictions on free expressions are lifted.

Uncertainty is a prominent feature in such contexts. Hybrid regimes are characterised by a distinct combination of institutional and informational uncertainty (Schedler 2013). Institutionally, multiparty elections fuel competition between political forces that lack confidence in democracy's robustness and fear their contenders may annul or manipulate future elections if they lose. In terms of communication, open public debate is the source of informational uncertainty, as issues, frames and narratives can take unexpected turns and be exploited by different groups in the power struggle. Schedler (2002) argues that elites have recourse to a 'menu of manipulation' to manage this pervasive uncertainty, and media instrumentalisation is one such tool. By co-opting or coercing media organisations and journalists to support their personal agendas, they can build a line of defence against attacks in the media and influence the interpretation of contentious events.

In this chapter, we analyse how the coexistence of democratic and authoritarian practices – what we call hybrid politics – shapes media and journalism in Lebanon and Tunisia. First, we introduce the political contexts and the challenges of fragility, informality and volatility. Then we provide a brief trajectory of the media in each country before discussing how instrumentalisation affects pluralism and press freedom.

The Hybrid Politics of Tunisia and Lebanon

The openness of media and politics has different origins in Lebanon and Tunisia, respectively. Lebanon has a nearly eighty-year history of political pluralism in a society organised around faith communities represented (willingly or not) by the feudal/religious/business elites in each identity group. With important exceptions caused by the civil war in 1975–90 and the ensuing occupation by Syria until 2005, clear-cut authoritarianism never existed in Lebanon, since elite competition has always produced a lively public sphere. Tunisia, on the other hand, was one of the Arab region's most repressive regimes throughout the entire postcolonial and post-cold war era. Then it suddenly embarked on a process of democratisation after the 2010–11 revolution. As we wrote this book, it ranked as a democracy (although a flawed one) on the most influential democracy indexes, and the quality of its post-revolutionary elections and civic freedoms surpassed that of Israel. In what ways is politics hybrid in each of these countries?

The Lebanese Republic was created under French mandate rule, adopted its constitution in 1926 and declared independence in 1943 (Traboulsi 2012). It is, nominally, a parliamentary democracy where the main political positions are divided between representatives from different religious communities by convention (Salibi 1990). There are eighteen officially recognised religious communities, but the most important groups are the Shi'a, the Sunnis, the Druze, and Maronite and Greek Orthodox Christians. Religious cleavages overlap with deep political conflicts, which are played out in the context of a weak state (Najem 2012). The country is a textbook example of what Ian Lustick calls 'deeply divided societies' where religious identities have high political salience, leading to 'antagonistic segmentation of society' (Lustick 1979: 325). The governing model that Lebanon's political elites adopted in 1943 to handle this situation was *consociationalism*, in which a 'cartel of elites' makes efforts to mitigate the destabilising potential of a fragmented society (Lijphart 1969). Hence the distribution of key political positions as well as the distribution of parliamentary seats among the religious groups according to sect. For example, the president is a Maronite Christian, the prime minister is a Sunni Muslim, and the speaker of parliament is a Shi'a Muslim.

In theory, consociationalism results in a stable and even democratic polity, and diversity has had the positive effect that no group has been strong enough to deny the other groups a voice (Salamé 1994). However, a historical heritage of feudal politics, internal conflicts and meddling by foreign countries has ensured that Lebanon has never experienced long periods of stability (Fisk 2001). Its history is peppered with near-collapses and complete state breakdowns (El Khazen 2020). To the extent that the consociational system was ever democratic, Lebanon's civil war and the post-war developments resulted in more entrenched and less accountable elites that vie for power in a 'politics of sectarianism' (Salloukh et al. 2015). The current system rests on competition and compromises between leaders composed in large part of the parties and militias that emerged from the civil war (El-Husseini 2004; Leenders 2012). While the country does hold (irregular) elections, it is the confessional elites that decide how to draw the boundaries of the electoral districts and in practice share power. The leaders use access to the state to sustain clientelist ruling strategies, distributing services in exchange for political support (Corstange 2016). As a result, civil liberties and associational freedom are compromised, infrastructure and public services are poor, and corruption is a major problem (Salloukh et al. 2015: 175–6).

Clientelism in Lebanon has deep roots and became pervasive with the feudal organisation of Mount Lebanon in the eighteenth and early nineteenth centuries (Khalaf 1977; Hamzeh 2001; Harik 1965). The Ottoman rulers controlled the population with the help of local notables (Hourani 1968). For their part, the notables offered protection to their own clients and redistributed a part of their wealth in return for political support (Gellner and Waterbury 1977). After capitalism and the territorial state became the bases of economic and political organisation, a new category of patrons emerged, who could influence access to government services and provide clients with capital, employment and contracts (Johnson 1986). Although patronage networks have changed and in part eroded due to factors such as demographic developments, the civil war and the Syrian occupation (Gade 2018), they continue to exist. Media instrumentalisation also incorporates their logic.

Another long-standing trait of Lebanese politics is external intervention (Khalaf 2002). For multiple reasons including the openness of society, the weakness of the state and a strategically important geographical location, international powers exert deep influence in the country. During the civil war, Israel and Syria were the most heavily involved external actors (Evron 2013; Picard 2016). After Syria's withdrawal, Iran and Saudi Arabia played out their differences in Lebanon (Geukjian 2016). Their interventions shaped the political fault lines as Lebanese elites gravitated toward one or the other. The Sunni establishment aligned with Saudi Arabia and other conservative Arab states whereas the Shi'a movement Hizbullah supported Iran and the Syrian regime. Starting in 2011, the Syrian revolution and the resulting inflow of refugees added new layers to an already complex situation, not least when Hizbullah decided to enter the war to support Bashar al-Asad (Salloukh 2017). As one experienced television journalist put it, 'Lebanon is always [the] prisoner of what happens in the region' (L13, 30 January 2018).

The continuous bickering between the political blocs has led to long periods of political paralysis. Before the election of Michel Aoun as president in 2016, the country was without a government for two years. Popular discontent soared and led to widespread demonstrations. Matters came to a head in the autumn of 2019, as we will discuss at more length in Chapter 8. In sum, Lebanese politics exhibit all the fragility, informality and volatility that Zielonka, quoted above, considers as potential warning signs of media instrumentalisation.

Turning to Tunisia, it is a republic like Lebanon, and was also colonised by France, gaining its independence in 1956 (Perkins 2014). In contrast to Lebanon, however, Tunisia has a homogenous population: around 98 per cent of Tunisians are Sunni Muslims. Its first president, Habib Bourguiba (1956–87), set Tunisia on a path of state-led secularisation (Salem 1984). Both Bourguiba and his successor, Zinedine Ben Ali, ruled in authoritarian fashion and were backed by a single party.

After the 2011 revolution, Tunisia charted a course toward a multi-party democracy (Alexander 2016). The 2014 constitution installed a semi-presidential system based on free elections, fundamental human rights and the separation of powers (Maboudi 2020). The constitution also guaranteed personal and public freedoms and defined Tunisia as 'a civil state based on citizenship, the will of the people, and the supremacy of law' ('Constitution de La République Tunisienne' 2015). The elections that have taken place since the revolution have been free and fair, and they have also shaken up the political landscape. In the presidential election of 2019, the two front runners were new to politics and ran on anti-establishment tickets. Tunisians ended up electing Kais Saied, a jurist who made the fight against corruption a central theme in his campaign and who had no affiliations with any of the political parties in Tunisia. The institutions of a functioning democracy were in place in Tunisia, and they mattered (Yerkes and ben Yahmed 2019).

However, democratic progress was uneven and the ghosts of the authoritarian past had by no means been put to rest. The security establishment remained largely unreformed and the state administration was still populated by a generation of bureaucrats who believed in the paternalistic, strong state (Boukhars 2017; Tripp 2015). Important provisions in the constitution, such as the need to devolve administrative power to local authorities and the creation of a Constitutional Court, had not come into force. High level bureaucrats and politicians capitalising on the old regime's clientelist networks repeatedly blocked decentralisation reforms (International Crisis Group 2019). Parliamentary bickering stood in the way of designating members to the Constitutional Court. In the absence of a Constitutional Court, the democratic order remained fragile (Günay and Sommavilla 2020).

On the systemic level, the revolution resulted in an elite circulation that was 'sudden and coerced, but narrow and shallow' (Stenslie and Selvik 2019). In other words, powerful actors who had enjoyed benefits under the authoritarian regime found themselves outside the political process after the Tunisian revolution, but their economic resources and social networks were not necessarily affected. Soon, they were able to re-enter the scene, either as members of new political parties such as Nida Tunis, Tunisia's largest, or via informal channels and behind-the-scenes politics. By 2017 much of the pre-revolution elite was back on centre stage: according to *Le Monde*, eighteen of the forty-three ministers and secretaries of state in Youssef Chahed's cabinet had been ministers, ruling party officials or affiliates under Ben Ali (Bobin and Haddad 2018). The political reintegration of the old elites was facilitated by a behind-the-scenes compromise between ex-President Beji Caid Essebsi and al-Nahda leader Rachid el-Ghannouchi (Boubekeur 2015). The two men tamed spiking polarisation between secularist and Islamists and managed to avert a serious crisis, but they also installed an 'opaque consensus' and a politics of 'closed doors' (Bobin 2018).

Corruption continued to plague the economy, politics and society; some have suggested that it became even more pervasive after the revolution (Yerkes and Muasher 2017). Businessmen lobbied politicians in the shadows and built clientelist networks throughout the administrative apparatus (International Crisis Group 2017). Public figures warned against the rise of a 'Mafia state', while the informal economy was estimated at around 60 per cent of the GDP in 2017 (Lefèvre 2017). Anger at this situation and the lack of economic progress resulted in widespread socio-economic protests. There were demonstrations and unrest across the country in January 2018 and again in January 2021.

Thus, the Tunisian political context in the 2010s was ambiguous. On the one hand, democratic practices based on the rule of law were supported by the existence of a functioning parliament, a new constitution, a vibrant civil society and freedom of expression. Free elections took place in Tunisia, and they had real political consequences. On the other hand, elite networks reappeared in public while at the same time manipulating the political game from the shadows, and the Islamist current joined this game. Politics in Tunisia was still very much a top-down process dominated by powerful men who lorded it over a population that was largely young, marginalised and disaffected.

To sum up, while the histories of Lebanon and Tunisia are very different, throughout the 2010s both countries had systems of political bargaining and conflict whose dynamics were hidden behind the formal political channels. The result was a hybrid kind of politics. Voting, parliamentary politics and public debate were not devoid of purpose in either country. However, democratic institutions coexisted with autocratic practices: hidden competitions between and within networks of politicians, business actors and state officials. Pluralism and formally democratic institutions were undercut by clientelism and elite-driven politics. The overall balance, however, was more favourable for democracy in Tunisia. Moreover, Tunisian political structures were still in the making. Whereas the Lebanese had been living between democracy and autocracy for decades, Tunisians were just beginning to familiarise themselves with hybrid politics. This difference was reflected in the history and state of their media.

The Contrasting Trajectories of Journalism in Lebanon and Tunisia

Lebanon has occupied an important role in Arab media since the appearance of print news media in the mid-to-late 1800s – a long time before the country gained independence in 1943. Its heterogeneous population, open urban culture and location at the intersection of East and West were factors that contributed to this role. Lebanese journalism was politicised from the beginning. The early newspapers had a rocky relationship with the Ottoman empire, which ruled the area today known as Lebanon until the First World War. During the French protectorate of 1918–43, the many and short-lived newspapers that emerged engaged in attacks on each other, on the various Lebanese political factions and on the French occupier. Steeped in factional conflicts and run by talented individuals, some Lebanese newspapers were willing to expound the views of those willing to pay, be they individuals or governmental bodies. Other papers were deeply ideological (Ayalon 1995: 82–91). This formative period led to a tendency that has persisted ever since: a journalism of *views* instead of a journalism of *news* (Dajani 2019: 23).

Older observers wistfully refer to a golden era of journalism in the 1950s and 1960s, when relaxed laws and Lebanon's vibrant politics made it a hub for journalism relevant to much of the Arab world. Towering editors such as Kamil Muruwwa (*al-Hayat*), George Naccache (*L'Orient/Le Jour*) and Ghassan Tuwayni (*al-Nahar*) emerged as icons of Arab journalism. At the same time, this was a period when various Arab governments began influencing the Lebanese press to propagate their own interests by sponsoring equipment, paying salaries and placing ads. The journalism of views became more entrenched, and as the different media aligned with regional and national political forces, a strong tendency towards political parallelism became apparent. One observer who witnessed this period described two kinds of media:

> The first group was made of media which were created by the political parties and published the political parties' views. The second group included media which were quasi-independent but which defended the interests of parties which funded them. (L35, 3 May 2018)

The Lebanese civil war ushered in new, partisan media and made journalists more dependent on political actors, which in turn exacerbated political parallelism and polarisation in the press. As a result of the war, the operations and finances of the newspapers were severely strained. Still, the main newspapers such as the right-of-centre *al-Nahar* and the leftist and Arab nationalist *al-Safir* commanded continued respect and played important roles in the public sphere.

The end of the civil war marked a watershed in the evolution of the Lebanese media. It resulted in a cementing of sectarianism as the principle underlying the political and media order, a point we will return to shortly. It was also the point where private television definitively became the most important mass medium. During the civil war, the different militias had either appropriated the ineffectual public television channel (Télé Liban) or set up their own television and radio channels, such as the Lebanese Broadcasting Corporation (LBC), established in 1985 by the Lebanese Forces (a Christian militia). After the war these channels continued to broadcast, and some new ones were established. In the period covered in our empirical investigation, there were eight major television channels, six of which were associated with specific religio-political groups. These were al-Jadid, al-Mustaqbal (which shut down in 2019), LBC, al-Manar, al-Mayadin, MTV, NBN and OTV.

Traditionally, Lebanon's newspapers were the pride and joy of the country's journalism. The most important Arabic-language newspapers until recently were *al-Nahar* and *al-Safir*. They were known for high-quality journalism and clear political affiliations. *Al-Nahar* has always been critical of Syrian interference in Lebanon and championed Lebanese nationalism. *Al-Safir* was Arab nationalist, and later provided sympathetic coverage of Hizbullah and Syria on account of their struggle against Israel. Both newspapers were known for their strong editors and independent views. In recent years, their fortunes waned, a fate they shared with the plethora of lesser newspapers and political magazines in Lebanon. Part of the reason was the global downturn for legacy media. Another factor was decreased involvement in Lebanese media from powerful regional actors such as Saudi Arabia, which used to contribute to the financing of newspapers they saw as supporting their interests. As a result of these difficulties, the newspaper scene changed in the 2010s. The venerable *al-Nahar* was reduced to a shadow of its former self, while *al-Safir* shut down in December 2016. The only newspaper that appeared to be thriving financially and that enjoyed wide readership was the hard-hitting *al-Akhbar*, a recent addition to the landscape which adopted a provocative editorial line: socially liberal but staunchly pro-Hizbullah and pro-Iran in terms of regional politics.

While traditional news media struggled, the digital landscape was and is dynamic and varied. In the late 2010s, all the important media organisations had websites and in some cases smartphone applications. Alongside the established media houses, the digital revolution enabled small, independent publishers to come to the fore. Without the right connections, licenses to publish are hard to come by in Lebanon, but the Internet is not included in this licensing regime. Consequently, alternative media proliferated. These ranged from short-lived, one-person ventures to more sustained operations, such as *al-Janubiyya* (The Southern Post), a website that featured news from southern Lebanon and was critical of Hizbullah. Local news seemed to experience a boost in this period; it might perhaps be said that the Internet replaced local radio as the main source of local news. According to the analytic tool Alexa, in 2021 three of the top news sites in Lebanon focused on news from southern municipalities: yasour.org (in Tyre), bintjbeil.org (in Bint Jubayl) and saidaonline.com (in Sidon). The Internet also provided opportunities for media that were all about transparency, such as *Daraj* (Steps), a website dedicated to independent, investigative journalism that openly stated its sources of funding. There were also various news crawl sites that just reproduced content from elsewhere and provided an arena for comments. In addition to edited news sites, social media apps like Twitter, Facebook and WhatsApp were a means of spreading news and commentary.

State-owned media is an important part of the media landscape in most countries. In Lebanon, however, it was and is irrelevant. The public broadcaster, Télé Liban, suffered blows during the civil war from which it never recovered. Although it was still in operation when we were writing this book, its productions were marred by outdated technical equipment and poor professional standards. To a large extent it aired nostalgic reprises of pre-civil war content.

Tunisia's recent media history is a narrative about a sudden rupture with a dictatorial past and coming to terms with a chaotic new political reality after

2011. The media situation before 2011 was described to us succinctly by the veteran journalist Murad: 'Under Ben Ali we did not have journalism, but we had some journalists' (T3, 7 April 2016). The profession languished, but gifted individuals kept journalism alive.

When Ben Ali came to power in 1987, the regime took tight control of the entire media sector. Outwardly, Tunisia appeared to have a pluralist private media sector, comprising television and radio channels as well as newspapers – especially during the 2000s, when the authorities allowed the establishment of some new private television and radio channels. But appearances were deceptive. In fact, licenses went to members of the ruling family or their close circle of friends (Haugbølle and Cavatorta 2012). The owners of the private media were often friends or family of Ben Ali or his wife; their finances were dependent on state-controlled advertising; and owners had to sign clauses that explicitly forbade them to air political commentary or even any political news at all (Chouikha 2015: 34–41).

Political journalism at that time was more akin to propaganda, and the only place where some freedom was allowed was in the culture and sport sections. State informants were recruited from among working journalists and from Tunisia's main college for journalism, Institut de Presse et des Sciences de l'information (IPSI), to ensure that even in-house discussions did not transgress the boundaries of accepted discourse. Journalists exercised strict self-censorship, and very few were willing to test the limits and engage in coverage even remotely critical of the regime's policies. A newspaper running headlines that crossed the line would simply not be distributed that day (the national press and distribution company was controlled by the regime). Private radio and television channels stayed focused on apolitical entertainment. All of these factors resulted in educational and professional standards that were very low.

The revolution changed everything virtually overnight. Several new television and radio channels were established, some of which have become fixtures of the media scene today. New digital news outlets appeared, and existing newspapers were revitalised. The national television and radio organisation, which dwarfs private media in terms of budgets and employees, embarked on a journey to shed its authoritarian heritage and become a modern public broadcaster. Journalists as well as politicians and bureaucrats had to come to terms with unprecedented freedoms.

Private news media burgeoned after the revolution. In 2021, Tunisia had fourteen television channels, forty-one radio channels, 228 paper print publications and a large number of news websites. Television and radio were the most important private media. Businessmen who made their fortune during the Ben Ali regime figured prominently among the owners. Three television channels shared most of the viewers between them: Nisma, al-Hiwar al-Tunisi and Channel 9. The print media also contributed to public debate, and the private newspapers were often family-owned, much like the traditional Lebanese newspapers once were. Newspapers catered to a smaller segment of the population, and they had clear editorial tendencies: *al-Shuruq* was affiliated with Tunisia's powerful labour union, *al-Damir* was the only well-known Islamist publication and *al-Maghrib* was a liberal, highbrow newspaper.

Digital media formed one of the drivers of the revolution. Some of the critical blog collectives that criticised the regime before 2011 quickly transformed into investigative news outlets, supported to some extent by western NGOs. The two best-known were Nawaat and Inkyfada. Besides these activist media outlets, regular for-profit digital media outlets also made their mark, particularly in the business news segment (digital news sites such as Kapitalis and Business News).

As for public media, the state-owned newspaper *al-Sahafa* and its French sister publication *La Presse* continued to be state-owned, but were, at least in theory, editorially independent. However, they were of relatively little importance compared to television. Tunisia's national broadcaster, al-Wataniyya, made up an important part of the political communication of the Ben Ali regime. It comprised several television and radio channels, all housed in a massive complex on the outskirts of the capital. A cornerstone of Tunisian media even after the revolution, it was a colossus on clay feet. On the one hand, its employees were guaranteed a decent salary; on the other they complained of a pervasive and inefficient bureaucracy, and a lack of financial resources in the organisation to cover basic operating costs such as public transportation for reporters in the field. Al-Wataniyya was severely overstaffed and underfunded, relative to the number of employees. A prominent commentator for one of the main private radio outlets noted that the public broadcaster employed between 1,200 and 1,300 journalists, when it could have managed well with 300 (T15, 3 May 2018). Still, al-Wataniyya occupied a central position in the Tunisian public sphere. For example, in the 2019 presidential election, it was al-Wataniyya that organised and aired the widely viewed debate between Kais Saeid and Nabil Karoui. One recent assessment concluded that the broadcaster remained important, but needed 'structural reform in its editorial policy, journalism practice, and professionalism standards before it can serve [the] crucial role of watchdog' (Miladi 2021: 282).

The media that were owned by the Ben Ali family or their associates were in a third category, one that lay between private and state-owned. Entire media enterprises or the shares that had been controlled by Ben Ali associates were confiscated by the state after the revolution. Most important among these were some national radio channels, such as Mosaïque FM and Shams FM, but some television and print media were also affected (Haugbølle 2013; Haugbølle and Cavatorta 2012). They continued to be subject to the logic of private media, relying on advertising for their income, but various actors associated with the post-2011 Tunisian state tried to influence them, a point we will return to below. This is important because the radio channels Mosaïque FM and Shams FM were among the main agenda-setters in Tunisia after the revolution in 2011.

So far, we have argued that Tunisia and Lebanon exhibit two different versions of hybrid politics, and that a positive aspect of hybridity is a level of media pluralism uncommon in the Middle East and North Africa. The flip side of this pluralism is uncertainty, which elites seek to minimise for themselves and maximise for their adversaries by using the media as a political tool. Pluralism and freedom are marred by clientelism, which takes the form of media instrumentalisation. This notion is central to understanding the ways in which Tunisian and Lebanese journalists we interviewed thought and acted.

Media Instrumentalisation

Media instrumentalisation is a global phenomenon, but it manifests itself in different ways. The most straightforward exploitation of the media for political purposes is when investors own one or more news outlets and exert influence through their ownership, to the point of instructing editors about what to cover and how. Another, less direct form of clientelism is when powerful businessmen (they are mostly men) tie advertising for their companies to the content of a news outlet, withholding advertising if they are displeased with a news report or commentary. In both examples, we see an asymmetrical relationship between, on the one hand, media professionals, and on the other, the people who effectively control the purse strings of the organisation and decide if the journalists have a job to go to or not. As in other forms of clientelism, it is an arrangement that works well for both parties, as long as the weaker party – the journalist – is prepared to play the game. However, professional standards suffer, since instrumentalisation encourages hidden deals, corruption and fake news.

Media instrumentalisation is particularly common in hybrid regimes and flawed democracies where a measure of media freedom necessarily exists. By contrast, in fully authoritarian states the rulers simply dictate what the media say, reducing them to propaganda outlets. No other Arab countries have moved as far in the direction of freedom as Tunisia and Lebanon, and to find comparable experiences we must look further afield, specifically to Eastern and Central Europe.

Natalia Roudakova has chronicled and analysed the rise of instrumentalisation in post-1990s Russia, providing a gloomy benchmark for the study of other cases of media capture (Roudakova 2017). When the Soviet Union collapsed, after a brief period of celebrating newfound freedoms, newspapers began experiencing financial problems in the new, unbridled capitalism that characterised post-Soviet Russia. Many went bankrupt, and editors started to realise that journalism could be conceived of as a commodity to be sold. Newspapers gravitated to various powerful political individuals and groups and offered them positive election coverage, to the extent that the role of the neutral, critical watchdog was rendered impossible – journalists were always taken as supporting one side or the other. The consequence of these processes was journalistic fragmentation. Boundaries between news and advertising were blurred, and camps of journalists who supported competing politicians became hostile to each other. One particularly visible aspect of instrumentalisation was the introduction of *kompromat* – commissioned, 'black' PR pieces built on real or fabricated rumours about politicians and journalists, written for the purpose of character assassination. Russian journalists referred to their own work using phrases and words associated with prostitution (Roudakova 2017: 98–146).

To a similar or lesser degree, journalists in other Eastern and Central European states have felt pressured to dance to the tune of their paymasters. *Advertorials*, or positive news paid for by politicians through a PR company, are common, and the aforementioned practice of *kompromat* has also been well-known in countries such as the Baltic states, the Czech Republic and Bulgaria (Örnebring 2012; Dobreva et al. 2011: 187–8). In this region, 'clientelist ties have led to the subordination of the journalists to the political elites' (Camaj 2016: 242).

The conditions for political communication in Lebanon and Tunisia are comparable in several respects to those of Eastern and Central Europe, but in other respects they differ. Let us start with Lebanon. An obvious difference is that instrumentalisation in Lebanon is not a new phenomenon that resulted from a dramatic political upheaval, as happened in Eastern and Central Europe after 1989. Formally, the Lebanese media system is based on two media laws from 1962 and 1994. In theory, this set of laws, and institutions including professional unions, secure a well-regulated media sector, comprising a limited number of licensed publications, radio stations and television channels that rely on advertising and subscriptions for their operation. According to the letter of the law, these media organisations are monitored by the state to ensure that they do not accept funding from political sources. In practice, however, the media system is shaped by the sectarian reality of Lebanese politics. The Lebanese polity is composed of strongly bounded religious communities, and it has long been an openly acknowledged fact of public life that media organisations act as mouthpieces for sectarian leaders. Using informal influence in the media organisations, the security services and the state administration, these leaders can reduce access to employment, airtime and information for journalists who threaten their interests. The competition for work opportunities is stiff and 'connections' (*wasta* in Arabic) are required to enter the field. The media organisations prefer to hire politically loyal reporters and writers. 'Everyone I know came into media through connections', explained a programme host on a television channel, who also gave the following account of how clientelism interfered with media work:

> The politician may exercise pressure on the journalist by calling the media organisation where he or she works. I know many cases where journalists

have lost their jobs due to pressures from a politician. The politician can also use another journalist to work against him. And there is security blackmail (*ibtizaz*), letting the journalist feel that he is under surveillance or threats. (L14, 31 January 2018)

According to a survey from 2018, 78 per cent of the major Lebanese media were politically affiliated at that time, making Lebanese media an intensely politicised field (Samir Kassir Foundation and Reporters Without Borders 2018). Media organisations were and are owned or co-owned by government ministers, MPs, political parties and powerful individuals involved in politics in some way. To cite some well-known examples: the al-Manar television outlet and website is a mouthpiece for the Shi'a Islamist party Hizbullah and enjoys very little editorial freedom. Al-Mustaqbal TV and the *al-Mustaqbal* newspaper, owned by the Hariri family, were the main media outlets associated with the Sunni elite until they closed down in 2019, while the television channel OTV is owned by supporters of Lebanon's Maronite president Michel Aoun and consistently provides coverage sympathetic to his agenda. Another major television channel, MTV, is named after its owner, Elias Murr, a Greek Orthodox Christian with a long political career. The Murr family offers a good example of the Byzantine nature of the connections between politics and the media in Lebanon. Elias Murr's brother Gabriel Murr owns the newspaper *al-Jumhuriyya* (The Republic), and the two sides of the family are bitter political enemies, having contested the same electoral district.

Information about exactly who owns how many shares of the various media outlets is often difficult to come by, but our interviewees agreed that the media is mostly owned and/or funded by political factions, parties or individuals with vested political interests. The term 'political money' (*mal siyasi*) came up again and again in conversations with Lebanese media professionals:

A big problem is the whole business model of Lebanese media. It doesn't rely on sales and advertisement. In the present market, it is very hard for the media actors [. . .]. So they rely on political funding, either by Lebanese politicians or other countries. This business model kills the development of quality journalism. It's an impediment to freedom and independence and keeps the journalist on a leash held by the funder. (L38, 6 March 2019)

Adding to the tangled mass of media and political actors, foreign governments have long invested in the Lebanese media scene to make their voice heard or support currents to which they are sympathetic. Saudi Arabia, Qatar, Iran and Libya have all injected money into various Lebanese media, thus fuelling a polarised pluralist public sphere (Kraidy 2011).

Tunisia provides a closer parallel to Eastern Europe, in that it experienced a sudden political change that completely upended the media scene, a process that is still ongoing. However, a notable achievement of Tunisian civil society and politicians is that they succeeded in putting in place a quite powerful regulating regime that has played an important role in post-revolutionary media life.

Since the Tunisian revolution, an objective and neutral media ethic was nurtured by political and media institutions alike. At the same time, figures connected to the previous regime tried to assert their influence, and rising political stars tried to increase theirs. As a result, political instrumentalisation was a public secret in the 2010s: disliked and stigmatised, but acknowledged by all. For example, several of our interviewees mentioned the example of a political fixer from the Ben Ali era, Kamil al-Latif, who was believed to pull a lot of strings behind the scenes:

> You cannot make a survey on journalism in Tunisia without hearing about the controversial Kamil al-Latif. He was very influential under Ben Ali, like a Rasputin, with a lot of relations in the police and in journalism. [. . .] After the revolution he came back very strongly. Many people hate him, but he has a big lobby and a lot of journalists belong to him. Several media [. . .] write on demand for him. He takes them on holidays, pays their apartments, buys them cars, etc. (T45, 4 May 2018)

In the same vein, we interviewed journalists who had been approached by up-and-coming politicians, wanting them to host programmes in new media set up by the same politicians. In turn, the politicians were often viewed by journalists as clients of more powerful, hidden interests that operated outside of formal politics (T23, 20 November 2018). One often heard complaints along the following lines from media professionals: 'The media field in Tunisia is like the Lebanese one: local political parties have control over 90 per cent of the media sector' (T24, 21 November 2018). Such statements are difficult to verify, but they point to a general impression shared by many journalists.

The economic basis of Tunisian media is weak, since the market is small, just like in Lebanon. The money to run the operations must come from somewhere, but exactly who funds and controls the media in the last instance is often a matter of rumour or hearsay. Among the people we interviewed, it was a common assumption that business capital, political parties and media funding were closely related:

> Those who own capital are those who own media outlets and they are politicians at the same time. [. . .] Channel 9 is a big [television] channel funded by Nida Tunis party and then the party Tahya Tunis after some politicians seceded from Nida Tunis. Those who are in the parliament are also businessmen. There's a mixture between all these. You could find [the same kinds of ties] in Europe or the USA but in Tunisia it lacks transparency. (T32, 18 June 2019)

Such assumptions are supported by research as well as events on the ground. A study by Reporters Without Borders found that politicised ownership was most obvious in television, where six out of ten private channels were affiliated with a politician (Media Ownership Monitor 2019). All the major channels had such connections. Tahar bin Husayn, the founder of al-Hiwar al-Tunisi, was a founder of the political party Nida Tunis, which gathered many members of the Ben Ali-era elite. Usama bin Salim, who founded the religious channel Zaytuna TV, is a member of the Islamist party al-Nahda and the son of one of the founders of that party. Both men sold their shares in the channels before entering politics, in compliance with post-revolutionary regulations, but there is no doubt that political figures continued to influence content (Miladi 2021: 277). The clearest case of politicised ownership is Nabil Karoui and his television channel Nisma. The channel received its license under Ben Ali. After the revolution, Karoui joined the new political party Nida Tunis together with many other elite figures from the Ben Ali period. Nisma provided support to Nida Tunis's chairman Beji Caid Essebsi in his successful bid to become president. Later, however, Karoui left the party and then used Nisma to support his own political career. In 2017, he started the daily show *Khalil Tunis*, which covered the activities of his charity organisation of the same name (established in memory of his son, who died in a car accident). From that year forward, the show featured Karoui and other volunteers of the charity distributing food, clothes and other essentials to poor people in Tunisia's many marginalised regions, earning him wide support in the country. As Nisma aired daily footage of Karoui distributing Ramadan meals to the poor in May 2019, Karoui gave an interview to the channel in which he announced his intention to run for president in the elections later that year (Jeune Afrique 2019).

The politics of private media in Tunisia are murky, but public media are also subject to political influence. After all, for decades, much of their *raison d'être* was to be propaganda instruments in the hands of the regime. Despite the revolution's important gains, political culture can be difficult to change, among both state officials and the journalists they employ. Successive governments of different colours have seen themselves as being above the media, thinking they should have the power to curb it if it suited them, in flagrant contravention of the post-revolutionary Tunisian constitution (Joffé 2014).

If Tunisian media as a rule were less overtly manipulated by politicians and businessmen than their Lebanese counterparts in the 2010s, this was in large part thanks to the more successful regulatory regime. A by-product of the 2011 revolution was the High Independent Authority of Audiovisual Communication (HAICA), which proved to be independent-minded and combative. HAICA describes itself as 'a constitutional body . . . that seeks to implant a regulatory culture laying down the independence of the media. It necessarily leads to a new way of governing the media and strengthening the freedom of expression' (HAICA n.d.). HAICA regulates licensing for radio and television, and during election campaigns, it has monitored content to ensure that media silence periods are respected and that candidates from all the main parties are given fair coverage. In 2019, the regulator forcibly closed the offices of Karoui's television channel Nisma, Tunisia's second biggest, because the channel had failed to comply with more than twenty requests to make public its sources and means of funding (France24 2019). The Journalists' Syndicate, which we will return to in Chapter 4, is another institutional pillar of the media. The syndicate was outspoken even under Ben Ali, and since the revolution it has become a cornerstone of media politics in Tunisia. Unlike its Lebanese counterpart, it is a vocal defender of journalists' rights and has a loud voice in public debate, and its headquarters has often been a rallying point during demonstrations. The existence of an independent regulator and a professional syndicate that did not hesitate to speak out against the powerful ensured that the Tunisian media scene was not a free-for-all, as occurred in Russia after the downfall of Communism.

Conclusion

Throughout the 2010s, the media scenes in Tunisia and Lebanon combined freedom and pluralism on the one hand and political instrumentalisation on the other. In Tunisia, post-revolutionary democratisation resulted in a proliferation of media outlets, freedom of expression, an active regulator and a vocal journalism syndicate. The Lebanese context was less democratic, but both its historical heritage as the Arab world's most free country and its consociational political system ensured media pluralism and a lively public sphere. At the same time, the political and economic elites in both countries successfully exerted wide-ranging control over the most important media, sometimes overtly and at other times covertly. Media ownership was highly politicised, resulting in hybrid structures where political, economic and media power converged. In several media institutions, journalists experienced that pluralism existed, but at best limited independence. The result was a media sector that contributed to real political competition while at the same time limiting the agency of journalists and editors. In the remaining chapters, we investigate how this hybrid reality marked the day-to-day work of journalists, how they carved out a professional working space and a measure of autonomy, and how the tensions inherent in instrumentalisation affected politics in these two countries.

3

BEING A JOURNALIST IN THE GREY ZONE

Institutionalised hybridity has consequences that go deeper than the political configuration of the media, which we explored in Chapter 2. It also affects the daily working life for journalists in multiple ways. In this chapter, we step inside the hybrid system and ask what it is like to be a journalist in the grey zone. Our account is based on experiences recounted by Lebanese and Tunisian journalists in interviews we conducted in 2016–19. Like the broader political picture itself, the environment for journalism consists of mixed and ambiguous conditions. On the one hand, most journalists affirm that they have freedom of expression. On the other hand, their ability to use that freedom as they wish is undermined by structural constraints. Speaking about Tunisia, Murad summed up the paradox:

> All agree that among the most important fruits of the revolution – and there are not many – is the freedom of expression and of the media. The question is just how to maintain this achievement, this freedom, in the shadow of very bad professional and economic conditions. (T3, 7 April 2016)

Both countries can look back on a recent past during which restrictions on the freedom of speech were harsh. In Lebanon, the civil war and the ensuing Syrian occupation constrained the exercise of journalism and left journalists vulnerable to attack. Those who went too far, like Samir Qasir and Jubran Tuwayni, paid for it with their lives. According to one senior journalist, Adam, 'self-censorship ended in 2005 when Syria left. The margin of freedom became a lot better' (L2, 27 May 2016). Kamal, Adam's junior by some twenty years, confirmed Adam's impression, saying: 'Freedom of expression is there for sure. I have never experienced someone calling to instruct me what to say or not. If the army, security forces or someone tried to interfere, I could yell at them' (L8, 27 January 2018). Similarly, in Tunisia, the turning point was the fall of Ben Ali's regime. The editor-in-chief Musa was emphatic about its importance, saying: 'Tunisians have enjoyed freedom of speech since 14 January 2011. Nobody can control the freedom of speech because Tunisians won't allow it' (T27, 22 November 2018).

One implication of this freedom of expression is that journalism has potential. Unfettered by directives from the Ministry of Information, it can develop as a force of its own. To an extent, journalism has become what journalists make of it. Journalistic agency matters as never before. In the everyday run of things, however, many of our interviewees felt inhibited. Why is that?

Before we delve into the empirical analysis based on testimonies from Lebanese and Tunisian journalists, it is worth looking at some of the general constraints on journalists' agency that have been identified in the literature. A long-standing body of work on the sociology of journalism and the news has documented constraints on the interactions of journalists, even in firmly democratic countries (Fishman 1988; Gans 2004; Gitlin 2003; Schudson 1989; Zelizer 2004). This literature argues that news making is conditioned by social, economic and political structures in deep-reaching ways. Under the influence of factors such as cultural conventions, market forces, institutional dynamics and the political system, the autonomy of journalists is necessarily imperfect. Consequently, as the media sociologist Waisbord (2014: 16) affirms, 'media studies need to be grounded in the analysis of social process and forces that shape the dynamic interaction between structures and agency'.

Globally, the conditions for free journalism have been deteriorating for a while. This is due not only to the fact that democracy in the world is in decline but also to major changes in the industry. The financial foundation of the news media is strained, mainstream audiences are fragmenting and the authority of journalism is eroding (Peters and Broersma 2013). The professional development of journalism is also under pressure (Witschge and Nygren 2009). In this context, journalistic autonomy appears even more out of reach. Journalism in many countries finds itself in a precarious state and therefore exposed to external influences. One comparative survey of journalists in eighteen countries asked which factors most reduce the latitude that practitioners have in carrying out their occupational duties. It found that political conditions and the individual's position in the news hierarchy were the most consequential. Interestingly, as pertains to our study, hybrid regimes were perceived to infringe professional autonomy more than authoritarian ones, a finding the authors ascribe to 'hybrid regimes probably attract[ing] higher expectations for professional autonomy' (Reich and Hanitzsch 2013: 152).

Studies of the sociology of the news have often pointed to the fact that the news is made on the terms of the elites. As Schudson (2003: 150) puts it, 'journalism, on a day-to-day basis, is the story of the interaction of reporters and government officials, both politicians and bureaucrats. Most analysts claim officials have the upper hand.' However, McNair maintains that the ever-growing pluralism of modern news media makes ideological domination, in the classical Marxist sense of the ruling classes enjoying a monopoly on the means of ideological production, nearly impossible to attain:

> [T]he content of these media is now so diverse and multisourced [. . .] that no ideology can be truly 'dominant' for any length of time if it does not correspond on some level to what ordinary people feel to be, and experience as, true. No account of events stands unchallenged anymore. (McNair 1998: 29)

Hence, although power and privilege in the journalistic environment are highly present, McNair insists that the production of the news remains a 'chaotic flow'. Journalism may be instrumentalised by elites seeking dominance in the public sphere, but there are always opposing tendencies.

Fragmentation

We shall see that the global constraints mentioned above are highly relevant for Lebanese and Tunisian journalists. However, we will begin our examination of why these journalists feel inhibited from a different point of departure, one having to do with the degree of professional integration and cohesion. Barbie Zelizer (1993) once described journalists in the United States as an 'interpretive community' that is 'united by its shared discourse and collective interpretations of key public events'. She argued that journalists create a shared understanding of events through informal channels, in their contacts with one another, and by building and reflecting on the prior reporting of their colleagues. When we embarked on this research, we were curious to see if Lebanese and Tunisian journalists also constitute a community and how they interpret events. We set out to investigate the question sociologically and in discourse. Throughout our interviews, we asked journalists about their sense of community and their interactions with peers. How strong is their professional identity? Is there group solidarity? What common ground exists? The answers we received all pointed in the same direction. Journalists in Lebanon and Tunisia are fragmented, and any sense of professional solidarity is weak. Few subscribe to the idea that there is *one* journalistic community. For example, the Lebanese print-media journalist 'Umar said that in his estimation:

> Community is a big word. I think there are groups (*shilal*) along sectarian and political divisions. There can be more than one group in every newspaper. The Muslim group, the Christian group and so forth. They are not united by ideals or commitment to the profession. (L3, 28 May 2016)

The experienced television journalist Nasim agreed, pointing that the audience was also fragmented. Journalists reached out to distinct and opposing communities. Thus, a journalist appearing on pro-Hizbullah channels such as al-Mayadin or al-Manar would be known in Beirut's Shi'a neighbourhoods. In Sunni neighbourhoods such as Tariq al-Jadida, however, ordinary people would not know him, because he works for 'the other team's TV' (L13, 30 January 2018).

Tunisia does not have the same sectarian divisions as Lebanon. Nonetheless, our North African interviewees described a fragmented scene in Tunisia as well. The union representative Rafiq refuted the idea that Tunisian journalists constituted a community:

> I think the only thing that unites them is their belief in the value of freedom. Nobody wants to go back to the time of dictatorship and closure. Apart from that, everybody sings their own tune. The Union has tried to gather people by organising conferences and such, but there is fragmentation. There are cantons of journalism corresponding to the various channels. As for a shared

identity, you find it among a small group of professional journalists, while the majority does not care much about the profession and its development. (T37, 10 October 2019)

Rafiq described a cantonised journalistic environment in which each media channel forms a separate community and cross-professional identity is weak. He explained that it was rare for journalists to socialise across their respective media outlets. Tunisian journalists came together in clusters but rarely as a corps. One reason is that they had few common spaces for socialising. In front of the Ministry of Interior there is a club called the 'Club of Journalists in Tunis', but journalists rarely met there. The 'House of Journalism' (*dar al-sahafa*) had more guests – it was jokingly called the 'Bar of Journalism' (*bar al-sahafa*) – but only appealed to a certain segment of the profession. In the view of the well-established television journalist Brahim, local journalists did not 'mingle and get to know each other' and this 'create[d] mistrust among them' (T20, 7 May 2018). In Lebanon, social compartmentalisation was even stronger. When we asked where journalists in Lebanon met, a common answer was 'they don't'. In contrast to Tunisia, Lebanon does not have a functioning syndicate, a point we will come back to. The barriers formed by sectarian and political cleavages are also difficult to overcome. Adam felt that journalists lived in parallel worlds from the day they entered university, because the sects have separate schools, clubs and welfare organisations: 'The media department has two buildings, one in the Christian area and one in the Muslim, and there is little interaction between them' (L2, 27 May 2016). This fragmentation is rooted in historical events.

Legacies of the past

The legacies of the past weigh on the journalistic environments in both Lebanon and Tunisia, albeit in different ways. Lebanon's deepest wound is the civil war that took place in 1975–90 and ripped the social fabric of the nation. After Syrian intervention, the war ended, but it was never genuinely resolved, and no national reconciliation process followed (Ghosn and Khoury 2011). For the most part, the media outlets of the warring parties lingered on into the post-war era. During the fifteen years of armed conflict, the capital of Beirut was split along the so-called 'Green Line' that separated the mostly Christian East from the predominantly Muslim West. Separate newspapers and journalistic communities existed on each side. Even after the militia checkpoints along the Green Line were dismantled, the boundaries it created between people have remained and continued to impede social and professional integration among journalists.

In Tunisia, the main source of division in recent history has been the authoritarian rule of Ben Ali from 1987 to 2011. This rule, although imposed from above, also created barriers and conflicts between ordinary people. In standard fashion for a police state, the regime perpetuated itself by obstructing the self-organisation of society, undermining trust and sowing fear. Ben Ali used the media to conceal and suppress opposition to the predatory behaviour of his clan. He curtailed freedom of expression and used the media to manipulate the public. State-controlled newspapers such as *La Presse* and *al-Sahafa*, as well as the public broadcasting service, were reduced to transmitters of regime propaganda. Within the slightly more open private newspapers, radio stations and television channels that were allowed to operate, Ben Ali directed cronies such as his son-in-law, Sakhr al-Matiri, to take ownership control. Journalists were kept under constant surveillance. Police expected them to prove their loyalty to the leader, and tailor-made rules and regulations kept them on a short leash. The Press Code listed such potential crimes as 'offence to members of the government and public officials' and 'the publication of non-accurate news that might be a problem for the public order' (Barata 2013: 124). Punishments for infringement were severe. In 2010, the World Press Freedom Index ranked Tunisia as the fourteenth least open country in the world (World Press Freedom Index 2010). Ripple effects on journalism included a decline in professionalism and widespread suspicion among colleagues. The media journalist Rafiq explained how the current 'fragmented' media sector was a result of the Ben Ali regime:

> It's a heritage from the old regime. It terrorised the journalists so much that they did not show solidarity with colleagues.
>
> [Interviewer: Why did they not dare to show solidarity?]
>
> Being a journalist was very hard under Ben Ali. The regime promoted mediocrity in the field and fear of one another. [. . .] It did not want the journalists to unite. (T37, 10 October 2019)

Stymied by this repression, Tunisian journalism failed to develop organically. Authorities interfered in every aspect of journalists' work (Lutterbeck 2015). The Ministry of Information was the ultimate news producer, calling journalists and instructing them about what to say and write and when to keep quiet. Making matters worse, some journalists acted as informants, reporting recalcitrant colleagues to the Ministry of the Interior. Distrust was ubiquitous in the sector (T12, 9 March 2018). Moreover, the regime controlled the sources of revenue and would pay for loyalty while letting dissenters starve (T9, 8 March 2018). One of the few opposition actors that emerged, Tawfiq bin Brik, minced no words about the net effect on his profession. Commenting on the 'dark decade' in neighbouring Algeria in the 1990s, he said: 'In Algeria, journalists are being killed, but in Tunisia, it is journalism that is being killed' (L'Obs 2000).

Journalism in both Lebanon and Tunisia has lasting problems that can be traced to these taxing experiences of the past. Besides a lack of social interaction and trust between individuals, our interviewees also reported a lack of agreement on what the practice of journalism implies. A history of civil war and subordination to repressive regimes propped up by divide-and-rule policies has retarded the development of shared professional norms. On a range of issues, from the rules of collecting information to verification procedures and the protection of sources, journalists disagreed. The Lebanese television reporter Kamal deplored what he saw as a failure by his colleagues to safeguard the dignity of the subjects of their news reporting, saying: 'Too many journalists will spread whatever they have' (L8, 27 January 2018). In the same vein, the Tunisian television profile Murad spoke regretfully about

> journalists interviewing the families of terror victims just moments after they have been told their loved ones have been killed: 'How does it feel to have lost your son, who was just a little boy?' Even on such issues we don't agree. And we don't agree on how to deal with the political powers that be. (T3, 16 April 2016)

Murad connected the problem of professionalism to the internal organisation of the media sector, arguing that the sector needed to build better structures to free itself from its authoritarian past. He deplored the persistence of a 'sultan-like management inside the media institutions' (T3, 16 April 2016). A prominent member of the syndicate of journalists named Zakariya made the same observation, reporting: 'Routines like daily editorial meetings are not in place, the infrastructure is poor, there is no editorial board, no ombudsman, and the owner intervenes in the editorial work' (T40, 6 April 2016).

Other subjects said journalism suffered from a deficiency of professional skills. Habiba, a Tunisian television journalist, blamed the educational system, arguing that it failed to teach journalists proper Arabic, diligence in checking sources and preparedness for the field. 'Young journalists are not qualified to write good articles', she said. 'The basic things are not in place. So, how can we talk about professional ethics?' (T4, 8 April 2016). Several of our interviewees laid blame at the door of the Institute of Press and Information Sciences, known under its French acronym, IPSI (T19, 3 May 2018; T20, 7 May 2018; T22, 20 November 2018, T15, 3 May 2018). Founded in 1967, IPSI is Tunisia's state-sanctioned journalism academy (IPSI n.d.). It is frequently criticised for being ossified and detached from the practical reality of news work. In Lebanon, too, the quality of the journalism being practiced came under question. Isma'il stressed that professionalism meant being familiar with the issues and the important questions to ask. He criticised journalists for not doing adequate research, saying:

> We desperately need that in Lebanon: journalists who know about electricity production, water distribution and internet infrastructure. [. . .] You have a lot of these 20-year-olds going into fields that they know nothing about and pushing a microphone into the official's face: 'Well, what's wrong here?' (L4, 30 May 2016)

Mirrors of political divides

The current political struggles are another source of fragmentation in the journalistic environment. Journalism in Lebanon and Tunisia has little autonomy from politics. In Tunisia, the struggle between revolutionary forces and old regime elites is the strongest source of friction in the journalistic community. Many journalists perceive themselves as part of the movement for democracy that was energised by the fall of Ben Ali. Several of our young interviewees pointed to the revolution as their reason for entering journalism in the first place. Far from everyone, however, self-identified with the revolutionary struggle. Some journalists owed their prominence to positions they held under Ben Ali and had ties to the old regime elites. A few, like Burhan Busays, spoke openly in favour of the old political order. Even some journalists new to the profession argued that to fulfil the imperative of getting the economy going for all Tunisians, the 'old' and 'new' guards had to unite. The television journalist Shawqi in al-Hiwar al-Tunisi was among those who felt the interpretive framework of revolutionary versus counter-revolutionary was a dead end. He said journalists 'who use[d] ideology' took the campaign to expel people from the old regime too far. He explained:

> Some see themselves as heroes of the revolution. They work in media that consider themselves revolutionary media. The contact was difficult with them because they see things as black or white. But now there is often a mix of new and old journalists in some media. There are journalists who were not in favour of propaganda under the old regime. When they got the chance to do other things and got liberated from the old regime, they did that. The mix of old and new journalists gives good and positive results. (T5, 8 April 2016)

Shawqi further said that some Tunisian journalists sought to 'cleanse' the media of colleagues from the Ben Ali era. During the Marzuqi presidency (2011–14), they referred to al-Hiwar al-Tunisi, Nisma and some radio stations, such as Shams FM, as 'the media of shame' (*i'lam al-'ar*). For Shawqi, such ideological divisions were the opposite of what Tunisia needs. He called for pragmatism in the media and asked journalists still making revolutionary demands to turn the page.

In Lebanon, the principal fault line after 2005 was a stand-off between the supporters and the opponents of 'resistance' – the 8 March and 14 March alliances. Activists who worked to unite journalists across this divide faced an uphill battle. Our interviews provided many examples of how politics had driven a wedge into the professional journalistic community. The first of two examples we will cite is that of a journalist, Karim, who had been physically attacked by supporters of Hizbullah. We asked him if his colleagues in other media institutions expressed support for him after the assault. Karim confirmed that they had, saying they had written more than ten opinion pieces and organised a sit-in in Beirut. We then asked if Karim saw this as a sign that Lebanese journalists had a shared professional identity. On this point, however, he demurred, saying:

> To be objective, the reactions were not for professional reasons or an expression of professional solidarity. The professional solidarity has retreated. There is a kind of solidarity that is sparked by personal or political reasons. Because the perpetrator was Hizbullah the solidarity comes from Hizbullah's opponents. [. . .]
>
> [Interviewer: So, you did not find that journalists who disagree with your political views stood with you for the sake of professional solidarity?]
>
> Publicly, no. It is very rare. But personally, a couple of people called me. (L18, 9 May 2018)

Karim's experience says a great deal about the subordination of journalism to politics in Lebanon. When a Hizbullah critic and journalist was exposed to violence, in the response of his peers, the former identity took precedence, not the latter. Instead of sympathising with a fellow journalist, they saw a Hizbullah critic and adjusted their reaction according to their political compass.

In our second example, a journalist for the pro-8 March newspaper *al-Akhbar* commented on the role of two non-governmental organisations, the Samir Kassir Foundation and the Maharat Foundation. The NGOs were credited by journalists in the 14 March camp with working for press freedom and media development. From the point of view of the *al-Akhbar* journalist Yusuf, however, they actually exerted a negative influence. Yusuf was critical of activists who promote the liberal–internationalist human rights agenda against community leaders in Lebanon. He argued that they became the pawns of Western powers and international NGOs, and lost connection with the local context. Speaking about media support programmes that receive funding in the name of women's rights, he railed:

> The Samir Kassir Foundation and Maharat bring people together and [. . .] train them on certain skills or topics like digital platforms, social media, etc. They take them out of their societal contexts, the public opinion, election

> campaigns and local conception of human rights. How can American NGOs help us to stop violence against women when US politics is based on violence, poverty and the plundering of our resources? [. . .] We have no idea about the creation, funding, and recruitment of these websites, organisations and associations. [. . .] In my opinion they defend Western interests in Lebanon under the cover of the defence of freedom and human rights. (L32, 7 March 2019)

Yusuf's mistrust mirrors a political environment in which supporters and opponents of resistance are miles apart. It offers a clue as to why journalists in Lebanon are disunited and the struggle for shared professional norms is so hard. Prima facie, one would expect journalists to unite behind NGOs that work for media pluralism and the freedom of expression. But Lebanese realities are different. When trendsetting journalists suspect that the NGOs have hidden agendas, the potential unifying effect is lost.

In sum, the fragmentation of the journalistic environment prevents Lebanese and Tunisian journalists from acting together and realising the full potential of their power. It precludes collective agency because there is little they agree on, beyond the need for freedom of speech. We have argued that this fragmentation has its roots in a troubled past and is magnified by current political divisions. Subordination to politics impedes the emergence of a shared identity and consensus on professional norms. According to Hallin and Mancini (2004), autonomy is both a prerequisite for journalistic professionalism and an expression thereof. Because of the instrumentalisation we described in Chapter 2, journalists often end up echoing the disputes of political elites.

Life as a Journalist

Working conditions

When we zoom in on the everyday challenges of individual journalists, additional drivers of fragmentation appear. Working conditions, first of all, leave much to be desired. Wages are low and short-term contracts common. There are few available jobs, and many journalists are laid off as the media lose funding. Employees are often not paid on time. With audiences migrating to social media and the advertising market in free fall, few journalists are able to make demands. In one case, a journalist at the Lebanese al-Mustaqbal

TV complained that she had worked for fourteen months without receiving her salary (L22, 20 October 2018). Just months after we did that interview, al-Mustaqbal TV closed down. It should be added that female journalists are significantly worse off than men in Lebanon. A 2016 study shows that their job security is lower, and they almost never attain senior positions. Sexual harassment is a serious problem, particularly by government officials and other politicians (Melki and Mallat 2016).

In Tunisia, job security and salaries for journalists working for the state-owned media are relatively better. Employees of privately owned media companies, however, which also boast the greatest viewer shares, face similar challenges. Marwan, a correspondent for an international newspaper, described the situation as follows:

> The working conditions in Tunisia are harsh. A journalist may work long hours but will not be paid for the extra time. If you complain or tell your boss that you are tired, you could be removed. Journalists are paid 300 to 400 US dollars per month. It is a very difficult situation. (T12, 9 March 2018)

According to one union representative, a salary as low as 250 USD per month was not unusual for journalists. He estimated the national average monthly salary at 500 USD (T40, 6 April 2016). Many journalists have to supplement with an additional job to make ends meet. Furthermore, the private and confiscated media seldom provide for social security and health care (T24, 21 November 2018). For the ageing news editor Musa, the problem was concrete:

> I take thirteen medications per day and only two medications are covered by the social insurance. I am diabetic and need to buy medicines which are not covered by the insurance. Those who work for the media do not have social coverage anymore. (T27, 22 November 2018)

In Lebanon, the story is the same. Most journalists work in private media that provide no insurance coverage or pension for their employees. As Nasim related:

> I have been a journalist for thirty years, but I don't have a pension. I cannot retire. If I stop working, I will find myself without a home or anything. I don't even have health insurance. Had I been a university professor my situation

would have been better. I am better known than the university professors, but what can you do with fame? (L13, 30 January 2018)

Unsurprisingly, these conditions gave rise to frustration and anger against the elites. When our interviewees expressed discontent, they often took aim at politicians. Musa accused the government of using economic strain as a crowbar in its stand-off with journalists. He saw the reduction in employment and social benefits as a 'strategy to control the media' (T27, 22 November 2018). Nasim was upset with the media owners who made windfall gains from the political influence of their companies while outsourcing the costs of the crumbling advertisement market. 'The owners never invest their own money', he lamented. 'Income from advertisement is for the newspaper. Political money is for the owner' (L13, 30 January 2018). Perceptions of corruption in the sector added to the discontent. Journalists who curried favour with the elites enjoyed some respite from the difficult conditions. The co-optation of some fuelled the annoyance of others. Nasim gave the example of the late Prime Minister Rafik Hariri, who surrounded himself with a group of loyal journalists. He argued that Hariri had built his relationships with journalists on mercantile grounds, thereby deepening class divisions among media professionals:

> We started to have a class of rich journalists, close to the prime minister. Other politicians adopted similar practices. Today when you visit a politician, you take an envelope when you leave. For this reason, you see some journalists with big houses while others who work night and day live in one-room apartments. You find journalists driving Mercedes and BMW. Houses on the beach. There is a class of journalists that is . . . I don't want to say 'hired', but it's very strange. (L13, 30 January 2018)

This example illustrates an important point: political instrumentalisation is a potential conduit for political dissent. Politicians in Lebanon and Tunisia use selected journalists to advance their agendas but end up provoking the anger of other journalists in turn. The flip side of co-optation is relative deprivation, because it works by differential treatment. In Tunisia, a manifestation of this tension is the relation between journalists and the television and radio commentators known as *chroniqueurs*. For ordinary journalists, the privileged state of the *chroniqueurs* is a palpable source of irritation, as they are often judged to be defending the agendas of hidden paymasters in politics and business. We will return to the phenomenon of the *chroniqueurs* in more depth in Chapter 4.

Editors or owners' interference

Another source of frustration among journalists is the interference of editors and owners. Interference is the everyday manifestation of political instrumentalisation. Given the shortage of and competition for funds in the sector, media owners are like 'kings'. They expect coverage by their media organisations to reflect their interests and rely on the chief editors to enforce their will. Jad Melki has described the internal hierarchy of Lebanese television stations using military metaphors. He refers to the news directors as the 'generals', the newscast producers as the 'lieutenants', the anchors and show hosts as the 'sergeants' and the correspondents, reporters and writers as the 'foot soldiers' (Melki 2008: 258–308). These metaphors reflect the top-down culture that habitually prevails in the Arab newsroom. In another telling sign, the news directors are often referred to as 'political directors' or 'political supervisors' by their subordinates. The news directors communicate closely with the owners and are politically aligned with them. In Melki's assessment, 'the news director is not simply an employee who runs the production machine, but rather a partner and political crony' (Melki 2008: 263).

Political control in the newsroom is enforced in different ways. As part of the daily work routine, the news director sets the agenda and allocates resources for the coverage of events. They also head and direct the editorial meetings. Melki argues that the news director 'pre-frames' the reporters' stories by deciding the angle from which to observe the news. Moreover, they check and approve the story after it has been written. Depending on the topic, the channel's policy and the management style of the individual editors, the amount of room for journalists to put their personal touch on the stories varies. Overall, however, the pressure from above is significant. For the individual journalist, this may or may not be perceived as a problem. Employees who agree with the channel's editorial line have little reason to complain. But for those who want to pursue a 'party-free' agenda, critical journalism feels shackled.

In our interview data from Tunisia, complaints about interference from editors and owners are widespread. In fact, journalists there appear to be particularly upset by this problem. Of course, in Lebanon, the pronounced political parallelism means that journalists tend to work in a media organisation that reflects their points of view. In Tunisia, there is no similar 'filter' in the recruitment of journalists. Many of our interviewees spoke negatively about the prevalence of directives and interventions from above. The young correspondent Marwan identified the political instrumentalisation and internal hierarchy of the Tunisian newsroom as sources of trouble, saying:

> There are many conflicts between journalists and chief editors. In many cases, the editor-in-chief has a friendly relationship with the owner of the media company. The owner relies on the editor-in-chief to maintain the editorial line. The big boss ties relations with the people in government. It is a chain that starts with the authorities on top and ends with the journalists' work. (T12, 9 March 2018)

Similar to Melki's observations about Lebanon, Marwan concludes that Tunisian journalists are controlled by editors and owners. Moreover, there is friction between them. Marwan described the relationship between journalists and the editor-in-chief as 'tense'. Sometimes, he said, 'the journalist comes to work and refuses to produce the requested stories' (T12, 9 March 2018). Other interviewees confirmed this view. For television journalist Najim, 'the owner of the channel is a kind of semi-god who can do whatever he wants with journalists' (T34, 8 October 2019). Again, we observe that political instrumentalisation fuels discontent among journalists in the grey zone. Many see the orders they get from on high as being in conflict with their professional ideals. In one case, a television journalist said he decided to quit his job after being pushed not to publish an interview with an influential politician (T24, 21 November 2018). We also heard anger at the news media's wilful suppression of troublesome positions and voices. An activist with the journalists' union expressed dismay about the two leading television channels in Tunisia, which he contended had instituted a ban on union stewards in their programmes:

> The propaganda is real [. . .] Those who control the newsrooms are editors-in-chief, supported by the media owners who refuse to host some guests. They have blacklists, especially in the private media. For example, we are blacklisted by Nisma TV and al-Hiwar al-Tunisi. (T37, 10 October 2019)

In the same vein, journalists for the e-media outlets Nawaat and Inkyfada criticised Nisma and al-Hiwar al-Tunisi for marginalising dissident voices in their programmes. In their view, the dominant media did more than simply set the agenda, because they actively worked against civil activists who criticise the political and economic elites. Such is media instrumentalisation in practice.

Freedom of Expression

Where does this leave freedom of expression? Is the journalist's voice unrestricted? Our interviewees had differing opinions on this matter, and the situation between Tunisia and Lebanon also differed. As a benchmark, Tunisia was ranked as the seventy-second freest country in the world in the World Press Freedom Index for 2020, whereas Lebanon stood at 102 (Reporters Without Borders 2020a). We will discuss journalists' perceptions of their level of freedom for each country in turn.

Tunisia

Thanks to the 2011 revolution, the right to speak one's mind in Tunisia was radically strengthened. It was constitutionally grounded and safeguarded by a strong set of institutions and actors. The life of journalists changed as the country moved out of its repressive past. Some of our interviewees insisted that freedom of expression had been fully achieved. In the judgment of Katya, an employee of the public broadcaster al-Wataniya, there were 'no longer any sacred persons and [. . .] no red lines' (T19, 7 May 2018). The radio journalist Khaldun was equally categorical, describing the level of freedom as '100 per cent'. He dismissed the idea that no-go areas existed (T28, 17 June 2019). For others, the picture was more nuanced. Whilst acknowledging the gains of the 2011 revolution, Murad argued that the day-to-day constraints on journalistic work impinged on freedom of expression (T3, 7 Avril 2016). Lamin maintained that freedom of speech remained 'conditional' because the media refrained from criticising its owners (T24, 21 November 2018). Rafiq made a similar point referring to the wide-reaching power of investors, saying:

> In the past, politicians used to break our balls and beat us up. Today, we are facing the advertisers. For example, we cannot criticise Qatar because the telecommunication company Oreedo is the number one advertiser and sponsor of newspapers in Tunisia. (T37, 10 October 2019)

Rafiq was not alone in arguing that investors continued to restrict freedom of expression where, previously, the regime had exerted pressure. Several interviewees stated that 'capital' posed the biggest threat to journalism nowadays. They reasoned that a lack of resources rendered journalists vulnerable to financial pressures or enticements. Without job security and proper pay, it is difficult to criticise investors and owners. By the same token, the temptation to accept a bribe is greater. The print media journalist Saʻd made this very point, concluding that 'Tunisia's private media liberated itself from the grip of political power, but was taken by the power of capital' (T18, 4 May 2018). He stressed that healthy journalism in Tunisia will have to be built on a sound economic foundation and argued that social and economic precarity left journalists vulnerable to 'blackmail and temptations'. Ultimately, he said, a journalist was also 'a normal citizen with a family and a life' (T18, 4 May 2018).

During a roundtable we co-organised with the NGO al-Bawsala in January 2020, an interesting discussion about censorship took place among a group of four journalists from Tunisia and one from Norway. The question was whether censorship had been defeated with the 2011 revolution, or whether it continued to place limits on freedom of expression. Luma, a female radio journalist from the public broadcaster al-Wataniyya, argued the latter position against two other participants: Muhammad, a journalist from a private radio station, and ʻAdil, a member of the press agency Tunis Afrique Presse (TAP). We will quote the exchange at some length:

Luma:	The system [of censorship] has not gone, the system is here, it exists [. . .] the surface has changed, the façade has changed, people have started to speak out. If you were a victim of censorship before 2010, you just had to accept the reality and be silent. Now you are censored while you are shouting. You can speak out as much as you want, but in vain. Censorship exists.
Muhammad:	Maybe in some media outlets . . .
Qays:	We don't have it.
Muhammad:	In the public media outlets . . .
Luma:	Not just public media, it's everywhere to some extent.
Muhammad:	Maybe . . .

Qays: [...]	Honestly, Luma, we don't have censorship.
Luma:	Censorship can take many forms and can be used for different means. There are soft methods, and maybe harsh methods, and it can become brutal when you say that an institution will face closure, or that half of the journalists will be sacked. This is a brutal kind of censorship. That a programme is not aired, or when only a part of it is aired, or is aired in a soft way: this is also a form of censorship.
Norwegian journalist:	Excuse me, I am a bit confused. It is a bit difficult to understand the way this censorship manifests itself. Because when I previously asked you if there were any limits or subjects that one cannot write about, you said no. But then, if censorship exists, concretely speaking, what is this system of censorship?
Luma:	It's complex. But it is felt through the practicalities. For example, a journalist can be prevented from working, which is one form of censorship. [. . .] I will take the example of [. . .] a confiscated media outlet. It needs working capital to finance its journalists and its everyday expenses. But the executive department may withhold the funds, and your money is not deposited because in one way or another you have refused to 'comply'. It lies in the small details. But it becomes a form of censorship as well. This is one form of pressure that is exercised on you, and on the institution, to work in this or that direction. They somehow try to influence the editorial choices. They can ask a journalist to be a bit more lenient with a political figure, for example. (Roundtable, Tunis, 25 January 2020)

This discussion illustrates the ambiguities of journalism in the grey zone we referred to in the introduction to this chapter. From Qays' vantage point in TAP, the activity of journalists is no longer censored, as the press agency has liberated itself from the surveillance of the state. However, Luma sees another form of censorship, which operates even 'while you are shouting'. Its logic is that you are free to speak your mind, but your voice will not be heard unless the message concurs with the interests of the media organisation's funders. You must fine-tune and adjust your position to get the news story on air or in print. Hence, journalists in a context of pervasive media instrumentalisation may feel simultaneously free and shackled, and the variation in their subjective experience is great.

Sometimes, journalists' freedom to exercise their profession is also restricted in more direct ways, as the Tunisian journalists' union (National Syndicate of Tunisian Journalists, SNJT) has reported. On its website, the SNJT issues monthly press releases about violations of media freedom. According to its annual report, more than 200 Tunisian journalists reported a total of 139 such violations between 1 May 2018 and 30 April 2019 (SNJT 2019). The most serious of these were fifty-four assaults that in the judgment of the SNJT required legal follow-up. These comprised eighteen physical attacks, twenty-three verbal assaults, eight cases of incitement (*tahrid*) and five cases of threats. The remaining complaints concerned violations of the right to access information or in other ways carry out the duties of the profession, and different forms of harassments in the field. The union judged that state officials were responsible for seventy-three out of 139 attacks. The remaining sixty-six were carried out by civilians (twenty-one), trade unionists (ten), sport supporters (six), politicians/media organisations (five) and others (six). In the SNJT's assessment, attacks by unofficial parties were the most dangerous because they included acts of violence. During periods of popular unrest, the frequency of citizen attacks on journalists increases.

Lebanon

In Lebanon, threats to journalistic freedom of expression were graver than in Tunisia, and the situation deteriorated over the period we cover. The constraints that derive from media instrumentalisation were the same, but Lebanon had additionally experienced both authoritarian regression and large-scale street confrontations. The mass demonstrations that kicked off in October 2019 greatly increased the strain on journalists, a point we shall return to in later chapters. But even prior to that, the kinds of violations that Lebanese journalists suffered were more severe. An activist with the Maharat Foundation for the freedom of expression and journalism informed us that in 2018, his organisation registered twenty cases of journalists being either detained, interrogated or subjected to investigation by the Office for Combatting Information Crimes. He observed that recourse to intimidation and legal pressures had increased since 2017. According to this activist, it was common practice for Lebanese authorities to hold journalists for days without charge. 'They typically detain them on Friday to let them wait until Monday. They often confiscate their laptops and sometimes force them to delete their Facebook accounts', he remarked (L46, 20 October 2020).

In our interviews, the journalists' unease with this situation came through clearly. The absence of both physical and economic security was a cause of concern. The radio host Taha perceived an increasing pressure on journalists that was stoking fear in the professional environment, saying: 'Journalists have been prosecuted legally for things they write on their Facebook or Twitter pages. This creates an atmosphere of terror (*irhab*)' (L14, 31 January 2018). Financial difficulties were also steadily increasing, in part because the 'political money' on which the Lebanese media run was drying up. With less money around, competition for remaining resources increased. According to the print media journalist 'Umar, the crisis struck junior members of the profession particularly hard. It also affected their professional ethics. 'Umar believed they had been forced to lower their professional standards to find work:

> It stands in glaring contrast with what you usually hear, that the youth have dreams and these kinds of things. They enter a field where people eat each other alive. There are hundreds of graduated students every year who end up doing anything to get attention. The situation is harsh and especially for the young people who thought they could use this work to discover secrets, defend the truth and so forth. No – you must adapt to the rules of the market! (L3, 28 May 2016)

'Umar explained that the market for Lebanese journalists abroad had shrunk in parallel with domestic funding cuts. The monarchies on the Arabian Peninsula had become less welcoming and wealthy than previously, and hundreds of exiled journalists had returned home, where they found themselves with fewer options and facing stiffer competition for headlines and funds. Arguably, one consequence of such a situation is decreased bargaining power for journalists vis-à-vis patrons. Moreover, when the future of their professional positions is in question, freedom of expression is also threatened.

'Freedom in Lebanon is a big lie!' exclaimed Nasim. 'You are free to criticise the other team but not your own' (L15, 3 May 2018). He cited the examples of journalists working at the Greek Orthodox-dominated newspaper *al-Nahar* or Hizbullah's television channel al-Manar. From what he had observed, the first group could attack anything but the Greek Orthodox Patriarchate, the latter everyone but Hizbullah. Rula made a similar remark about editorial restrictions for Lebanese employees in media organisations with Saudi Arabian ownership or funding. Commenting on the coldblooded dismembering of Jamal Khashoggi inside the Saudi Arabian consulate in Istanbul in October 2018, she described a sense of frustration at being unable to speak out, saying: 'You are a Lebanese, living in Beirut, you don't have any other source of income, and then Jamal Khashoggi is brutally killed, and you cannot write about it, and you are actually being expected to defend the Saudis!' (L22, 20 October 2018).

Compared with their Tunisian colleagues, journalists in Lebanon referred more often to such perceived red lines. Corruption, the army and the security apparatus and Hizbullah were all mentioned as particularly sensitive subjects. If journalists ventured into that terrain, they had to weigh their words. The experienced e-media journalist Samir described corruption as a 'very risky topic'. In his assessment, if you went too far in mentioning names and exposing details of certain economic crimes in Lebanon, your 'head [would] be cut off' (L19, 9 May 2018). The radio host 'Asi described talking about the army, the police and the security services as 'forbidden' (L17, 7 May 2018). Overstepping the agreed-upon boundaries imposed by the multiple branches of the security apparatus put a journalist at serious risk. In Nasim's view, the ultimate no-go area was Hizbullah (L15, 3 May 2018). Given the party's pre-eminence in Lebanese politics and the unrivalled force of its militia, no journalist could expose its hidden activities without consequences. The television journalist Zayn summed up these limitations in this telling and worrisome remark:

> All Lebanese journalists and media actors are deeply aware that there is a 'law of silence', a mafia law, that prevents us from saying what everybody knows.

There are truths as clear as day that most Lebanese know, but no one can say them. Especially when it comes to the deep corruption among the officials and the governmental and private institutions. [. . .] There are limits that people will decide personally not to cross, not necessarily imposed by Hizbullah. People treat this issue carefully. And everything that concerns the military or security apparatus in Lebanon – the army and the various intelligence agencies, the judiciary. Journalists treat these very carefully and purposefully ignore the bitter truths that we know exist. (L20, 9 May 2018)

The 'law of silence' that Zayn describes defines the boundaries of free speech to which all local journalists must relate. As open as the public debate in Lebanon appears, there are things that remain unsaid. Key reasons include the volatile security situation in the country and the above-the-law status of security agents. Additionally, Zayn's reference to a 'mafia' evokes the presence of armed groups that have no formal authority in the state. Limitations on the liberty of expression come, in other words, from both state and non-state agents in Lebanon. The legal framework is the regime's first line of defence. According to Reporters Without Borders, 'Lebanon's criminal code regards defamation and the dissemination of false information as crimes and defines them very broadly', and 'the courts are used to prosecute media outlets and journalists' (Reporters Without Borders 2020b). On top of this is the mafia law, to which Zayn refers. Journalists cannot push the boundaries of acceptable criticism without bearing in mind the price they may have to pay.

Conclusion

In this chapter, we have dissected the problem of journalism in hybrid political settings where pluralism and the appearance of free speech go hand in hand with instrumentalisation and obstacles of different types. We have shown the professional vulnerability of journalists in these settings, stemming from such factors as professional fragmentation, historical legacies, precarious working conditions, pressure from editors and owners, and de facto restrictions on the freedom of expression. Because of these weaknesses, it is difficult for Tunisian and Lebanese journalists to defy the wielders of economic and political power. The structure of the 'playing field' favours journalists who comply. The Tunisian radio journalist Nawfal summed up the situation thusly: 'the journalists who keep their jobs and do not have problems are those who are dependent and have no objections on this or that' (T15, 3 May 2018).

However, as we may gather from Nawfal's comment, not all journalists are equally happy to fall in line. There is more to the story of journalism in Lebanon and Tunisia than its underlying structural conditions. First, journalists have ambitions for, and ideas about, their profession that may lead them in different directions. Second, they have ways to deal with 'capture' that give them some leeway vis-à-vis the instrumentalisation of elites. It is to these manifestations of journalistic sense-making, and to the individual and collective responses of journalists to the conditions under which they work, that the following chapters now turn.

4

FINDING A ROLE: TUNISIAN JOURNALISM AFTER THE REVOLUTION

In 2013, the office of Tunisia's first democratically elected president, al-Munsif al-Marzuqi, published an investigation, based on the archives of the presidential palace, entitled *Black Book: The Propaganda System under Ben Ali's Rule* (Tunisian Republic Presidential Office 2013). It claimed that 376 journalists had taken money from the old regime's communication agency and named ninety of them as 'friends' of the regime ('Le Livre noir des "journalistes amis" en Tunisie sous Ben Ali' 2013). The book stirred controversy and was criticised for factual errors and its political agenda. Nonetheless, it gave an indication of the scale of collusion between journalists and politicians under the old regime. One of the main aims of the 2011 revolution was to get rid of such corruption and to dismantle the state propaganda machine. Henceforth, the country's journalists would have to reinvent their role. As we have argued in the preceding chapters, this reinvention took place in a context of continuous political turmoil: a hybrid political situation in which both political and business elites were eager to use the media for their own purposes. What kind of journalism emerged from the ashes of Ben Ali's propaganda system? What aims and ambitions did Tunisian journalists have? In this chapter, we focus on how post-revolutionary journalistic ideals clashed with a political reality in which politicians and businessmen sought to instrumentalise the media. We analyse the tensions this clash created among journalists, and the means that critical journalists deployed to retain their professional identity and resist meddling by those with power.

The study of journalistic roles has widened its scope in recent years and increasingly looks beyond the Western experiences that influenced its early thinking. This progress is in large part due to survey-based studies enabling researchers to compare journalistic cultures across the world (Hanitzsch et al. 2019; Mellado 2020b). However, for the sake of deepening our understanding of the norms, ideals and practices that characterise journalism outside the West, sociological case studies are also important (Waisbord 2016). Mellado, Hellmueller, and Donsbach (Mellado et al. 2016) distinguish between journalists' *role conception*, denoting 'the purposes of the profession that journalists conceive as more important at the individual level', and their *role perception*, meaning 'a followed script that has been internalised and is located in the larger social structure'. Journalists negotiate their roles between their personal convictions, the expectations of the media organisations and societies in which they work, and the performance of their everyday practice (Mellado 2020a).

Ideas and Ideals of Journalism

As an introduction to the ongoing debate among Tunisian journalists about their role in a transitional democracy, the following exchange is instructive. It took place among four Tunisian journalists and a journalist educator on the second day of a roundtable we co-organised with al-Bawsala, a transparency NGO, in January 2019:

> Nasima: In a new democracy, I think that the role of a journalist is to educate . . .
> 'Usman: Not really, Nasima.
> Nasima: And to give the correct information –
> 'Usman: Yes, to inform, to inform.
> Nasima: Not just to inform, one must also provide cultural content, and [. . .] I think that our role as journalists today is also to educate. Even the new generation – I give talks in schools to provide them with information about the industry of journalism.
> Tamir: This is not your role as a journalist, but the role of civil society. The journalist's role in a piece of writing is not to educate people, but to inform them. [. . .]

Nasima: I also think that if we were in a democracy that is established, my role would be only to inform, but we are in a new democracy, in a democratic transition. So our other role as journalist is to also bridge this gap between the public and the media. And only then can we work comfortably. So, I think that just arriving to this stage only, no, of only playing the role of informing . . . we are still too far from this. I think that my role is also . . .

Ihab: Isn't your mistake here that you are idealising the public? [. . .] You have a romantic approach to the public. [. . .] You consider Tunisians as people who are in a situation where they want to receive the 'lights of truth', in a situation where they are not polarised, and that they are somewhat waiting for the journalist to show them the path to follow.

Nasima: No, it's not this. It's not this at all. [. . .] I think that we need to have a new generation. Because now we are living with an old generation that depends on dictatorship. We are in the process of creating a new generation that is well educated in the correct way of practising journalism. Then we can work comfortably. Now we are building these things, building the pillars. We are one part of this building process. (Roundtable, Tunis, 26 January 2019)

This exchange clearly shows two opposing schools of thought. On the one hand there is the idea, defended by 'Usman and Tamir, that journalists have a responsibility to inform the public and ought to keep their opinions aside. Neutrality, fairness and detachment are the watchwords. Journalists should leave activism to civil society. The contrary idea, adopted by Nasima, is that it is not enough simply to pass on pieces of information. A journalist should also *educate* the public. In the exchange above, Nasima argues that Tunisia's situation as a nascent democracy places a special responsibility on journalists to cultivate awareness and values in the post-revolutionary generation. Journalists should lead the way out of the past and break with the corrupt way in which journalism was understood and practised under the old dictatorship.

The interventionist ideal

The discussion between Nasima, 'Usman and Tamir reflects a fundamental professional disagreement between 'educators' and 'informers' among Tunisian journalists after the revolution (Hammami 2017). In several of the interviews we conducted, Nasima's argument was reiterated in various forms. For example, the veteran journalist Murad held that journalism was a 'mission', not merely a job. He said he could not maintain a separation between his profession and his responsibility to society. As he put it:

> Some of my colleagues think that it's enough to do good work that conforms to a given editorial line, even if it is the yellow press. This may work in an established democracy, but we have not reached a stage that allows us to deal with journalism only in a technical sense. We have a role and we must assume it. (T3, 7 April 2016)

Both Nasima and Murad argue for journalistic interventionism. According to this role conception, journalists take an 'active, socially committed, and assertive role in their reporting, and in so doing they involve themselves in social and political processes to the extent that they become participants' (Hanitzsch et al. 2016: 3). Journalistic interventionism can take different forms but is characterised by the will to participate and promote change. Interventionism is uncommon in Western journalistic cultures but is a frequent feature of the media in transitional democracies, including Tunisia.

The interventionist ideal appears in three different forms in our research data. Nasima and Murad represent the first, in which a journalist should play the societal role of 'educator'. Murad argued that Tunisians suffered from a systematic suppression of information under the Ben Ali regime. This, he said, had left the Tunisian people in the dark: 'The Tunisian citizen does not know how decisions are taken. He does not know how to defend himself against the men of influence. He does not know how much a minister earns. Such simple matters' (T3, 7 April 2016). For Murad, the implication was that journalists should help ordinary men and women understand how the country works. They should use the insights they have acquired to educate the public.

We found a second form of interventionism among journalists who saw their role as strengthening and broadening democracy and fighting corruption in the elite. This is in line with global trends, where a lack of transparency has been found to be the single most important factor leading journalists to embrace an interventionist role (Hanitzsch et al. 2019: 193).

A certain segment of Tunisia's journalists entered their profession to continue the battle for dignity and justice they began in 2011. The revolution changed the career plans of some young people who saw journalism as a promising domain where they could strive to realise the power of the people. For example, Bilal, an e-media journalist, studied engineering prior to 2011 but recalled feeling a lack of motivation for that profession. 'When the revolution occurred, I had the opportunity to do what I wanted' (T14, 10 March 2018), he said. Journalists in independent, non-profit media are overrepresented among those who think of journalism as a conduit for grassroots pressure and a check on the elites. We also found sympathy for this position among Tunisian representatives in the international press corps. The e-journalist Sadiq described how the news website Nawaat worked in symbiosis with the civil society community in Tunis. The e-media outlet provided the NGOs with publicity, and in return, the organisations alerted Nawaat about issues to cover. He explained: 'Tunisia is not very big, especially the capital. The NGOs that work to improve the state's accountability help each other' (T9, 8 March 2018). In the conventional media, by contrast, it is rare to hear expressions of this critical activist ethos. Mainstream journalists will claim to advance the revolution's democratic ideal by educating the public. But they seldom express determination to deepen Tunisia's democracy through fighting corruption among the elite.

The third form of interventionist journalism we observed is practically oriented and aims to help citizens solve problems in their everyday lives. It builds on the idea that journalists can use their agenda-setting powers to unblock bottlenecks in the bureaucracy and help ordinary people vis-à-vis the state. Journalists who see this as their role could perhaps be characterised as a kind of 'service provider' because they seek to fulfil their audience's wishes (Meyen and Riesmeyer 2012). However, contrary to the common understanding of this label in the West (Hanusch 2019), these journalists extend their services beyond the domain of entertainment. Consider the following illustration.

Nadim, a radio host, invited us to attend one of his studio performances before our interview. He led a phone-in programme where people aired their everyday worries in the hope that the media might help. The programme consisted of two parts. The first was a legal consultation, in which listeners asked questions about the rules for issues like house renting and divorce and received advice from a legal expert. The second part of the programme was dedicated to bureaucratic hurdles. Nadim explained that, to prepare for the show, his team studied cases submitted by listeners to assess whether they were entitled to assistance. If they found that the person was being deprived of some right, they intervened and put pressure on the bureaucracy (T26, 22 November 2018). Nadim gave several examples of what he and his colleagues had achieved. In one instance, they mobilised support from the Minister of Health for an infant with a heart defect to undergo life-saving surgery outside Tunisia. They managed to have the Tunisian National Health Insurance Fund prioritise the case so that the operation could take place, and the child survived. Nadim stressed his belief that the media should help people by solving their practical problems. Elaborating on the idea behind the phone-in programme, he specified what he meant by helping:

> It's about speeding up things because we suffer from bureaucratic problems in Tunisia. We are there to catalyse. We have solved a lot of problems for people who apply to get connected to the electricity grid. It may take many weeks but goes faster when we intervene. We have also helped people in the remote areas get roads with proper quality. We call the governors and the local authorities. (T26, 22 November 2018)

In Nadim's experience, Tunisian journalists could serve as mediators between the state bureaucracy and citizens, intervening by mobilising their personal connections with politicians and officials. His programme became very popular, receiving hundreds of calls every week. Other radio stations had similar phone-in programmes. The popularity of such journalism was an indication of the state of the Tunisian bureaucracy as well as the media's potential for creating waves. This interventionist journalism can only work in contexts where the rational–legal authority is weak.

The disinterested informer

Many journalists disagree with the interventionist position, however. In the exchange quoted at the beginning of this section, 'Usman and Tamir argued against the view that journalists should take an educative role. They made the case that journalism is essentially about passing on accurate information. Moreover, Ihab, a journalism teacher at the university level, criticised Nasima for 'idealising the public'. For Ihab, the premise that Tunisian citizens look to the media for education was mistaken.

In our interview data, the disinterested ideal of neutrality and objectivity in journalism finds significant support. Several of our interviewees complained that there was 'too much noise' in Arab journalism. They saw a tendency for opinions to trump the value of both news and information. The television journalist Najim, for example, believed that journalistic work should be measured according to the ideals of balance, precision, non-partisanship and objectivity. For him, a good journalist was 'a mediator who relays but does not exert influence on the news, and gives people alternatives to choose from' (T34, 8 October 2019). Najim was concerned that the newfound liberty in Tunisia had led journalists to 'ride popular waves and overdo their zealousness'. He believed this got in the way of proper journalism, which should be governed by professional standards and the ethical code of the press:

> The journalist is not a hero and should not appear as one. Especially now, in the time of buzz [. . .] everybody thinks that he is some kind of news agency that relates news through the social media. This is not what is demanded from a journalist. He should be precise and relate news checked for its verity. (T34, 8 October 2019)

Najim warned that Tunisian journalism was at risk of losing the role of the illuminator and adopting the role of instigator instead, which he believed was a threat to both journalism and society. He perceived an urgent need to maintain a separation between fact and personal opinion.

The ideal of autonomy

The principle of separation applies to more than facts and opinions, however. Tunisian journalists, whether of the interventionist or disinterested persuasion, are wary of getting too cosy with politicians after decades in which the media functioned as the extended arm of the regime. Our interviewees strongly hewed to the ideal of journalistic autonomy. Tunisia is very different from Lebanon, where the system of political parallelism makes connections between journalism and politics an assumed and tacitly accepted feature. In Tunisia, journalists are expected to keep their political affiliations to themselves. Political neutrality is the norm, and most educators as well as the journalists' union push for it. A prominent news anchor summed up the prevailing wisdom as follows: 'A good journalist should never be influenced by other people's views' (T25, 21 November 2018).

Tunisian journalists are uncomfortable exposing their political connections. Such connections do exist, since Tunisia is, after all, a small country. The journalist and union representative Maymun admitted: 'To be honest, I have three or four friends in the current government. We have been friends for years. The government spokesman is my friend' (T32, 18 June 2019). Maymun nonetheless argued that the nature of relations between journalists and politicians was different in Tunisia than in Lebanon. When visiting Lebanon, he was surprised at how openly and closely Lebanese journalists cooperated with politicians. He personally preferred not to call his friends to obtain contacts or special information, because he felt more comfortable keeping some professional distance to those in power.

As journalism reinvented itself in the transition from Ben Ali's police state, the nature of journalists' relations with politicians also shifted. From a situation where journalists took orders and bribes, and fear accompanied any interaction with the regime, the relative strength of journalism grew, and journalists gained a certain leverage. Politicians could no longer take media subservience and support for granted. One of Tunisia's most prominent political talk show hosts commented: 'I have good relations with politicians. Some politicians consider themselves more important than journalists. But journalists have gained influence in the public sphere. So there is competition between them post-revolution' (T25, 21 November 2018). One veteran editor we interviewed in 2018 felt that politicians had actually started fearing journalists to some extent and noted approvingly that there were 'sometimes heated exchanges', 'mutual respect' and 'reasonable relations' between the two groups (T22, 20 November 2018).

However, other interviewees contested the depiction of journalists and politicians as actors on an equal footing and observed that, overall, Tunisian journalists were closer to politicians than they liked to say in public. A prominent news host explained that it had become a source of humiliation for journalists to spend time with politicians openly:

> I will tell you why journalists and politicians are discreet. They know that people have an eye on them. The Tunisians who have a good culture and follow politics do not tolerate informal interactions because they experienced it under Ben Ali. Spending time with politicians is a kind of humiliation for the journalists because we want to be transparent now. (T21, 19 November 2018)

Whatever their disagreements about the actual state of affairs, those we met agreed that journalists who are seen as mouthpieces for the government lose credibility and respect with their audiences. The reputational costs of collaborating with the centres of power can be high. Politicians and journalists alike must take heed of the fact that public opinion matters.

Post-revolutionary Realities and Tensions in the Journalistic Field

How does Tunisian journalists' perception of their role square with the realities in Tunisia after 2011? It is not an exaggeration to say that after the revolution, Tunisian journalism was born again after having died a slow death over decades of autocratic rule. The strong orientation towards autonomy that we have seen above went hand in hand with robust legislation and regulation to safeguard the freedom of expression and a pluralist public sphere. However, ghosts from the past continued to haunt the post-revolutionary media landscape, and the opportunities offered by a more open society could be used for good or ill. What happened when revolutionary aspirations and ideals met post-revolutionary realities?

Naturally, the revolution did not change Tunisia overnight. People who were part of the Ben Ali regime, including people who were responsible for arrests and torture, still populated the bureaucracy, and many corrupt businessmen escaped justice and continued to play important roles in the Tunisian economy. The verdict of one Tunisian media scholar in 2017 was that the revolution had been 'lenient towards the private media that acted as trumpets for the Ben Ali regime' (Hizawi 2017: 138). His assessment was in accord with many of our informants, who claimed that post-revolutionary politicians were not able or willing to pursue deep-rooted change. They succumbed to the great 'machine' which is the Tunisian bureaucracy, as one journalist put it (T14, 10 March 2018).

Let us start by looking at the experience of Hisham, a legal scholar who played a central role in reforming public media before being abruptly removed from his position by the government in 2015. He explained the difficulties of reforming the media system:

> Things won't change just because there are new laws. It is a more complicated question, concerning culture, mentality, practices, style, etc. [. . .] The media worked in tandem with the hegemonic political system and the security, so it was a media of one colour and one direction only [. . .] [with] a culture of loyalty and submission. It was difficult to change this mentality in a public institution that was the trumpet [*buq*] of the family of tyranny and dictatorship . . . people had been raised within the mentality of submission and obedience. (T47, 7 May 2018)

As the new director of a major public media outlet, Hisham saw both journalists and administrative staff react with astonishment when he talked about independence and neutrality in the public media. High-level officials had always had strong ties to political actors who gave them political cover and protection. People were used to a clientelist system, to searching for a political umbrella that would protect them, whether an individual or an organisation. In Hisham's experience, it was difficult to make them realise that they were expected to build a new, independent culture of neutrality, objectivity and professionalism. In his view, the public media establishment he was working to reform was still striving to achieve independence, because the political elite were not happy with a critical and objective media, and private media were to a great extent controlled by lobbies. Hisham remained in his leadership post for only a little more than a year before the government intervened directly to remove him. He believed the reason was his refusal to accept political meddling in editorial policies in the public media.

We met other public radio and television journalists who, like Hisham, were frustrated with the obscure, top-down processes by which directors were appointed, and who spoke of 'tension' within their organisations (T8, 7 March 2018; T19, 7 May 2018). Larbi Chouikha's account of the media transition shows that the country's first democratically elected government, dominated by the Islamist al-Nahda party, tried to impose its own candidates on several media organisations in 2011–12, without consulting with the sector first. This line of action engendered deep mistrust against the Islamist trend among journalists in the public media (Chouikha 2015: 85–6).

In other words, there was no neat fit between the ideal of free journalism and the political realities in the new Tunisia. The post-revolutionary situation presented journalists with difficult professional and moral choices regarding their role in the public sphere. Tunisian media professionals were arrayed on a continuum that ranged from those who rode the wave of instrumentalisation to those who fiercely resisted it. Let us look at this continuum.

Riding the wave

In Chapter 2, we used the example of the television channel Nisma and its owner Nabil Karoui to describe the instrumentalisation of private media. Karoui used Nisma to promote himself as a philanthropist, helping him reach to the second round of the presidential elections in 2019.

Seen from the outside, this is a clear case of media instrumentalisation, and Nisma has been targeted by the audiovisual regulator HAICA. In April 2019, HAICA forcibly and temporarily closed Nisma's editorial offices for failure to comply with the broadcasting law. It has also fined the channel for airing illegal political advertising. Journalists at other news organisations tend to be severely critical of Nisma. Anais, a reporter with a large network and long experience at a private radio station, claimed that Nisma peddled fake news and its journalists felt compelled to play along. She referred to a conflict between Karoui and the transparency NGO iWatch, which accused Karoui of tax evasion in 2017:

> There was an audio leak where you can hear how he demands that the journalists create a story to hurt the reputation of this NGO – he even demanded that they defamed the friends and families of the NGO workers in a very dirty way. [. . .] Some of my colleagues there have done this kind of work, and when I ask them why they have made this or that unprofessional report, they say that they are obliged (*mujbar*) to do it – they will find themselves without a job if they don't. (T33, 19 June 2019)

However, journalists we interviewed who worked for Nisma saw themselves quite differently: not as instruments of a media magnate, but as active participants in a media operation that defended the people against the elite. They talked about the channel in terms of advocacy journalism rather than instrumentalisation. Nadim, a prime time talk show host for Nisma, quit his job in public media precisely because he thought Nisma and other private media gave him greater freedom. Likewise, Fakhriya, a journalist and veteran of several news outlets, asserted that her ideal was critical journalism that gives ordinary citizens a voice. Nisma gave her the freedom she wanted as a journalist, and she did not feel that anybody controlled her. Both Nadim and Fakhriya took the politicisation of the entire media field for granted. There was no escape from working for some political interests and against others; it was just a question of which camp to join.

> There are owners and there are editorial offices. It's like that across the world. Why not accept it in Tunisia? [. . .] Nisma is a private channel that defends the people and is considered to be opposed to the government. But I ask people: have we ever spread fake news? No. [. . .] If I'm uncomfortable working for Nisma, I leave, that's all. (T26, 22 November 2018)

In an interventionist vein, Fakhriya prioritised what she saw as a progressive, liberal project over the ideal of neutrality. To her, HAICA was a tool used by the state to silence Nisma because the channel was close to the people. In this scheme of things, everything becomes political, making the idea of autonomous journalism a moot point.

Instrumentalisation goes hand in hand with corruption. During the roundtable we conducted with Tunisian journalists in 2019, corruption was a prominent issue. The participants observed that those who disregarded the ideal of autonomy often got the best jobs: '[They] are present in the forefront of the most popular programmes because they are [. . .] "instrumentalised"', as one of our interlocutors commented (Roundtable, Tunis, 26 January 2019). Luma, a journalist for the public broadcaster al-Wataniyya, put the matter simply: 'We all know that there are corrupt individuals on the media scene, who actually control the scene. This is part of the disagreements that exist in the sector' (Roundtable, Tunis, 25 January 2019). Luma's 'we all know' leaves little doubt about the journalists' awareness of the problem, and her views were echoed in several of our interviews. Officials of the National Syndicate of Tunisian Journalists as well as investigative reporters emphasised corruption and impunity as 'big problems' in the media, in business and in the state bureaucracy (T14, 10 March 2018; T32, 18 June 2019).

It is a symptom of widespread media instrumentalisation that corruption gets relatively little attention, considering how serious a problem it is for a young democracy. Since 2012, Tunisia has hovered around the middle of Transparency International's Corruption Perceptions Index, composed of 198 countries (2020). When Youssef Chahed was prime minister (2016–20), he called the fight against corruption a priority of his government. Media owners and influential businessmen, however, can easily suppress news about corruption in the private media. For example, in 2018, a public controversy arose when the government sought to lift the asset freeze on Marwan Mabruk, a Ben Ali-era businessman under investigation for corruption. Journalists in several private media were instructed by their owners not to cover the case. As one of them sardonically commented: '[Mabruk] happens to own four major commercial brands in Tunisia, including Monoprix and Orange, so he's an advertiser of the first degree. If the media had persisted, he might have stopped advertising' (T33, 19 June 2019).

Journalists are not always on the receiving end of corrupt practices, which adds to the seriousness of the problem. Some exploit connections established either before or after the fall of the Ben Ali regime to enrich themselves or obtain powerful positions in the media and outside it. Naturally, corruption is an issue shrouded in secrecy and rumour, but two high-profile examples indicate that journalism in the post-revolutionary period may be used to cover up rather than expose wrongdoing. The first is the example of the programme host and *chroniqueur* Samir al-Wafi. He has been apprehended on corruption charges several times since 2015 and has served time in prison, under suspicion of exploiting ties to a public official and accepting illicit gifts and privileges (Middle East Monitor 2017). Specifically, he was convicted for accepting a large sum of money from a businessman to help him obtain a license to sell alcohol in Tunisia. He has also been accused of offering to help a Ben Ali-era businessman evade charges – for a fee, of course. During all this time, he has remained a prominent political talk show host on two of

Tunisia's biggest private television channels, al-Hiwar al-Tunisi and Channel 9 (Tunisie numérique 2018).

Sometimes the dubious connections between politics, business and media can become almost a caricature of themselves, as in the adventures of the *chroniqueur* and political talk show host Burhan Busays. Busays was a familiar face during the old regime, since he defended it in pan-Arab media outlets such as the television channel al-Jazeera. After the revolution, he retreated from the public sphere because of his association with Ben Ali, but he reappeared in 2014 and relaunched his journalistic career. At first, he worked for Nisma, which was owned by Nabil Karoui. Karoui was at this time a prominent member of Nida Tunis, which gathered much of the pre-revolutionary elite. Just as Karoui left Nida Tunis to establish his own political party, Busays quit Nisma, citing disagreements with Karoui, and joined Channel 9, which had close ties to Prime Minister Youssef Chahed. Shortly thereafter, Busays was appointed party spokesman for none other than Nida Tunis. Then, in a dramatic turn of events, in 2018 Busays was arrested, tried and convicted for having held a fictitious position (while drawing a very real salary) in a telecommunications company for six years under the Ben Ali regime. After two months behind bars, he was pardoned by President Essebsi, who was incidentally also the founder of the Nida Tunis party. Essebsi did not state any reasons for the pardon, but merely cited his presidential privilege. Perhaps not completely by coincidence, all this happened at the height of a conflict between the president and the prime minister, Yusuf Chahed. The example of Busays is admittedly toward the more parodic end of the Tunisian media-politics scale but is nevertheless instructive as an indication of the lack of transparency in connections between journalists and politicians. Tellingly, one of the veteran journalists we interviewed referred to such practices as *labnana* – the 'Lebanonisation' – of Tunisian journalism. (T22, 20 November 2018)

Celebrities and entrepreneurs

> The political landscape that was created after [the elections in] 2014 was a very complex landscape for Tunisia, for the political actors and also for the media. We weren't really ready for the great plurality (*tanawwu'*). In addition, as a result of the lack of political experience, the political actors joined or created

alliances that we didn't understand at the time, or we didn't accept them, judging them unprincipled. The result of this was that a chasm appeared between the political community and the Tunisian society. Some journalists leaned towards the former, while others leaned towards the latter. New kinds of clientelist or mercantile relations (*'alaqat zabuniyya*) were created. This made the politicians and the media alike lose much of their glitter and the respect of public opinion. (T30, 17 June 2019)

These words belong to Murad, the veteran journalist and public figure, who tried to sum up the fraught relations between politics and journalism under Tunisia's new, democratic regime. Along with most other journalists, Murad was critical of instrumentalisation and blamed some of his colleagues for allying with a political current, a party or even individual politicians, thus becoming part of a propaganda apparatus rather than serving as critical watchdogs or information providers.

However, Murad himself was part of a controversial category of media professionals: the commentators, or *chroniqueurs*, as they are known in Tunisia. The *chroniqueurs* may be described as 'news celebrities', and they emerged along with the post-revolutionary media. Associated chiefly with television and radio, they are part of political and entertainment talk shows, where they comment on political and social affairs. They are relatively few (and most of them are men), but their importance far exceeds their small number, since they have access to many of the most popular spots on radio, television and print media. According to the programme host Shawqi at the television channel al-Hiwar al-Tunisi,

a good *chroniqueur* should comment, analyse and provide new information. He has precise information that we may not have. He uses information to confront guests and establish the truth about a subject. The most important thing is that the *chroniqueur* has a clear voice, is persuasive, and defends his ideas. (T5, 8 April 2016)

While this description evokes an image of independent, critical analysts, media funders expect such 'talking heads' to defend their political agendas, and some commentators willingly accept this tacit expectation; the above-mentioned Burhan Busays is a well-known *chroniqueur*.

But the role also allows for a measure of autonomy. As communication has become an ever more important part of the political game, so the market value for *chroniqueurs* has increased. During our research, we saw that well-known journalists could leverage their market value to secure more autonomy for themselves in the private media sector. Prominent media professionals could 'shop around' to secure the highest possible degree of independence for their own work. Experienced journalists who had made a name for themselves could leave one media outlet for another when they found their freedom unacceptably constrained. This was precisely the professional strategy Murad used to secure a prominent, yet independent role. He described his move from one of the big television channels (Nisma) to its competitor (al-Hiwar al-Tunisi) as follows:

> We transformed Nisma into a political channel. I was promoted until I became responsible for news. After a while the channel's position changed in a way that did not correspond to my convictions. So I left, and I engaged in a new experience to defend a modern society based on gender equality, the peaceful transfer of power and the right to disagree. (T3, 7 April 2016)

Journalists such as Murad often possess an entrepreneurial spirit, giving them multiple options in the media industry. Another of our interlocutors, Lamin, was both a journalist and the founder-owner of several companies. The latter occupation gave him enough financial leeway to simply quit a top job at Channel 9 when the channel's funders wanted him to support the prime minister:

> My previous collaborators are businessmen and the sponsors of the channel. We had some disagreement on the media's editorial line. Their economic interests were threatened because under my direction, Channel 9 was not aligned to the government. I can fully understand that my decisions caused trouble to my collaborators. They are businessmen and need to secure their income. (T24, 21 November 2018)

Lamin was soon contacted by another television company that wanted him to host his own programme on their channel.

'Shopping around' as Murad and Lamin describe, however, was a luxury only a minority could afford. For most Tunisian journalists, the fear of losing their job was their Achilles heel, which political actors could exploit. Journalists who struggle to make ends meet are vulnerable to corruption. Highly committed journalists solved this problem by escaping to the digital domain and establishing their own media outlets. We will return to them shortly. Suffice it to say here that a small segment of entrepreneurial and highly idealistic journalists were able to nurture their autonomy and, often, a critical impulse in their journalism. However, for the large majority who did not have access to foreign funding or alternative sources of income, it was very difficult to step outside the dependency relations that exist in the private as well as the state-owned media.

Disgruntlement of the rank and file

While the *chroniqueurs* enjoy the opportunity to play an influential public role, they belong to a dubious category in the eyes of most of their colleagues. The journalists we interviewed often criticised them for their connections to political actors and for constantly giving their opinion on every conceivable issue, as well as for their polarising style. They were not viewed as autonomous commentators; instead they were accused of exacerbating the phenomenon of instrumentalisation:

> [T]he *chroniqueurs* are trumpets (*abwaq*) for the politicians, and this is a real problem because they have great impact on public opinion. We are talking about a small group. When I watch the BBC, I find *chroniqueurs* who are political scientists, media scholars and the like. This is not the case in Tunisia. You find journalists who are good at talking – 'word-peddlers'. Suddenly they have become commentators. You turn on the radio at home and in the car, and there they are. You do the same in the evening, and the same persons are still talking. (T6, 6 March 2018)

Some journalists accused the *chroniqueurs* of being hired 'attack dogs' rather than analytical commentators and imposing their opinions on issues they knew little or nothing about (T14, 10 March 2018; T17, 4 May 2018). An editor for the national broadcaster al-Wataniyya summed up views expressed in many of our interviews when he criticised the 'cosy' relationship between the commentators and the political class: 'They might even be spokespersons for specific political parties. [. . .] When a *chroniqueur* becomes more like an official spokesman for the party of the owner of a channel, that's a real problem' (T34, 8 October 2019).

The veteran television journalist Najim took issue with the polarising style of many *chroniqueurs*. He argued that a commentator should present his views in an objective manner 'to clarify and explain the alternatives for people'. Around him, however, he described seeing 'media stars who scream and weep and make dramatic scenes and clashes'. There was, he regretted, a 'culture of the clash' (T34, 8 October 2019). Added to such criticism was the belief that these journalist celebrities earn easy money. This perceived injustice aroused anger in the journalist corps. Luma complained that a 'class division' had been created in the media:

> You have the stars who create and influence public opinion [. . .] those who work for a few hours and show up to deliver a message for certain agendas and then get huge sums of money [. . .] while the real journalists work day and night and are deprived of their economic rights. (Roundtable, Tunis, 25 January 2019)

Another journalist likened the media rank and file to the infantry in an army in which the commentators had the rank of 'generals'. He cited a well-known Tunisian proverb: 'Like soldiers of Zwawa, [we are] advancing in the battle line, but falling behind in payment' (Roundtable, Tunis, 26 January 2019). The Zwawa were fighters of Algerian Berber tribes that the Ottomans used as foot troops in Tunisia. Both examples point to a clash between ideals and realities in the profession. The 'real journalists', to use Luma's term, were paying the price.

In contrast to the 'real journalists', the *chroniqueurs* might appear more like media entrepreneurs and celebrities than journalists. It was not unusual for them to work for several different media organisations simultaneously. The host of one political talk show would appear regularly as a guest on another programme – not days but hours after his own show ended. Some of the most well-known talking heads often invited each other to various radio and television programmes, thus creating a small community of media professionals who knew each other well and constantly appeared in television and radio studios. Their own public personas even became news: search for the name of one of the well-known *chroniqueurs* in Tunisia, and you will find many news items about the latest spats/controversies/social happenings they have been involved in.

In a way, the post-revolutionary phenomenon of political commentary became a media ecosystem all by itself. A prominent example is that of Muhammad Bughallab, a Tunisian public radio journalist who has also worked as a *chroniqueur* for two of Tunisia's most important private media outlets, Shams FM and the television channel al-Hiwar al-Tunisi. On top of this, for a time he held a prominent position in Tunisia's *Cité de la culture*, a prestigious organisation for supporting music and the arts, owned by the Ministry of Culture. In the fall of 2019, Bughallab suddenly disappeared from his regular radio and television posts, and the Ministry of Culture terminated his contract, citing a law that makes it illegal for state employees to accumulate positions in private media. At the time, rumours circulated in the media that Bughallab had also been accused of corruption in his capacity as a Ministry of Culture official, but he was not convicted. After his acquittal, he was invited onto a colleague's television show, where he sat comfortably on a sofa talking about his hardships, in an appearance that underlined the celebrity status and camaraderie of prominent *chroniqueurs*. Bughallab's case is hardly unique. Reporting on the story, the news site Kapitalis laconically noted that accumulating positions in the private sector while working for the state has become 'a national sport in Tunisia' (Kapitalis 2019).

Resistance

Tunisia's post-revolutionary freedom of expression meant that disgruntlement with instrumentalisation, corruption and dubious professional practices was translated into public resistance on the collective and individual levels. Some of the most combative journalists were the young revolutionaries who worked for independent, online media. In April and May 2016, one of these media outlets, the aptly named Inkyfada, published a series of investigative articles on the Panama papers. The papers – leaked documents from a legal firm in Panama – were obtained by *Süddeutsche Zeitung*, which invited an international consortium of journalists to investigate the trove of information the papers contained about offshore companies and tax evasions (Inkyfada 2017). Inkyfada delved into the leaks relating to Tunisian affairs and created a stir in Tunisian media and politics. It soon became clear that the journalists posed a threat to some obscure networks of media, business and politics. Usama, who worked on the dossier, recounted the reactions they faced:

> When we had published the Panama papers [. . .] we were really in big shit. Everyone was after us, because we had touched the interests of the media advertisers. There was a campaign against us that you cannot imagine. They insulted us and said we were agents for the CIA, Israel, working against Islam, seeking to destabilise the country. (T11, 9 March 2018)

Usama and a colleague were invited to appear on the private television channel al-Hiwar al-Tunisi, where they confronted a hostile panel that attacked them for working for foreign interests and targeting specific individuals. Afterwards, however, they received a great deal of support from journalist colleagues:

> I made sure to explain what is a tax haven, what is tax evasion, and people started to understand that our work was not about throwing out names [. . .]. We gave the people the right to speak and defend themselves. [. . .] Many, many journalists were with us. They published supportive posts on Facebook and even organised a press conference on tax evasion, the Panama papers, the new independent media etc. [. . .] The syndicate of journalists published a statement with Reporters Without Borders (RSF) and Deutsche Welle and the International Federation of Journalists I believe, to defend us because we were really lynched. (T11, 9 March 2018)

Inkyfada nurtures a profile as provider of critical, investigative journalism, something which is in short supply in Tunisia – at the time of our research, only one privately owned television channel featured a programme based on investigative reporting, and the public broadcaster had no such programme (T13, 9 March 2018; T34, 8 October 2019). Inkyfada is part of the non-profit foundation al-Khatt (The Line), which comprises various media-related projects. It describes itself as a 'counterforce' and part of 'the alternative media' that 'challenges the dominant media flow, which does not reach the proper level of covering the situation we live in today' (Inkyfada, 2020).

The 'progenitor' of Inkyfada and the pioneer in critical journalism is Nawaat ('Kernel'), which was established as a blog collective in 2004 and operated illegally until after the revolution in 2011. It describes itself as an alternative to the 'dominant' media in Tunisia, and in its reporting and commentary it focuses on democracy, transparency, good governance, justice and citizen rights (Nawaat 2020). When confronting a state bureaucracy that is still close-minded and secretive, the strategy of Nawaat's journalists is to nag, expose unwillingness to release information, and cooperate with likeminded NGOs:

> [Nawaat] enjoys the sympathy and respect of many other organisations. Tunisia is not very big, especially the capital. The NGOs that work to improve the state's accountability help each other. We provide publicity. They alert us about things that happen and we rely on them in the quest for information. (T9, 8 March 2018)

Both Nawaat and Inkyfada avoid taking money from Tunisian sources and are partly funded by Western NGOs such as the Open Society Foundation and International Media Support instead. A sympathetic observer pointed out that critical reporting is upheld by these outlets as well as international journalists, because they are not beholden to Tunisian business interests and are thus 'a pain in the neck for the establishment' (T6, 6 March 2018).

Setting up an Internet-based media operation is comparatively cheap and easy, something that aids media entrepreneurs who are more interested in the message than the money. However, combative journalists are found in legacy media as well. Sami, an employee of a private pan-Arab television channel, entered journalism out of revolutionary zeal, because he saw men from the old regime returning to retake the reins of control. For him, media change was paramount, because he did not trust those raised under the old system to help the transition to democracy. Sami said there were many people like him:

> You'll find many others in Tunisia who invaded (*iqtahama*) – note the word – the field of journalism, practising it without an academic degree. We invaded the field with lots of zeal, then training came gradually afterwards, and the field opened to us. It opened to a new mentality coming from outside the narrow journalistic community. (T6, 6 March 2018)

Journalists like Sami are found across the media industry. The best-known is the *chroniqueur* Haytham Makki, who hosted the talk show *Le Midi* on the radio station Mosaïque for several years. Makki's lively and sarcastic style went hand in hand with a politically combative attitude and a strong sense of journalistic freedom. This earned him enemies among politicians. The leader of the Karama party called him a 'dog' live on air after he accused the party of toeing the line of the Islamist movement (Business News 2020). (Ironically, the name *karama* translates as both 'generosity' and 'dignity'.)

In the public media, too, journalists put up a fight against politicians who attempted to influence coverage. Musa, a senior editor at a state-owned newspaper, accused actors as various as the Islamist al-Nahda party and Prime Minister Youseuf Chahed of trying to control the editorial line of the newspaper when they were in power. In his interpretation of events, the government consciously underfunded his newspaper because of his independent, critical editorial policies:

> If I quit, the financial problems [of the newspaper] will be solved. This is due to the editorial line. [. . .] [W]e have financial troubles because of the media's editorial line. This is not against me as a person but due to my editorial line choices. (T27, 22 November 2018)

As employees working under state or private owners, critical journalists were obviously at a disadvantage in this struggle. However, Tunisian journalists wielded a weapon of resistance of which journalists in many other instrumentalised contexts are deprived: a professional syndicate with real power. The National Syndicate of Tunisian Journalists (SNJT) was independent-minded and combative even under the Ben Ali regime and earned its credentials when it broke with the regime in 2008. The head of SNJT, Naji Bughuri, estimated that there are about 2,000 journalists in Tunisia, and SNJT organises 1,400 of these. The syndicate considers it an important task to improve the standards of Tunisian journalism and fight for better working conditions: an environment that accepts and encourages press freedom, transparency in private media ownership structures, and a salary that enables journalists to get by with one job. It is a clear sign of SNJT's position in the media landscape that Bughuri's comments on media politics echo those of the independent media professionals we cited above:

Democracy and institutions today are decoration. Behind this is a culture of tyranny. As for the opposition, its culture is one of not accepting the other. Both the opposition and the government will crack down on journalism they don't like. There is a big difference between the rhetoric of democracy and the daily practice: Tunisia is in the yellow area, neither green nor red. (T40, 6 April 2016)

The SNJT headquarters in downtown Tunis is a lively hub of media and politics. They organise training sessions and debates on politics and the media, and when conflicts with politicians or media owners arise, SNJT officials can be seen surrounded by a throng of journalists, giving interviews to various media outlets about their position and grievances. SNJT's most important political role is to sound the alarm whenever it feels that the conditions of free journalism are being threatened. It has organised sit-ins when corrupt officials have been appointed directors of state-owned media, demonstrations against the harassment of journalists by security forces, and media campaigns against politicians and media owners who blatantly try to curtail press freedom. A particularly graphic example of its combative attitude was the huge banner draped over most of the building during an official visit by Saudi Arabia's strongman Muhammad bin Salman in November 2018. The Saudi regime was under heavy attack at the time, as its agents had killed the journalist Jamal Khashoggi inside the Saudi consulate in Istanbul and then dismembered the body. The banner made by the syndicate showed Muhammad bin Salman from behind, resting his hand on a giant chainsaw. The text above the image read: 'No to the sullying of revolutionary Tunisia's soil.'

SNJT was part and parcel of the revolutionary movement in Tunisia, and so it was naturally contested. Journalists associated with powerful business interests or politicians from the Ben Ali era were not enthusiastic about it, dismissing it as a politicised body, a tool for leftist forces. However, few would dispute that it had enabled Tunisian journalists to play a much more relevant role in society than they did previously.

Conclusion

Even as they debated whether to adopt an interventionist or neutral stance, Tunisian journalists were, in a sense, overtaken by events. Corrupt businessmen and politicians attempted to instrumentalise the media and some professionals played along, acquiring prominent positions as a result. As in many other transitioning countries, the conditions for journalism in post-revolutionary Tunisia are a mixed bag of opportunities and vulnerabilities (Høigilt and Selvik 2020). The newfound freedom of the press that lets journalists cover and comment on contested events is offset by job insecurity and contests over the new 'rules of the game'. An important asset in the struggle for critical, autonomous journalism is nonetheless the strong culture of independence that we have documented above on both the individual and the collective level. The revolution led a new generation of young, combative journalists into the profession and energised the SNJT and older journalists in public and private media. These forces were fierce protectors of journalists' professional integrity. In contrast to other countries where instrumentalisation of the media is rife, there was little cynicism to be found among Tunisian journalists; a spirit of earnestness pervaded most of the profession. The question is how long that spirit could last, faced with a political culture that encouraged instrumentalisation. One answer to this question is found in Lebanon, to which we now turn.

5

NAVIGATING A FIELD OF TENSIONS: JOURNALISM AND POLITICS IN LEBANON

In August 2011, when the popular uprising in Syria was at its peak, the left-leaning Lebanese journalist Khalid Saghiyah resigned in protest from his position as associate editor of the newspaper *al-Akhbar*, of which he was a founding member. A long-standing supporter of Hizbullah's resistance agenda (*al-muqawama*) and champion of the Arab left, he nonetheless broke with *al-Akhbar* over its negative coverage of the Syrian uprising (Dot-Pouillard 2012). Saghiyah stated that, although the cause of resistance was just, the time had come to support reform and democracy. As he put it, the revolutionary wave had shown that the Arab people's priority was 'freedom, dignity and bread' (Saghiyah 2011). Saghiyah found a new job as news manager at the centrist-right private TV station LBCI (Lebanese Broadcasting Corporation International) without relinquishing his political ideals. He used the channel as a platform to promote issues such as the conditions of workers, domestic violence, racism and human rights. In the fall of 2019, an aspiring revolutionary movement spread through Lebanon, and Saghiyah threw his experience behind it. He co-created the activist e-media platform Megaphone, which became a bellwether of the protests.

Khaled Saghiyah is a 'change agent' who puts journalism at the service of democratic aspirations. He is also one of the first Lebanese journalists we met. Saghiyah introduced us to a social activist strand of journalism, which resists the pull toward instrumentalisation. It defines itself through opposition with the journalists who speak for the country's politicians. Lebanon harbours a fascinating mix of such change agents and 'trumpets'. Many high-profile journalists are closely aligned with specific political blocs and positions. In the words of one veteran news editor, all the main political parties have journalists who 'speak in their name' (L13, 30 January 2018). Opposed to them one finds an undercurrent of activists like Saghiyah who openly challenge the powers that be (Hanitzsch 2007: 373). They made their mark in the 2019–20 protests, as we will show in Chapter 8, but were active in the media long before that.

In this chapter, we trace the existence of these opposing journalistic types to contrasting influences in the Lebanese media context and the choices individuals make. We combine an innovative perspective on the country's media system with sociological observations of how journalists navigate within it.

Instrumentalised Political Parallelism

The Lebanese media system is characterised by a combination of political parallelism and instrumentalisation. According to the media studies literature, these two phenomena push journalists in opposite directions. The concept of political parallelism refers to stable forms of media/politics connections that reproduce political cleavages within the media landscape. It manifests itself at the twin levels of content – 'the extent to which the different media reflect distinct political orientations' – and organisation – connections between media organisations and various parts of the political establishment, whether on the individual or the collective level (Hallin and Mancini 2004: 28). Hallin and Mancini argue that parallelism affects journalistic role expectations and practices. In systems characterised by alignment between the media and specific ideological, political and cultural views, the journalistic ideal is not to be a neutral provider of information but to actively defend a cause and influence public opinion. Political parallelism invites opinion journalism because journalists are expected to embrace a political project and report from a partisan perspective (Mancini 2012).

Political parallelism may be a democratic asset insofar as it creates a pluralism where elites rooted in different cultural, ideological and political articulations of society argue in the public sphere. Outside of Western liberal democracies, however, media instrumentalisation tends to accompany political parallelism.

Instrumentalisation undermines journalism's autonomy since journalists are, to one degree or another, coerced into clientelist relationships with powerful people (Roudakova 2008). The elites monopolise the public discourse and use media organisations and individual journalists to achieve their narrow aims. The result is a manipulated form of pluralism in which the space for negotiating different points of view disappears because spirited debate is replaced by attacks and counter-attacks. We call this situation *instrumentalised political parallelism* (Selvik and Høigilt 2021).

Journalism in Lebanon bears signs of these competing influences. As we explained in Chapter 2, the country has a history of both a 'journalism of views' and a 'journalism for hire'. On the one hand, the journalistic ideal has traditionally been to have a strong voice and sense of mission. The historical heroes of Lebanese journalism are figures like Samir Qasir and Ghassan Tuwayni, who combined professional integrity with political commitment; Qasir was a prominent leftist academic, while Tuwayni was a member of the Lebanese parliament. Their examples continue to inspire journalists who aspire to an active societal role today. On the other hand, the media ownership structure and prevalence of clientelism favour journalists who remain subservient to their political masters. The competition for work opportunities is stiff and 'connections' (*wasta* in Arabic) are required to enter the field. Currying favour with the rich and powerful is the easy way for journalists to succeed.

Political leaders also exert considerable control over journalists in Lebanon. Using informal influence in the media organisations, the security services and the state administration, they can reduce access to employment, airtime and information for journalists they dislike. Troublesome detractors become targets of repression. Political and business leaders rely on vague statutes in the criminal law to prosecute journalists, on thugs to attack individuals or entire media houses, or on security forces to systematically harass critical journalists – all of the above are well-documented tactics for silencing independent, critical coverage (Maharat Foundation 2019). A seasoned journalist summed up:

> The Lebanese journalist faces three obstacles to freedom. The first is the shortage of funding. Most journalists lack money, and those who have it have often

been bought. [. . .] The second is fear. They harass you on the phone, follow you to your home or distribute disinformation about you on social media. The political parties and the authorities . . . They ask why you criticise this and that. [. . .] The third is the instrumentalisation of your sectarian affiliation. They say your community is threatened and use it to push you. The community is like God: you cannot betray it. (L28, 5 March 2019)

Loyal interventionists and aspiring counterpowers

The media owners and politicians' leverage over journalists has resulted in partisan forms of interventionist journalism, in which journalists act as mouthpieces for groups or individuals within the political elite. Lebanese journalists are expected to advocate for the politically powerful, who decide or strongly influence the media organisations' editorial lines. There are many examples of such *loyal interventionists*, from a variety of media and political persuasions. To name a few that were prominent in the years we have focused on: the managing editor of the online newspaper *al-Mustaqbal*, Georges Bakasini, is a staunch supporter of Prime Minister Saad Hariri. He hosts a daily morning talk show on LBCI where he discusses political and security affairs. The *al-Nahar* journalist (and brother of veteran politician Marwan Hamadah) 'Ali Hamadah is also close to the prime minister. He was a confidant of the late Rafik Hariri and member of the Future Movement until 2020. Future is often described as the party of Lebanese Sunnis, but Bakasini is Christian and Hamadah is Druze. That is an asset for Saad Hariri, who, like all Lebanese politicians, is eager to demonstrate his national vision and appeal.

President Michel Aoun's party, the Free Patriotic Movement, has been represented by journalists such as Jean Aziz, Joseph Abu Fadil and Scarlett Haddad. The latter writes for the French-language Lebanese daily *L'Orient-Le Jour* and is a frequent guest on political talk shows on various channels. The fact that she is a woman, Christian and often defends the positions of Hizbullah (the president's strategic ally) increases her appeal on television. There are few women in the upper echelon of partisan interventionist journalism. Jean Aziz was a close aide and communication advisor to Aoun and the managing editor of OTV. However, he resigned in 2018 following a dispute with the president's adviser for international affairs (L'Orient-Le Jour, 2018) and has turned into a critic of the president. Joseph Abu Fadil has long been a fierce defender of the Free Patriotic Movement and its president Jubran Basil. In the context of the economic collapse that hit Lebanon in 2020–1, however, also he became more critical (Lazkani 2021). The Lebanese Forces, which competes for the Christian communities' votes, has its spokespersons as well. One of them is Charles Jabbur, who is called a 'freelance journalist' but who heads the Lebanese Forces' communications and media department. Toni Abi Najim, the editor-in-chief of the e-media outlet IMLebanon, is another.

Hizbullah can count on the support of many hard-hitting journalists. The CEO and editor-in-chief of the newspaper *al-Akhbar*, Ibrahim al-Amin, is a prominent voice. He does not speak as often on television as the above-mentioned commentators, but when he intervenes, observers of the Shi'a Islamist party listen carefully. Husayn Murtada is an al-Manar reporter who is famous for on-the-ground coverage of the Syrian war. He comments widely on geopolitical events and supports Hizbullah with passion. Murtada's opinions reach wide audiences: at the time of writing, he has 396.6K followers on Twitter. Another well-known example is Salim Zahran, who is controversial among some Lebanese because he is a Sunni Muslim who avidly supports Hizbullah and the Syrian regime. In keeping with the ethos of loyal interventionism, he has repeatedly attracted attention with statements that support the interests of these political actors.

An incident from 2018 illustrates how loyal interventionists are used in elite scuffles and how all actors are aware of it. In September of that year, in an interview with the Hizbullah-run television channel al-Manar, Zahran claimed that the emir of Kuwait (an enemy of Hizbullah and the Syrian regime) was under the heel of US President Donald Trump, who had allegedly forced the emir to cancel contracts with China. The emir and his Lebanese allies, including Lebanese Prime Minister-designate Saad Hariri, were incensed at this offense, and Hariri saw to it that the state prosecutor began investigating Zahran for defamation. (As an aside, this is an example of how politicians apply pressure to journalists. The Lebanese penal code includes several laws on defamation, and insulting a foreign head of state falls into that category, but these laws have historically been dormant. However, in recent years politicians have started making active use of these laws to silence voices they do not like [Human Rights Watch 2019].) The matter created something of a media stir in Lebanon. When Hizbullah leaders saw that

Zahran might have gone a bit too far, al-Manar quickly issued a statement saying that it was not responsible for and did not agree with all the comments of guests on its programmes. A report by the Lebanese news outlet Naharnet succinctly showed that all those concerned regarded Zahran's intervention as a political act on behalf of Hizbullah and the Syrian regime: Prime Minister-designate Saad Hariri condemned the remarks and tasked State Prosecutor Samir Hammud with probing the content of the interview. Kuwait's ambassador visited Hariri later in the day and stressed that Kuwait's relation with Lebanon would not be affected, while hinting that Zahran's backers had pushed him to voice such remarks (al-Nahar 2018).

Eventually, the case was quietly dropped; Hariri's intention was probably to send a message to Hizbullah and Zahran, and none of the competing elites in Lebanon would benefit from restricting the space for free expression too much. In fact, the politicians have an interest in letting journalists like Zahran continue to talk. Loyal interventionists enable them to influence the public debate and air controversial topics while maintaining an air of plausible deniability. As television journalist Nasim remarked, 'when Hizbullah talks about a scandal, people say "Hizbullah says that . . .". But when a journalist speaks about a specific political issue, it is only the journalist who says something' (L13, 30 January 2018).

Interventionism may be fuelled by political persuasion and ideology, as Shafiq, who writes for the Hizbullah-friendly newspaper *al-Akhbar*, illustrated. When asked about the role that journalists should play in society, he said: 'Here, in the Levant, the Mediterranean region, journalism is about contributing to rejecting the hostilities against our countries – economic, political or military. I cannot see a role for the journalist outside of a revolutionary frame' (L30, 7 March 2019). By 'revolutionary frame' Shafiq meant resistance against the regional agendas of the US, Israel and Saudi Arabia, a close fit with how the militia-cum-political party Hizbullah defines its rationale and mission. For as long as the Middle East is under US/Israeli occupation, and imperialism deprives Arabs and Muslims of genuine freedom, other concerns are secondary.

Conviction is not the only motive for loyal interventionism, however. Media instrumentalisation is a form of clientelism and therefore comes with special privileges. Journalists who prove their loyalty to politicians are rewarded with influence and responsibilities in the media organisations and may, for example, aspire to become news directors, as we explained in Chapter 3. Because their views correspond to the owners' opinions, all doors are open. Outright corruption is part of the picture, too. When talking to people familiar with the media landscape in Lebanon, one often hears caustic remarks about journalists whose living standard is far above the supposed level of their salary. Yusuf, a senior journalist with *al-Akhbar* told the following story:

> A colleague of mine was able to pay for his wedding through personal relations. He wrote nice articles about a few businessmen who then funded the wedding. How [. . .] can his friends and enemies respect him? [. . .] Then there is this journalist who was fired from a newspaper. One year later he was deputy editor in another news outlet and lived in a big, expensive house. How could he afford this? There is a lack of transparency here. (L32, 7 March 2019)

Few believe that journalists who live in expensive apartments and drive luxury cars have earned the money for them in honest ways. Some veterans are even more blunt than the leftist journalist we quote above; one print media journalist in his sixties described the relation between politicians and journalists as a relation between 'master and servant'. However, he then went on to relate a humorous story which suggests that servant-journalists do at least have some chutzpah:

> A journalist [who] owned one of the most important news magazines in Lebanon [. . .] used to criticise the United Arab Emirates under the rule of Shaykh Zayid. Zayid started funding the journalist, who then stopped criticising him. Once, the two met at a regional summit, and Zayid complained that the journalist did not publish any positive stories about the UAE. The journalist replied that he had received funding to stop criticising his rule but if he wanted him to praise the regime he would need to pay [more] for it! (L19, 9 May 2018)

The blatant instrumentalisation of journalism in Lebanon draws criticism from many media practitioners and prompts some to actively resist it. They profess belief that a journalist should be the citizen's voice against the political establishment and guard the public interest. Despite the 'journalism for hire' described above, there is high awareness of the rules and merits of professional journalism, thanks not least to a long tradition of media studies. Several Lebanese universities and colleges offer media studies programmes, the oldest of which was established in 1967. These programmes are all bilingual or even trilingual and strongly oriented toward professional values (Melki 2009). Instrumentalisation has not erased Lebanese journalists' convictions about what journalism *ought to be*. On the contrary, it nurtures the feeling that the present situation is wrong. Several of our interviewees expressed the belief that a journalist's responsibility is to reveal, denounce and prevent abuses of power, and – importantly – not only when these occur on the opposing political side. For example, Jamil at al-Jadid said:

> I belong to the school of thought that says that journalists should clash with the rulers. Our role is to be a strong force. According to the social contract, my role is to monitor on behalf of society. The more there is distance between me and the power holders and the security services the better, because it gives me a bigger room to constitute a strong force. (L29, 26 March 2019)

This public interest-inspired critique of loyal interventionist journalism illustrates the tensions in the Lebanese media environment and the contradictory impulses at work. Instrumentalised political parallelism entices journalists to be 'trumpets' for the politically powerful but also sparks a movement against this trend. As we explained in Chapter 1, journalists working in instrumentalised media systems are situated on two axes of political conflict simultaneously: one horizontal and the other vertical. The horizontal axis is the competition between various elites who seek to use the media (and by extension, journalism) to hurt their competitors and boost their own legitimacy in the eyes of the public. The vertical axis describes an unequal and conflictual relationship between the elites and the grassroots. Below, we analyse how journalists consciously play with these axes of conflict to carve out a professional space.

Journalistic Navigation

The opposing role orientations of journalists are intertwined with different ways of navigating the complex landscape of media and politics. In our interviews with Lebanese journalists, three navigation strategies stand out. The first is playing the relations game, the second is exploiting internal contradictions in the system and the third is connecting with popular grievances.

Playing the relations game

In countries characterised by political clientelism, the importance of 'knowing someone' – a power broker – is crucial. Social and professional life can be likened to a game in which the person who acquires the most influential connections wins. Journalists reduce their vulnerability to instrumentalisation by multiplying relationships with influential actors and activating them at the right moment. The need for connections is basically a weakness: journalists need political protection because they lack economic self-sufficiency and well-defined and enforced legal rights. 'A Lebanese journalist is unable to operate unless they have personal connections with politicians', affirmed one television presenter (L10, 31 January 2018). As the literature on political clientelism explains, clients seek protection from patrons in return for political support (Gellner and Waterbury 1977). However, in the context of a modern state and a complex media landscape, the number of potential patrons is high. Journalists may boost their relative strength by diversifying and counterbalancing political contacts.

Journalists are well placed to play the relations game for the simple reason that they know a lot of people. Over the years, they make contacts in different institutions and camps, which they mobilise for different purposes. By way of illustration, a popular writer in Beirut interchangeably works for different and competing Sunni Muslim politicians. It increases his room to manoeuvre because, if relations sour with one patron, he may switch to another. The same journalist also writes for a Saudi Arabian newspaper and has good contacts in that country. Since Saudi Arabia is the leading sponsor of Sunni Muslim politicians in Lebanon, his connections abroad increase his value in the eyes of Lebanese politicians (L27, 4 March 2019).

The relations game is part of how journalists operating under instrumentalised political parallelism exercise their profession. To access information, for example, personal contacts are a recipe for success. Sending a formal request to a ministry or another state organ will usually accomplish nothing.

A journalist with a leading newspaper explained how he gets around this obstacle:

> You can build special relations with people in the security services and the judiciary to get access to information. You can create a personal network of informants. You provide them with services such as helping someone enter the hospital, helping someone cross the border. You offer such favours knowing that this person will help you access information. You may, for instance, know the minister of health and give him a call about someone who needs to get his daughter to hospital. (L11, 29 January 2018)

Social connections mean influence. Taking advantage of their social capital, journalists may turn the clientelist system to their benefit. In the above example, the journalist trades information and services. Sometimes, a mere reputation for being connected to powerful persons is enough to get things done. At other times, the ability to push an institution or person unwillingly into the spotlight is a lever that journalists can use. Where corruption and mismanagement are common, attracting the public's attention is a credible threat. The journalist quoted above was frank about why the minister was likely to comply with his wishes:

> Let me tell you how it works. When I call the minister of health to ask him to open the hospital's door to a person that I know, I say, 'You have to take him in now, otherwise I will send someone to do a report about them'. (L11, 29 January 2018).

Exploiting internal contradictions in the system

The internal contradictions that accompany instrumentalised political parallelism give journalists another tool to play with. In countries where clientelism and political parallelism coexist, the state is often as divided as society. Lebanon is an extreme example because its confessional power-sharing system gives each sect a foothold in the administrative apparatus. A journalist with more than twenty years' experience explained:

> The irony is that because we have a sectarian system and because society is so polarised and there is so much division based on sect and each sect has its

own institutions, its own media, there is no one single [authority] or autocrat that is running it. This is a positive thing that comes out of this! (L22, 20 October 2018)

State fragmentation opens up opportunities for journalists to either ally themselves with one of the feuding parties or carve out a space to operate in between them. By way of example, let us return to Salim Zahran, the loyal interventionist who attacked the emir of Kuwait. Zahran supports Hizbullah and, by extension, Hizbullah's friends in the Syrian and Iranian regimes. He regularly appears on Hizbullah's channel, al-Manar, and he writes for the pro-Iranian website al-Mayadin. He is, however, not a party member but rather an enterprising journalist concerned with building a career, as is evident from his frequently updated personal website, complete with biography, profile and a news archive that includes all his media appearances (salemzahran.com). His loyal support for Hizbullah provides him with a platform that increases his public visibility. Even more important, it gives him the protection he needs to criticise his self-proclaimed enemy: Sunni Islamism, whether in the guise of ultraconservative Salafism or the modernist Muslim Brothers. When he wishes to create a stir, as he did with his comments about the emir of Kuwait, he can count on Hizbullah and its allies to protect him from serious consequences, as long as he does not go too far. Thus, nothing came of the state prosecutor's investigation of Zahran after his allegedly defamatory statements about the Kuwaiti emir.

There are several possibilities for journalists who seek wiggle room in horizontal conflicts. For instance, there are at least five parallel intelligence agencies, controlled by opposing identity groups (Rabah 2016). These agencies are charged with overseeing security developments in their own camp, but at the same time compete and spy on each other. Journalists are important sources of information for the intelligence agencies. Some have a reputation of working for the agencies directly. Co-opted journalists are made party to sensitive issues and serve as the agencies' mouthpieces. Others deal with the agencies on a case-by-case basis. In any given case, there may be overlap between the agenda of the journalist and that of the agency, as one part of the state may approve of the journalist digging up dirt about another. Such contradictions open a space for journalistic navigation, but this also requires journalists to walk a tightrope between different actors with the power to disrupt their professional and private lives. As an investigative journalist explained:

> I once obtained the file of an MP involved in providing weapons for the [Sunni Muslim] armed opposition in Syria. I published it. I received threats. I also exposed corrupt Shi'a Muslim leaders. I wrote about them and received threats. They said they would throw me from the sixth floor of a building and many other things. [. . .] I have been exposed to a lot of strain and threats. Nevertheless, I continue to find openings. If one side closes the door to you, another opens. It's always like that. You have to play on the contradictions. (L11, 29 January 2018)

Enterprising journalists have also learned to exploit weaknesses inside the state institutions. Identifying disloyal servants is their favoured way to proceed. One senior journalist described finding leaks in the bureaucracy as 'easy', explaining that it only required a network of informants and a bit of money:

> I can choose someone who works in a ministry. Let's say that this person serves drinks and food to people who attend meetings. I can ask the person to collect the papers and documents that were left by participants in the meeting. It is so simple. Journalists have different sources who have different positions and are paid according to their status. (L19, 9 May 2018)

Other interviewees confirmed and expressed no anguish about paying for such services. 'We commit a small crime to uncover big ones', was the standard reply. They rhetorically asked what the alternative would be. Jamil specialises in corruption cases and put the blame on the politicians, saying: 'They have created the chaos and must bear responsibility for that' (L29, 6 March 2019).

Connecting with popular grievances

The third strategy is to connect with popular grievances. Journalists may increase their relative strength by raising questions and agendas that pit ordinary people against the elite. In democracies, the ability to ignite public anger is the journalists' ultimate crowbar against the decision-makers.

Under instrumentalised political parallelism, the politically powerful use clientelism and polarisation to reduce the efficacy of this tool. Clientelism constrains journalists because it is costly to criticise 'the hand that feeds you'. Polarisation creates opportunities for the politically powerful to reframe and dismiss criticism of their governance as an attack by 'them' on 'us'. Nonetheless, the politicians' survival strategies do not erase the rank and file's grievances. On the contrary, they help perpetuate corruption and mismanagement and thereby increase societal frustration in the long term. An abyss of distrust separates the elites from Lebanese commoners who must live with the consequences of political wheeling and dealing (Dajani 2019: 107–9).

Journalists may connect with this vertical conflict to challenge the elites, not least on the issue of corruption. A television reporter who self-identified with civil society and worked with a hidden camera for six years said:

> [A]t that time very few journalists worked that way. I worked undercover to shed light on many things, like the municipal elections [in 2018] during which I sold my vote and recorded the operation. Many people were jailed following that [. . .] I confront every problem in society, report on it and denounce it. I report on corruption and fight against it as my mission, and I do it every day. (L25, 20 October 2018)

Whether or not a journalist is willing and able to defy the barriers of clientelism and polarisation depends on the person, the issue and the situation. Personal disposition plays an important role. Some individuals are more courageous or more driven than others to confront abuses of power. Some are driven by ideology and some get energised by going against the flow. The nature of the issue also impacts the room for manoeuvre. Certain themes are prone to getting stuck in sectarian politics: media discourse in Lebanon tends to be polarised when it comes to stories about identity and hegemony and more neutral in the socioeconomic realm (Fawaz 2013). Security-related themes are inherently sensitive, making scrutiny of the military, security services or Hizbullah a high-wire act. Corruption, too, becomes a bombshell issue when connected with specific names, parties, and institutions. Referring to the example of a Lebanese actor who spent five months in jail based on fabricated accusations that he had cooperated with Israel, an online journalist explained:

> Corruption is a very risky topic. I can report on an event like the accusation of the Lebanese actor Ziyad 'Itani [. . .] but I cannot criticise the people who saw to it that he was arrested. If I investigate and discover that the chief of police who arrested 'Itani is corrupt and protected by some politician, I cannot publish this because I would risk my life. (L19, 9 May 2018)

The situation or circumstances in which journalists seek to connect with the power of the grassroots also impact the likelihood of success. In periods of public protests or active civil society mobilisation, the effectiveness of playing the vertical conflict 'card' increases.

Illustrative Case Studies

We will now look at two empirical examples in which journalists tried to disrupt control by politicians over the flow of information. In the first example, a journalist acted upon grassroots-level discontent with the leadership within the Sunni community. The political elite damped down polarisation and succeeded in marginalising the journalist. In the second example, journalists from across the board mobilised under a cross-sectarian agenda and managed to put the political establishment under considerable strain.

Between jihadis and Hizbullah

The first story relates to Lebanon's entanglement in the Syrian war, and more specifically a prisoner swap in late 2015 between the al-Qa'ida-affiliated Syrian militia Jabhat al-Nusra (the Nusra Front) and the Lebanese army. In early August 2014, warriors of the Nusra Front and the Islamic State (IS) laid siege to the Lebanese town of Arsal on the northeast border with Syria following the arrest of a Syrian militia commander loyal to the IS. They clashed with the Lebanese Armed Forces (LAF), resulting in the death of 117 soldiers, militants and civilians. When they retreated into Syria, the fighters took captive some twenty-nine Lebanese soldiers and police officers. This was the beginning of a protracted hostage crisis, which also became a media event: for example, IS warriors beheaded a Lebanese soldier to build up its 'theater of terror' (Weimann and Winn 1994). As the fate of the remaining soldiers was negotiated, the Lebanese public held its breath.

The abduction threatened more than the lives of the individual hostages. It also put the domestic stability of Lebanon at risk. Since 2011, the Syrian uprising and war had been a source of mounting tensions in Lebanon. Many Lebanese, not least the Sunnis among them, sympathised with the revolt against the repressive regime in Damascus. At the same time, the powerful Lebanese Shi'a Muslim Hizbullah militia, a long-time ally of the Syrian regime, had entered the war on Bashar al-Asad's side. It was not implausible to interpret the Arsal crisis as a showdown not between the Sunni jihadis and the Lebanese state, but between the jihadis and Hizbullah. The Nusra Front fighters used the hapless soldiers of the Lebanese army as pawns to extract concessions from Bashar al-Asad's Lebanese allies.

The Sunni Muslim and Christian political elites that were normally fierce opponents of Hizbullah could not afford to interpret the situation this way, however. If they articulated the strong tension between the Sunni grassroots and Hizbullah, they risked igniting an open sectarian confrontation that might destabilise Lebanon and endanger their own political and economic interests. In addition, no Lebanese politician takes attacks on the military lightly, because the army is a national symbol amidst a welter of sectarian power games. Conscripts and officers from all religious communities serve side by side, standing as proof of unity in diversity. This symbolic function assumed greater salience than usual in the tense domestic climate after the outbreak of the Syrian war. Hence, all the elites agreed to lay their differences aside and treat the crisis as an attack on the Lebanese army and Lebanese sovereignty, demonising the Nusra Front as wild-eyed and bloodthirsty fanatics rather than rational actors involved in a game of extortion where the stakes were war prisoners on both sides (Gade and Moussa 2017).

In early December 2015, following sixteen months of difficult negotiations, a swap deal was reached between the Lebanese government and the Nusra Front, brokered by Qatar. The deal entailed the release of sixteen Lebanese servicemen in exchange for thirteen prisoners affiliated with the jihadi group, including the ex-wife and the daughter of IS 'caliph' Abu Bakr al-Baghdadi.

This event was a golden opportunity for Raghib, a Muslim journalist at the Christian-owned commercial television channel MTV. MTV opposed the Christian–Shi'a alliance between President Aoun and Hizbullah, and by extension also the Syrian regime. Raghib had started working for the channel as his own attitude to Syria and Hizbullah grew progressively more critical after the outbreak of the Syrian war. He had a background in religious studies and was closely familiar with the religious ideology and reasoning of the jihadis. Moreover, he had earned credibility among them through critical reporting on the Syrian war. Raghib was committed to showing the polarised reality of Lebanese attitudes to the Syrian war. He affirmed that he flew the flag of objective reporting high:

> The journalist's role is to simply describe, not to judge or argue a point of view. [. . .] As a journalist I don't belong to anyone. If I get a chance to interview the leader of Hizbullah or even Syrian president Bashar al-Asad, I would be happy to do it. But these people always want the media to be either with or against them. This is a mistake. [. . .] Journalism is about passing on the truth. (L9, 27 January 2018)

Raghib believed that journalists should show the facts as they are and act as a check on the authorities. If, in addition, he could get a scoop out of it, so much the better. He played the relations game to his advantage. MTV had given him the green light to cover news about the Nusra Front first hand. He had nurtured contacts with the media office of the militia for some time, and when the date for the prisoner swap drew near, they approached him and invited him to cover the event from their side – the only Lebanese journalist allowed to do so. This was obviously a scoop both for Raghib and for his employer, MTV. In addition, MTV's owners and leadership were happy to support a take on the swap that undermined Hizbullah's wish to depict the jihadis as the ultimate evil and threat against Lebanon.

On the day of the swap, the entire country sat glued to their screens. Before the cameras of Raghib and a team from al-Jazeera, the Nusra Front seized the opportunity to appear as professional warriors concerned with the welfare of not only ordinary Syrians, but also their Lebanese prisoners. The Lebanese soldiers were even recorded thanking their captors for treating them well. This was in stark contrast to the image of wild-eyed fanatics out to attack the entire Lebanese nation.

Raghib shared the view of many Lebanese journalists that the soldiers and the Lebanese army, in general, were the victims of the games played by the Lebanese elites and the Syrian regime. According to this logic, if Hizbullah had not intervened in the Syrian war and started attacking the jihadis, they would never have come to Lebanon in the first place and there would have been no casualties or hostages from the Lebanese army. Raghib sought to connect with a vertical axis of conflict between ordinary Sunni Muslims, who supported the enemies of Syrian president al-Asad, and the Sunni elite, who kept silent about al-Asad and Hizbullah's warfare against a Sunni-dominated Syrian opposition. He knew that many among the Sunni population of Lebanon did not perceive the Nusra Front as the enemy of Lebanon, but as the enemy of the Syrian regime and Hizbullah, which they detested.

Raghib's coverage of the prisoner swap contributed to a narrative about the Nusra Front not as a terrorist organisation, but as a civilised resistance group that served the interests of ordinary Syrians caught in a war. This narrative undoubtedly appealed to many ordinary Sunni Lebanese who deeply distrusted Hizbullah. However, in the view of Hizbullah loyalists and large parts of the Lebanese political elite, Raghib had gone too far in challenging the narrative about a united Lebanese nation facing bloodthirsty jihadi terrorists. The safety net he had woven by playing the relations game, exploiting political contradictions and connecting with the vertical axis of conflict, proved to be too weak to protect him against the onslaught that followed the prisoner swap report. In Lebanon's most important newspaper, *al-Akhbar*, fellow journalist Zaynab Hawi severely criticised Raghib's lack of critical distance in his reporting and described him as a propaganda 'hostage' of the Nusra Front (Hawi 2015). In the social media sphere, he was given the unflattering moniker of 'the official spokesman for terrorism'. The Hizbullah-affiliated television channel al-Manar went further: the host of the popular political talk show *Talk of the Hour* raised the question of whether Raghib might have committed treason against the Lebanese state by covering the prisoner swap from the jihadi side while they were occupying Lebanese land (*Hadith al-Sa'a* [*Talk of the Hour*] 2015). Such attacks from other journalists rendered visible a fact that most were very reluctant to discuss: that Lebanese were deeply divided on the issue of the Syrian war and Hizbullah's involvement in it. Open conflict on this issue was more than the Lebanese elites were prepared to accept. The Sunni leaders needed religious polarisation to be dialled down in order not to escalate tensions with Hizbullah, and attempts to portray the jihadis fighting Hizbullah in a more flattering light were not compatible with this. Hizbullah, for its part, could not tolerate that its narrative of being Lebanon's first line of defence against jihadist terrorists was being challenged. In other words, the media attacks on Raghib's coverage had strong political backing, and not long after the prisoner swap, his employer MTV was pressured to fire him, allegedly by Hizbullah. Raghib went overnight from an omnipresent figure on the country's television screens to a marginalised figure in the Lebanese media landscape. He had given voice to the silenced sentiments among many on the Sunni Lebanese grassroots, but at the cost of his own career, as the political elites saw to it that he was silenced. By actively engaging with the Nusra Front he entered a landscape that proved too difficult to navigate successfully.

You Stink

In July and August 2015, thousands of Lebanese from different religious and socioeconomic groups demonstrated in downtown Beirut to express their anger at garbage piling up in the streets (Abu-Rish 2016). A deadlock between Lebanon's sectarian leaders had paralysed the entire political system, so that the government had failed to renew its contract with the private garbage collector. The thousands who poured into the streets were angry not only about the garbage, but also about the general corruption and ineptness of the government, and because they felt the elites treated them like clients in a pyramid of power, or pawns in a political game, rather than like citizens. They soon began demanding an end to corruption, the holding of parliamentary elections and the resignation of the minister of environmental affairs. The demands amounted to 'nothing less than a radical reformation of the entrenched, sectarian, political system' (Kraidy 2016: 23). The political elites went into alarm mode and started smearing protesters in the media they controlled. Elite wrangling gave way to a cross-confessional effort to silence the grassroots protests, including the use of batons, water cannons and arbitrary detentions. All the while, political leaders across the spectrum did their best to discredit the protesters, suggesting that they were acting at the behest of foreign governments or that they were somehow immoral.

However, individual journalists and some news organisations chose to connect with the vertical axis of conflict (al-Jurayjiri and al-Shaluhi 2017). The crisis unequivocally showed the chasm between a self-serving political elite and ordinary citizens of all faiths, and both LBCI and al-Jadid covered the protests comprehensively during the first two weeks, airing embarrassing footage of the mistreatment of ordinary people by security forces. As a result, the state turned on the media. On 22 August, al-Jadid reporter Nawal Birri was injured when security personnel threw chairs at her. The following day a reporter from LBCI was attacked and beaten by security forces live on air as she was covering the protests from the perspective of the demonstrators. At least eight journalists were assaulted by security personnel during these two days alone (Committee to Protect Journalists 2015; 'LBCI' 2015).

The You Stink protests shook the establishment. As one analyst put it at the time, the protests were 'the beginning of a very slow process where you start chipping away at the ideological hegemony of the sectarian system' (Blanford 2015). To understand why the journalists who defied the elites during the garbage crisis were more successful than Raghib in the example above, three differences are essential to note. First, as we have explained, it is easier to mobilise cross-sectarian grassroots support on socio-economic problems than on security issues like jihadis and Hizbullah, which are sensitive and highly polarising. Second, the support of media organisations during the You Stink protests made a huge difference. LBCI and al-Jadid made a strategic choice to cover the garbage crisis. These two channels had branded themselves as critics of the system of sectarian power sharing and supporters of civil society, although their owners had their own political agendas.[1] In contrast, MTV bowed to pressure from the political establishment and threw Raghib under the bus. Third, the situations in which journalists tried

---

[1] The owner of al-Jadid is described as a 'rival' of the powerful Sunni Muslim Hariri family and is supported by the Qatari regime (El-Richani 2016: 76). As for LBCI, despite the pluralism of its staff it retains a 'sectarian and political inclination' associated with the Maronite Christian sect and a former Christian militia known as the Lebanese Forces (El-Richani 2016: 93; Nötzold, 2009: 147).

to connect with vertical grievances were radically different. During You Stink, journalists were both acting together and – crucially – amplifying an existing social movement. Raghib was acting on his own in trying to generate grassroots pressure. For all these reasons, the journalists' leverage vis-à-vis the politicians was considerably stronger in the You Stink case. But both examples speak to the potential for political disruption when journalists break with the elite-managed horizontal, sectarian polarisation and connect with a vertical conflict axis of citizens vs politicians instead.

Conclusion

To return to our conceptual starting point, political parallelism in Lebanon is instrumentalised because it works as a self-serving tool for the elite. Corrupt state leaders use media polarisation to distract attention from the shortcomings of their governance in a convoluted strategy of 'divide and rule'. Sociologically speaking, instrumentalised political parallelism works as a mutually beneficial arrangement between media owners and co-opted journalists. In this sense, the Lebanese media context is similar to that of post-1990 Russia, where journalists came to be regarded as 'prostitutes' for the political elites (Roudakova 2009; 2017).

Nonetheless, while instrumentalisation exerts a strong pressure on journalists, our findings suggest that journalists find professional elbow room. Their strategies are adapted to the context in which they operate and the specific mix of horizontal and vertical conflicts that apply. We found three main ways for journalists to navigate vis-à-vis politicians. They may play the relations game, exploit the internal contradictions in the system, and connect with vertical grievances. Playing the relations game and exploiting internal contradictions integrate and comply with the system of clientelism, although the power dynamics are reversed. The strategy of connecting with popular grievances is potentially more disruptive to the system.

The navigation strategies we have described in this chapter are normally accommodated within the political system, but in Raghib's case they did not work. Why? The Lebanese elites are often at odds over positions and policies, and so critical journalists can raise contentious issues. However, when the elites close ranks, as happened in the Arsal crisis, journalistic freedom is constrained. At such times journalists are deprived of the political protection that normally comes with working for a sectarian-based media outlet. A well-known television journalist who has walked the tightrope of journalistic navigation for many years put it succinctly: '[W]hen [the elites] are polarised the truth is saved . . . and when [they] are united, the truth is killed. That's the Lebanese case' (L22, 20 October 2018).

This is a rather bleak assertion, but the interesting question is how long such a situation can last. We have shown that the system of instrumentalised political parallelism is prone to instability. This is due, first, to the coexistence of opposing journalistic ideals and the tensions between many journalists and the elites who seek to instrumentalise them. Second, the latent conflicts between the grassroots and the elite represent an opportunity for media institutions and individual journalists. To the extent that important media organisations and individual journalists reject the entire game of instrumentalising political parallelism and instead latch on to the grievances of the grassroots, they can raise a serious challenge to the elites' communication strategy. This brings us back to Khalid Saghiyah, with whom we started this chapter. In 2019, Lebanon was rocked by contentious events that enabled Saghiyah and many of his colleagues to reconfigure the news media scene in Lebanon and shake the system of instrumentalised political parallelism to its core. We will analyse how this played out in Chapter 8.

6

NATIONAL SECURITY AND FREE SPEECH IN TUNISIA

It is a general dilemma in politics that the values of freedom and pluralism may collide with a regime's need to maintain security and stability. A prime example of this is the controversy around the Patriot Act in the United States in the aftermath of the 9/11 terror attacks on the World Trade Center and the Pentagon. The act gave the security establishment more prerogatives, and conservative libertarians and liberal leftists alike feared that individual rights, including the right to free speech, would be trampled on as a result (Etzioni 2005). The Patriot Act is a vivid example of how the right to free speech may clash with the need for security, but it is far from unique. The media in democratic states has at times relinquished some of its freedom in order to support the state's struggle against terrorism (for example, in West Germany during the terror campaign of the Red Army Faction in the 1970s); and whistleblowers such as Edward Snowden and Wikileaks have been prosecuted for leaking information that the state regards as sensitive for national security, but proves that governments breach their own laws pertaining to the freedom of speech (Nacos 2016: 173–90).

If established democracies are sometimes willing to jeopardise the right to free speech in the interest of national security, how does the tension between security and rights play out in countries where people are in the process of negotiating the rules of the democratic game? And not least: what wider political consequences does that tension have? Tunisia's most important gain from the revolution was perhaps freedom of expression. Journalists were given unprecedented space to act as interpreters of current affairs and arbitrators in public debate. However, press freedom and pluralism are brittle gains, always threatened by political forces that would like to control the public sphere as much as possible.

While we were doing the research for this book, the fragility of freedom and pluralism was highlighted by a dramatic event and what happened in its aftermath. On 18 March 2015, three Islamist terrorists infiltrated downtown Tunis, entered the Bardo Museum and killed nineteen tourists, one Tunisian citizen and one policeman. The attack was the first large-scale terrorism incident in Tunisia after the 2011 revolution, and it happened amid a political transition process fraught with crises. Soon afterwards, terrorists attacked again at the beach resort of Soussa, killing thirty-nine people.

In this chapter, we delve into the debate after the first attack, on the Bardo Museum, to tease out the connections between hybrid politics, security and press freedom. At the time, the Tunisian media sector itself was in the throes of change, as journalists and other media professionals were trying to come to terms with unprecedented freedom of expression and urgent questions of professional identity and political role. We investigate how Tunisian journalists managed the tension between a heightened sense of insecurity and the country's uncertain democratic development after the attack. The Bardo attack proved to have wider implications for Tunisia's transition, as the democratisation process was challenged by securitisation and a so-called 'authoritarian drift'. Shortly after the attack, President Beji Qaid Essebsi made a call for 'national reconciliation' and introduced a draft anti-terror bill. In hindsight, both initiatives have proven to impede Tunisia's path towards an open and inclusive society. The 'administrative reconciliation law' voted in September 2017 contradicted the ongoing process of transitional justice by letting corrupt businesspeople and state officials from the Ben Ali era off the hook. The anti-terror law, introduced a week after the attack and adopted by the national assembly in October 2015, gave security forces increased license to harass and attack journalists, as we will show in this chapter. Did journalists pose a counterbalance to the elite's authoritarian drift? Did they critically reflect on the acute social and political tensions that made Tunisia so vulnerable to attempts at political destabilisation? And how did they react to the infringements on press freedom in the years after 2015? In the following, we present a detailed study of the journalistic discourse in newspapers and television programmes just after the Bardo attack. The main focus is on how journalists interpreted the causes of terrorism, and how they contributed to the public debate about countering it. We end the chapter by explaining how the fraught relationship between the right to free speech and appeals to national security affected press–politics dynamics after 2015.

Terrorism, Media and Political Stability

The Bardo incident was an instance of what Cottle (2006a: 421) calls a *mediatised disaster* – an exceptional phenomenon that serves to sustain or mobilise collective sentiments and solidarities, often in ways that disrupt the political process. In a crisis or disaster that catches the government off guard, the media typically assumes a position of enhanced importance as the public seeks reassurance. In such a situation, journalism becomes an important point of reference to make sense of what is going on; journalists become interpreters on behalf of collectivities. Journalists' ways of explaining the issue and informing public debate 'variously sustain a subjunctive orientation to the "social good" (of how society could or should be)' (Cottle 2006a: 411). In transitional contexts, where there is uncertainty about the shape of the emerging political order, the shock provoked by an exceptional event may raise fundamental questions about the social good and the national interest. When revolution throws society into chaos and upsets people's habitual interpretive frameworks, the media's ability to shape public consciousness increases (Voltmer and Rawnsley 2009: 234–5).

However, existing research about terrorism and the media has little to say about transitional contexts in general and the Middle East and North Africa in particular, and those that do treat it tend to focus on structural properties of the media–politics nexus (Eickelman 2004). Most of the media and terrorism literature is informed by international terrorism and responses by Western countries, 9/11 being the defining case. One core concern in this literature is that corporate media with close ties to governments become 'cheerleaders' for a 'war on terrorism' or uncritical transmitters of various policies couched in such terms (Hess and Kalb 2003: 10–13; Kellner 2015: 65; Lewis and Reese 2009; Nichols 2005). Analysing the coverage of terrorism in a transitional context opens our view to the potential agency of journalists more than the critical research about Western media allows for. In transitional periods, the media system is typically less defined and the power of corporations over it less strong. At these times, as Voltmer notes, individual journalistic agency is important: what is needed, but rarely available, in such processes is moral leadership by media actors who can influence political culture in ways that are conducive to peaceful deliberation (Voltmer 2013: 38). By focusing on the discourse of influential journalists after the Bardo attack, we can assess whether they tried to assume such a role in the face of a security-oriented state apparatus.

We collected media coverage of the Bardo attack between 18 March and 1 April 2015. It is important to underline that what we analyse is the journalistic commentary after Bardo and not the journalistic coverage of the event. There was an enormous amount of coverage during this period, even when we restricted our analysis to Tunisia's most important television channel, al-Hiwar al-Tunisi (Tunisian Dialogue), and five newspapers catering to different audiences. On al-Hiwar al-Tunisi, we focused on political talk shows, where the *chroniqueurs* play an important role (see Chapter 4), and in the five newspapers, we focused on editorials. We collected all the political debates on al-Hiwar al-Tunisi that discussed the attack – twelve programmes in all, as well as the newspaper daily editorials. In addition, we analysed some particularly relevant opinion pieces that were not editorials but were written by prominent newspaper journalists.

The attack in context

In March 2015, Tunisia was into its fourth year of transition since the downfall of the Ben Ali regime, and its nascent democracy was brittle. Polarisation and conflict between secularists and Islamists had come close to derailing the transition process. The attack reinforced the fear of Islamism, which had roots in the survival politics of the old regime. During the Ben Ali years, the regime imposed what Beatrice Hibou called a 'security pact' on the Tunisia people (Hibou 2011: 183). The state was the guarantor of a certain level of material wellbeing, a progressive social order and security. In return, it demanded that Tunisians accept a high level of surveillance and a low level of personal and political freedom. This pact was sustained on the one hand by reference to nationalism and unity of the social body, and on the other by the ceaseless nurturing of a 'political culture of danger'. The danger here was the purported chaos that would ensue from an uncontrolled social situation, rebellion stirred by the dissatisfaction of the most underprivileged strata – and Islamism.

The regime-induced fear and mistrust of Islamism among many Tunisians survived Ben Ali. The victory of the Islamist al-Nahda party in the 2011 elections and its attempted reversal of certain secularist and gender-progressive laws and policies did nothing to dissipate the scepticism, and when two socialist leaders that were outspoken critics of Islamism were murdered in 2013 many blamed al-Nahda for having indirect or even direct responsibility for their deaths. The mistrust continued after al-Nahda agreed to political compromises and relinquished power peacefully when they lost the 2014 elections. Conversely, the brutal oppression of Islamists during the Ben Ali regime and the social stigma of being branded an Islamist had radicalised many young members of the movement. Anne Wolf (2017: 206) draws a causal line between this experience of isolation and the growth of Islamist radicalism in Tunisia in the years preceding the revolution.

The revolution added new fault lines to the long-standing confrontation between authoritarian secularism and socially conservative Islamism. At the time of the Bardo attack, four socio-political tendencies competed with each other: the paternalistic idea of a strong state populated by enlightened officials, prevalent among state administrators and a political elite increasingly concerned about security; a market-friendly, individualistic liberalism embraced by businessmen who had prospered under Ben Ali; an ideal of an egalitarian, secular republic, strong among the left and many ordinary people; and last the Islamic communitarianism of al-Nahda (Tripp 2015). When Essebsi was sworn in as president in December 2014 it was a sign that the first tendency had gained the upper hand. Importantly, he was elected with the support of al-Nahda, after Essebsi and al-Nahda's leader Rachid el-Ghannouchi had agreed informally to refrain from attacking each other during a meeting in August 2013 (Bobin 2018). In effect, it was a gentleman's agreement between the strong state current and the moderate Islamist movement, leaving the egalitarian revolutionaries out in the cold.

As we argued in Chapter 2, the Tunisian media was as coloured by the combination of new and old elements as many other institutions in society.

After the revolution, its role was contested. The journalists we interviewed repeatedly said that the most important gain from the revolution was freedom of expression and reported experiencing a completely new and exhilarating reality. At the same time, however, they were frustrated because of the meddling from stakeholders, whether these were private actors or, in the case of state-owned and confiscated media outlets, bureaucrats and government. In particular, they were wary of al-Nahda, which had been part of various governments since the revolution. The fear and mistrust of Islamism that was cultivated by the Ben Ali regime was a striking feature of many of our interviews, and the attempts by al-Nahda to dominate the state bureaucracy and the state-owned media only exacerbated the mistrust (Chouikha 2015: 92–3). There are only a few Islamist media outlets in Tunisia, and there seems to be a secular bias among Tunisian journalists.

Journalistic Interpretation of the Terrorism Problem

The journalistic commentary on the problem of terrorism after Bardo reflected the multiple political conflicts in Tunisia and was very diverse. One would perhaps expect that the shocking attack would give rise to a straightforward, nationally shared definition of the problem, focused on the alarming rise of jihadism on Tunisian soil. In fact, different journalists offered contrasting interpretations of what the exceptional phenomenon was an expression of.

Let us start with newspaper editorials, looking first at one of the few Islamist-leaning publications.[1] In *al-Damir*, the editorials directly related to the Bardo attack were all written by the editor-in-chief, Muhammad al-Hamruni, who almost immediately shifted the problem definition from the attack itself to the reactions among Tunisian elites, including other media. For al-Hamruni, the 'sacred Tunisian national unity' was threatened by vaguely defined media and political actors. Al-Hamruni used the Bardo attacks as a springboard to paint a political scene in which al-Nahda represented the transition towards democracy, which was under constant threat by dark, counter-revolutionary forces. In other words, the problem for al-Hamruni had to do with the Islamist-secularist divide in Tunisia.

---

[1] To facilitate the flow of reading, we do not refer with parentheses to the newspaper editorials we collected between 18 March and 1 April 2015.

The socialist paper *al-Shuruq* also focused on Islamism and secularism, but presented a narrative almost diametrically opposed to the storyline found in *al-Damir*. In *al-Shuruq*'s portrayal, Islamism was taken for granted as a threat to the country. The problem highlighted by the Bardo attack was a lack of preparedness, and this was in turn connected to a fundamental disunity in Tunisian politics. In its 26 March editorial, *al-Shuruq* laid the blame for this lack of unity squarely at the feet of

> parties, groups and organisations that refuse to enter this struggle [against Islamist terrorism] and that continue to cover up politically [. . .], and [. . .] radio channels, tv channels and newspapers and electronic news sites that [. . .] incite against the security and military men and portray the terrorists as victims!

For these two newspapers, situated at opposite ends of the secularist-Islamist spectrum, the problem was national disunity. For *al-Shuruq*, the terror attack was a symptom of the problem; for *al-Damir*, the debate about the attack was a symptom of the problem.

Like *al-Damir* and *al-Shuruq*, the other major newspapers took the problem of terrorism for granted and did not spend much space discussing it. For example, *al-Sabah*'s op-ed writer on 19 March noted that terrorism was a global problem that haunted countries far more stable and powerful than Tunisia. The writers in *al-Sabah*, *al-Sahafa* and *al-Damir* quickly turned to weak security policies as the main problem, given that terrorism is something Tunisia will have to contend with in any case. 'We have a long way to go before we are ready for a full-scale war on terrorism, and several deficiencies stain the security work [*al-'amal al-amni*]', Rafiq bin 'Abdallah noted in *al-Sabah* on 23 March. These newspapers also alluded to Islamism as a problem in society, but their main focus was on security policies and lack of preparedness.

Turning to television, let us start by considering the coverage on al-Hiwar al-Tunisi on the day of the attack. The channel broadcast a three-hour special edition of the political talk show *24/7* focusing on the crisis, led by programme host Hamza Bil'umi. It gathered politicians from the governing parties Nida Tunis and al-Nahda as well as the centrist-liberal Republican party, one former policeman and two *chroniqueurs*, Lutfi al-'Amari and Sufiyan bin Hamida. Lutfi al-'Amari is a hard-hitting commentator whose trademark is a tough interviewing style. He lashed out at the politicians with the posture of an angry layman. Dramaturgically speaking, he appeared to have a mandate to turn up the heat. The problem definition in al-'Amari's narrative was wide. Generally, things were bad and getting worse. Tunisia was assailed by enemies – from the inside and the outside – and was losing its reputation in the world. The politicians had 'worn us out' and were 'destroying the people's morale instead of destroying terrorism'. Al-'Amari lashed out at what he saw as the profoundly nefarious influence of the Islamist trend. He criticised al-Nahda's role in governance and accused mainstream Islamists of sympathising with the terrorists.

Sufiyan bin Hamida is a soft-spoken analyst who shies away from heated confrontation. Situated on the secular left, he is known to be critical of Islamism. However, in the special broadcast, he struck a conciliatory tone. He warned against politicisation of the crisis, arguing that 'the state, the country and the people must stay united against terrorism'. He praised the swift reaction of the security forces, tourist guides and others who were at the scene. Bin Hamida expressed confidence in the government's determination and ability to deal with terrorism in Tunisia and underscored that the carnage could have been far greater. He predicted that the attack would serve as a wake-up call, because the problem was that Tunisians had treated terrorism as something that was far away, in the mountains: 'as if we were watching a movie'.

In other words, two journalistic narratives were presented in Hiwar al-Tunisi's early coverage. The first narrative explained that the country and nation were in tatters due to political mismanagement and the treasonous deviance of the Islamist segment. The second narrative warned against internal divisions and expressed confidence in the prospect of national unity and in the organisational capacity of the state.

Blaming democracy or the revolution?

Knowing that the Bardo attack occurred against the backdrop of a recent regime change, a pertinent question is whether journalists faulted democracy or the Tunisian revolution for the flare-up of terrorism. Did the sudden instability lead journalists to throw doubt on the merits of a democratic transition or question the value of the revolution itself? In the special broadcast of *24/7* on Hiwar al-Tunisi on the day of the attack, Lutfi al-'Amari ventured into this terrain. Lambasting the political class for talking without acting, he stated that

> what is happening, whether in Parliament or even in government, is shameful and make the Tunisians regret a thousand times that they trusted a group of activists who betrayed them with slogans that have shown themselves to be empty and which they were the first to abandon. If they don't provide people that can govern and protect the people, what was all the fuss about?

In a later exchange in the same programme, host Hamza Bil'umi pressed 'Imad al-Hamami, a representative of the Islamist al-Nahda party, on his party's loyalty to the Tunisian nation. When al-Hamami defended the principle of human rights, the rule of law and the constitution, al-'Amari intervened: 'Iraq today has a constitution and democracy. See what good it has brought them!' The prominent *chroniqueur*'s argument was that Tunisia did not yet have a nation [*watan*] and could therefore not introduce democracy. Sufiyan bin Hamida, the other journalist commentator in the panel, strongly disagreed. 'For the first time I feel that the state, in its internal composition, is in a strong position', bin Hamida concluded.

None of the newspaper journalists blamed democracy or the transition as such for the instability. On the contrary, they described terrorism as a threat against Tunisia's path towards democracy, clearly judging the latter to be something positive. Given that terrorism was taken for granted as the problem, what did these journalists see as the main causes for terrorism? The editorial writers were remarkably silent on that point – most of them seemed satisfied with ascribing to the terrorists a 'culture of death', which reifies the phenomenon of terrorism as something inherently evil rather than explaining its causes.

The newspapers were more explicit about the secondary question of what caused the terrorist attack to succeed. They all agreed that the security sector had suffered from poor organisation, and that the previous government had taken the terrorist threat too lightly. The paper *al-Maghrib* opined that there had been a political 'culture of forgetting', when what was needed to counter terrorism was a 'culture of vigilance' (20 March).

Divisions and 'unity'

The attribution of blame has bearing on another question, namely the degree to which journalists highlighted divisions or unity in terrorism-hit Tunisia. Their framing could be expected to go either way: on the one hand, the country was severely polarised, but on the other, national catastrophes often induce the media to emphasise national unity. As we shall see, this assumption finds support in our data. The meaning of 'unity' was, however, not straightforward. It related to President Essebsi's initiative for 'national reconciliation' (*musalaha wataniyya*), presented two days after the attack.

In part, the journalistic commentary after Bardo was marked by polarisation. As we have shown the Islamist daily *al-Damir* and the secularist *al-Shuruq* quickly took up opposing views. In al-Hamruni's view, certain media and political actors (*atraf siyasiyya*) were exploiting the situation – 'trad[ing] in terror' and 'invest[ing] in blood' (20 March). His tone grew sharper in later editorials. On 27 March he denounced unnamed secular politicians and media people (*i'lamiyyin*) as mad, using expressions such as a 'sick political imagination', 'bacteria' and 'schizophrenia' (*marad al-wiswas al-qahri*) when talking about al-Nahda's detractors.

This mudslinging was, however, a sideshow to the more important blaming of the entire political establishment engaged in by the newspapers *al-Sabah*, *al-Maghrib* and *al-Sahafa*. These papers adopted a less populist version of *chroniqueur* Lutfi al-'Amari's condemnation of the general state of Tunisia's politics. They argued that terrorism was an inescapable threat, and that what caused the Bardo attackers to succeed was lack of preparedness and a weak security sector. The blame was not laid at the doorstep of the security forces, who were hailed as heroes, especially after they located the terror cell and attacked it, killing nine militants including the leader of the cell. Instead, the newspapers blamed Tunisia's politicians. They had had four years to deal with this problem, but they had failed miserably, concentrating on petty squabbles at the cost of forging a strong anti-terror policy, as Hayat al-Sayib wrote in *al-Sabah* on 21 March. In *al-Sahafa* the next day, Munawwar al-Maliti wrote that Tunisia's politicians had

> arrogantly refrained from making the struggle against terrorism a priority in their political programmes to save the country, appearing for [ordinary] Tunisians as the Andalusian petty kings [in the Middle Ages] who competed with each other for a seat in the palace of the kasbah.

His criticism concurred with Ghazi al-Ghuyariri's assessment in *al-Maghrib* on 19 March. He exhorted the politicians to leave behind their personal and party ambitions and focus on national unity. In short, the main concern of the newspapers was to blame politicians for the lack of a strong policy against terrorism and to exhort all Tunisians to act united and forcefully against it.

On Tunisia's national day, 20 March, President Essebsi talked about the need for 'national reconciliation'. When programme host Ilyas al-Gharbi interviewed Nida Tunis' Muhsin Marzuq on the talk show *24/7* that evening, he asked if the reconciliation would include 'persons with a connection to terrorism [. . .] or that seek to explain away terrorism'. The question echoed Lutfi al-'Amari's comment two days previously on the *24/7* special broadcast, that national unity required the Islamists to acknowledge their guilt in nurturing terrorist sentiments. Marzuq's reply was that anyone who had not committed murder would be part of the reconciliation, because this was a 'big war against terrorism'. The host asked what the president meant when he said, 'We are at war with terrorism'. Marzuq replied, 'War means that the person in front of you is the enemy. Everyone who takes up arms against the state is the enemy. In such situations human rights do not apply. When it comes to terrorism there is no left and right, only with us and against us. [. . .] There is no time for bickering. We are not against democracy, but we have to have enough strength to take decisive decisions.' The journalist raised no follow-up questions about the implications for Tunisia's transition.

The editors of *al-Sahafa* and *al-Sabah* dismissed critics who feared that this new initiative would come at the cost of the already established transitional justice process. They argued that transitional justice should not be about revenge, but rather about uniting the country. In the 24 March edition of *al-Sabah*, Muhsin al-Zaghlami went as far as saying that reconciliation was a 'national duty' at this time.

Civil society activists, however, did criticise the reconciliation initiative on al-Hiwar al-Tunisi. On 23 March, Amna al-Manif of the citizenship movement Kullna Tunis (We Are All Tunisia) debated 'national unity' with Nida Tunis leader Mundhir Bilhajj 'Ali on *24/7*. She criticised the idea that national reconciliation could be effected by a law and pleaded for a deeper process based on transitional justice. The next day on *24/7*, Siham bin Sidrin, the leader of the Truth and Dignity Commission, defended al-Manif's mission of investigating human rights violations committed by the Tunisian state since 1955. Strikingly, however, no journalists in al-Hiwar al-Tunisi criticised the reconciliation initiative because it might hamper transitional justice. *Chroniqueur* Muhammad Bughallab saved his critical comments for the civil society activists. He asked Amna al-Manif about the utility of 'holding people from 1955 responsible', criticising the travel ban imposed on businessmen with links to Ben Ali's regime. When al-Manif pointed out that the Truth and Dignity Commission was a constitutional body that should be protected, he raised his voice, saying:

> 'Constitutional', this is the ogre you always scare people with. Even the municipality is a constitutional body. Everything mentioned in the constitution is a constitutional body. [Drowning out al-Manif's voice:] The Truth and Dignity Commission is not mentioned among the independent bodies. It is a temporary committee. Why don't you call it a temporary body? You always say constitutional as if it was the holy Quran!

All in all, Essebsi's sidestepping of transitional justice did not run into resistance from the journalist commentators.

Debating the draft counter-terrorism law

The foremost threat that terrorism poses to democracy is, in most cases, an indirect one. Governments cut back on civil liberties at the request of security forces, which want fewer restraints in their pursuit of terrorism suspects. In transitional contexts, the threat is acute, because empowering security forces in many cases equals strengthening the institutions and networks upon which the old regime was built. It makes sense to assume that journalists in Tunisia, who as a professional community had benefitted from the newfound liberties and had been subject to pressures from the security forces in the past, would be aware of this risk. It is therefore interesting to look at how journalists in our sample commented on the government's introduction of a new counter-terrorism bill on 26 March, eight days after the Bardo attack.

In the case of *al-Sabah* and also *al-Sahafa*, criticism of Tunisia's politicians and the call for inclusive unity was combined with praise for the government's counter-terrorism bill. The new legislation was criticised by human rights activists for bringing back capital punishment, detentions without trial, increased police surveillance and several other authoritarian elements. In *al-Sabah*, however, it received wholehearted support. On 27 March, Muhsin al-Zaghlami argued that the law's controversial elements were necessary to the 'war on terror' that Tunisia was entering and that the law would not adversely affect ordinary people's legal rights. The editorials in *al-Sahafa* did not mention the law, but they emphasised the necessity for a full scale 'war on terror'. In effect, both *al-Sabah* and *al-Sahafa* praised the strongman Essebsi, who, as they saw it, rose above the trivial concerns of Tunisia's politicians. *Al-Maghrib* was, by comparison nuanced and liberal: it stated that the war on terror required media that were free, critical and responsible.

On television, al-Hiwar al-Tunisi broadcast a debate on the talk show *Kalam al-Nas* (Talk of the Town) on 25 March, the night before the government introduced the new law. In his opening remarks, programme host Nawfal Wartini noted that no terrorist had been sentenced in Tunisia since 2011. 'Is terrorism', he asked, 'a crime without punishment?' To discuss this and other questions, the programme had invited in three artists, the lawyer Sayf al-Din Makhluf and two *chroniqueurs*, Lutfi al-'Amari and Maya al-Qusuri, the latter herself a lawyer. The set-up was very polarising. As an outspoken defender of Salafis, Makhluf was a controversial character who was stripped of his licence to practice law in October 2015. All the other participants stood against him. Yet, the point he made was that stronger prerogatives for the state to defeat terrorism should not come at the expense of the rule of law:

Makhluf: Repressing freedom is a form of terrorism. What is freedom? That we hold our authorities responsible. That we say the truth and elect our politicians in free elections. That we hold criminals responsible but don't take freedom away from me.

[. . .]

al-'Amari: Freedom, how many crimes shall be committed in your name! What you describe is chaos, not freedom. You talk about the terrorist's freedom, but freedom is a universal value, which you have issues with.

Al-'Amari went on to accuse Makhluf's Islamist colleagues of murder, concluding: 'You practice freedom as chaos to destroy the state. If freedom is defiling the state, then we don't need this freedom!'

At this point the debate descended into a shouting match. There was no informed reflection on the difficulty of balancing security and democracy. Instead, spectators saw a circus, and acute polarisation around the secularist-Islamist divide. Al-'Amari and the other journalists seemed more concerned with protecting the state than with the principles of the rule of law and civil rights. The only voice on the show that was critical of increasing the prerogatives of the security was that of the Islamist lawyer.

Discussion

Journalistic commentary on the Bardo attack illustrated the newfound freedoms and pluralism in Tunisia after the revolution. While they praised the efforts of security officers, editorials were sharply critical towards the security sector as an institution and especially towards Tunisia's elected politicians, whom they accused of neglecting security in favour of petty bickering and personal settling of accounts. Opposition between Islamists and socialists was also on display: a clear sign of a vital and opinionated media.

Television is by far the most important media channel in Tunisia, and hence vulnerable to 'capture' by rich actors with political agendas. By 2015, however, it was already clear that the Independent High Authority for Audiovisual Communication (HAICA) was having considerable impact. HAICA monitors the diversity of views represented in all Tunisian audiovisual media and has the authority to sanction channels that fail to invite in different voices. In line with the regulator's demands for pluralism, sharply different views were on display during political talk shows, contributing to a pluralist public sphere during a very difficult and sensitive period in Tunisia's transition. Still, HAICA's regulatory power did not extend to individual journalists.

Pluralism and partisanship do not equate to critical journalism and a defence of civil freedoms. It is true that both in television and the print media, there were journalists who defended the importance of a liberal political order and the principles of human rights and rule of law in the struggle against terrorism. *Chroniqueur* Sufiyan bin Hamida was one of the few who directly criticised President Essebsi for his dehumanising of the terrorists, while the liberal newspaper *al-Maghrib* emphasised that transparency and civil rights must not be jeopardised in the struggle against terrorism. However, the main thrust of journalistic commentary on television as well as in newspapers was rather different.

Two tendencies are noteworthy in relation to the question of whether journalists provided space for critical reflection about the problem of terrorism and a counterbalance to the regime's authoritarian turn. First, there was little serious attention paid to the actual causes of terrorism and jihadism in Tunisia and how to deal with them. Many journalists contented themselves with denouncing terrorists as belonging to a 'culture of death' and contrasting this to the unity and inclusiveness of Tunisians, thus brushing aside the difficult fact that jihadism had been able to take root among Tunisian youth. Instead of using the Bardo attack as a point of departure for a critical reflection on why this was so, the incident was instrumentalised to launch attacks against ideological adversaries. While Islamist journalists were no less fierce than their secularist counterparts in this respect, the Islamist trend was clearly the weaker part in this confrontation. Despite their newfound freedom and possibility of creating new public discourses, journalists thus chose to draw on the Ben Ali-era 'culture of danger' of which Hibou speaks (Hibou 2011: 183–99), and as in that era, they homed in on the Islamist trend. The Bardo attack saw them jumping into the old trenches to reignite a war of words that did little to elucidate the terrorism problem at hand. The political situation in Tunisia at the time of the Bardo attack was radically new, but the journalistic commentary did not reflect this. Instead, it breathed new life into a pre-revolutionary discourse.

The second point is that a notable trend among journalist commentators was to support the president's authoritarian steps and connect them with national unity. His 'national reconciliation' initiative would rehabilitate businessmen with close ties to the Ben Ali regime, and the new counterterrorism law would curtail civil freedoms. Yet, prominent journalists embraced and supported them. Lutfi al-'Amari even questioned the value of political freedom if it did not come with security guarantees. This support for Essebsi's initiatives was connected to the theme of national unity. Journalists implicitly juxtaposed President Essebsi's resoluteness with the paralysis of Tunisia's parliamentarians, whom they accused of neglecting the country in their pursuit of petty squabbles. Some commentators described reconciliation as a 'national duty'. What is striking here is not the emphasis on national unity, nor the call for forceful political action; both are expected reactions to a terrorist attack. The surprising element is the celebration of the president's initiatives, the connection drawn between his policies and national unity, and the willingness to jeopardise important achievements of the Tunisian revolution. In her analysis of the Ben Ali political order, Hibou notes a widespread saying in Tunisia relating to the security pact: 'It is the price to be paid.' Corruption and the lack of freedom was the price to be paid for security against external (and Islamist) danger (Hibou 2011: 201–2). In their reactions to the Bardo attack, many journalists seemed to cheer on the strong leader and accept that the price to be paid for supporting him was a setback for civil liberties, a derailing of the transitional justice process and the rehabilitation of the cronies of Ben Ali.

This tendency was noted by the well-known Tunisian intellectual al-Safi Sa'id in a scathingly critical letter to the president:

> In times of revolutions, upheavals and wars, fear grips nations. Consequently, the Leader as Saviour is that man who has no fear and does not allow fear to sneak upon his people. [. . .] But he should walk on the democratic path, not outside it or on its edges! Otherwise his legitimacy will erode, regardless whether he earned it through elections or [historical events]. (al-Sa'id 2017: 66, 69)

What significant portions of Tunisian journalists seemed to lack during the Bardo crisis was the critical impulse evident in Sa'id's message to Essebsi.

In a sense, Essebsi's use of the Bardo attack to consolidate his grip on power, and the support given him by many journalists, are two sides of the same coin, in that they both point to the survival of the old political culture in the new political order. While the system had changed, many of the same men (and some women) continued to hold powerful positions in politics as well as in the media. The journalists who cheered on the strong president and scorned the bickering parliamentarians were raised under the Ben Ali regime and obtained their professional positions under that system. Many of them were apparently still beholden to the old discourse of security and the culture of danger nurtured by Tunisia's autocrats.

For Tunisia's transition, this 'time lag' in journalistic commentary poses a problem. Ben Ali's security discourse was designed to keep Islamists and especially the Nahda party out of politics. But democratic progress hinges on the ability to include all parts of society and communicate across ideological divides. The basic contradiction in the commentary we have analysed is that journalists call for national unity while continuously stressing how alien and dangerous the Islamists are. Thus, they fail to create a common ground where Tunisians of all ideological hues can debate the sources of violence.

As Cottle points out, journalists may play a role in the 'democratization of violence': that is, to facilitate and contribute to public, open deliberation about the issue of political violence (Cottle 2006b: 144–52). In the Tunisian case this did not happen. Journalistic commentary did not focus on the root causes of terrorism but treated the Bardo attack merely as a springboard to call for unity and strong leadership. In a context where these exact notions were being used by a Bourguiba-era president to rehabilitate pre-revolutionary elites and fasten the grip on power, journalistic comment served to cloud the political realities instead of contributing critically to further democratisation.

So far, we have zoomed in on a critical point in Tunisia's transition: a mediatised disaster where the role of journalists as sense-makers comes to the fore. The journalists commenting on the causes and consequences of the Bardo attack enjoyed unprecedented prominence and freedom of expression because of the democratic opening after the 2011 revolution. Yet they did not forcefully counter the regime's authoritarian drift in the wake of the terrorist attack. In fact, some actively contributed to it by praising strongman leadership and undermining respect for civil liberties. The journalists fell back on discursive habits they had acquired under Ben Ali's 'security pact'. How did the Bardo attack and the media coverage of it play into the political dynamics after 2015?

The Terrorism Debate in the Wider Political Process

Paradoxically, the real losers in the aftermath of the Bardo attack proved to be not the Islamists who were so roundly condemned, but liberal civil society activists and journalists. Rachid el-Ghannouchi, the leader of the main Islamist party al-Nahda, had already concluded an informal gentleman's agreement with President Essebsi when the Bardo attackers struck, thus securing al-Nahda's position in the political establishment. In 2016, al-Nahda disavowed the moniker 'Islamist', announced that it was a political party rather than a social movement and henceforth referred to itself as a Muslim democratic party. Tunisian journalists and civil society activists, however, found themselves in a more precarious situation. From 2015, repeated incidents of violence from the security apparatus were met with indifference from leading political figures.

President Essebsi succeeded in getting both the reconciliation bill and the counter-terrorism bill through parliament. The reconciliation bill was fiercely opposed by civil society activists and was not adopted until 2017. The law granted amnesty to civil servants accused of corruption under Ben Ali and overturned the sentences of others who were judged as part of the transitional justice process. Thus, it reversed the process towards increased transparency that had been ongoing since 2011 and trampled on the idea of justice that was so central to the revolution. The counter-terrorism law was adopted earlier, in July 2015, and worried civil society activists. It reinstated capital punishment, allowed the authorities to detain people without charge for fifteen days, and made it easier for investigators to tap the phones of suspects. Not least, public expressions of support for terrorism were made a jailable offence – a direct restriction on the freedom of speech in a situation where the definition of 'terrorism' may be fluid (The Guardian, 2015).

The new laws and subsequent actions by President Essebsi were inimical to the democratisation process, and many observers interpreted his policies as an attempt to strengthen the office of the president at the cost of other constitutional bodies as well as civil society. Essebsi was clear that he considered the independent watchdogs that had been set up after the revolution, including the media watchdog HAICA and the Authority for Access to Information, to be institutions that weakened the state and endangered the stability of the country (Nouira 2017). His preferred path to ensure stability was to boost the powers of the president to bypass the prime minister and the fragmented parliament. As part of this effort, he put in place a national security council in 2018 over which he himself presided (Gobe 2018). A further boost to the executive at the cost of other institutions was the declaration of a state of emergency after the terrorist attacks in 2015. The state of emergency grants wide powers to the security apparatus, allows for measures to control the press in the interest of national security, and makes it easier for the state to ban meetings and strikes that may create disorder. Essebsi passed away in 2019, but his successor, Kais Saied, has continued to claim that his powers as commander of the armed forces are not limited to the army, but extend to the internal security forces (Amara 2021). He also keeps renewing the state of emergency, which was still in force when we wrote this book.

The result of these policies is that the security forces zealously clamp down on protests with impunity and without bothering too much about whether their batons hit protesters or the journalists who cover the protests. When demonstrations over austerity measures broke out in early 2018, hundreds of protesters were arrested, and many were mistreated by the police (CNN Arabic 2018). Some of the journalists who covered the protests were wiretapped and threatened, prompting them to organise a 'Day of Rage' in early February. As the then-head of the Journalist Syndicate, Naji Bughuri, stated: 'Today, they want to create a press working according to orders; they want a press that does what they want it to do' (Jeune Afrique 2018). Bilal, a journalist in one of Tunisia's most critical digital news outlets, claimed:

> The authorities have allowed themselves to persecute journalists for terrorism-related questions; people have been tortured under the counter-terrorism law. It is very important to take a step back and say it is correct that this is a war, but we should not slip back into the situation we had under Ben Ali, because Ben Ali played a lot on these questions. Today, people are persecuted over a

Facebook post. This is a question about the freedom of expression. (T14, 10 March 2018)

The state has continued to come down heavily on journalists. In April 2021, security forces broke into the offices of the state-owned national news agency Tunis Afrique Presse (TAP) to disband a sit-in by employees. The employees were protesting the appointment of a new director considered to have ties to al-Nahda and the pre-revolutionary Ben Ali regime. Tunisian journalists noted that such violent behaviour by security forces against public media institutions was unheard of even in the darkest periods of the autocracy (Kapitalis 2021). A month later, the National Syndicate of Tunisian Journalists (SNJT) released its yearly report on press freedom, detailing 206 incidents of attacks on journalist, including twenty-four direct physical assaults (SNJT 2021). SNJT commented that these figures were the highest in three years, and that the security forces were the most frequent offender.

All through the 2010s, Tunisian politics and media were in an uncertain process of transition from authoritarianism to democracy, and it was at times difficult to decide whether the glass was half empty or half full. The overconcentration of power in the executive office that began under President Essebsi and accelerated under Kais Saied suggests that it was half empty. In 2021, the new president set aside the constitution, suspended the parliament and began to rule by decree. We have noted the paradox inherent in the fact that a considerable number of journalists supported a focus on security and a strong presidential office at the cost of transitional justice and civil freedoms after the Bardo attack as the president proceeded to assert increased control through a revamped security sector and a state of emergency. The security forces did not hesitate to attack journalists, and this trend has only worsened after Kais Saied took over.

Despite the fact that journalists are often the victims of authoritarian politics, the 'security-first' attitude and support to the powers that be crept into some editorial rooms. To give another example, we monitored Tunisian media coverage of the popular protests that erupted in early 2018 over the rising cost of living in Tunisia. Journalists for the national broadcaster al-Wataniyya insinuated that hostile forces seeking to destabilise the country lay behind the unrest (Watania 1 2018). Al-Hiwar al-Tunisi and its team defended the idea that traffickers and corrupted people had instigated the protests because Prime Minister Youssef Chahed had declared a war on corruption (Ministry of the Interior – Tunisia 2018). On the other hand, the e-media outlet Nawaat and Nisma TV aired sympathetic coverage of the protests. Journalists of Nawaat highlighted the socio-economic difficulties in peripheral areas and gave a voice to the local population (Nawaat 2018b). They denounced the 'demonisation' of civil society activists by the pro-government media and reported on the repression of protesters by security forces (Nawaat 2018a). A programme host on Nisma TV attributed the riot to the failures of the country's politicians. He accused the political class of being disconnected from the people, especially in poor areas, and of 'stealing public resources' (Nisma TV 2018).

As is evident from this chapter and other parts of our book, the picture of Tunisian journalists' contribution to the ongoing struggle for democracy is a mixed bag of principled defence and harmful opportunism. We stress that several media organisations have resisted the slide towards authoritarianism. In particular, the journalists' syndicate has consistently cried foul every time press freedoms and journalists are attacked: it remains one of the most combative Tunisian NGOs and has become an important national institution. A young newspaper journalist neatly expressed a sentiment we often heard in interviews:

> [The SNJT] is the house of all journalists. For me, the syndicate plays a key role for Tunisian media. Because when the syndicate is strong, the journalist is not afraid and does not retreat. Thank God, after the revolution, the syndicate has done great work and succeeded in many issues. It is up to the journalists now to be agents of reform. (T18, 4 May 2018)

And when journalists organise to protest, they are listened to. In the TAP incident in 2021, the government eventually yielded to the demands of the employees and withdrew their nomination of the controversial new director (Article 19 2021).

Conclusion

Terror attacks always pose a challenge to critical journalism. Still, when it comes to relinquishing media freedom in the interest of security, the stakes were even higher in post-revolutionary Tunisia than in established democracies. This is because the danger of security-induced authoritarian drift is greater in a country that is still in a transition phase, with only fledgling institutions to support democracy. After the 2015 attack on the Bardo Museum, the story about terrorism and security that some prominent journalists told eventually supported an ominous tendency to rely on security forces to deal with political and social dissension. President Essebsi and other politicians used the problem of security and the threat of terrorism to implement policies that impeded Tunisia's progress towards a consolidated democracy. A considerable number of media professionals supported the focus on security that made this manoeuvre possible. Prominent *chroniqueurs* and op-ed writers fell back on interpretive schema from the Ben Ali era after the Bardo terrorist attack, emphasising the need for a strong executive to push back against what they saw as the Islamist danger. The government's attempt at imposing a loyal, deeply unpopular director of TAP in 2021 shows that the spirit of wanting to keep media freedom 'under control' (Jelassi 2021) is alive and well among politicians.

The debate immediately after the Bardo attack and the subsequent controversies surrounding the freedom of the press show the importance of a well-developed professional journalistic community. The main gain of the revolution – freedom of expression – meant that journalists had the opportunity to tell a different story – which many did, with the support of the national journalists' syndicate. Their narrative focused on the sanctity of unfettered journalistic freedom based on professional, ethical standards. At no time is this combination more important than during elections, which are the focus of our next chapter.

7

ELECTIONS AND MEDIA CAPTURE

By coincidence, Lebanon and Tunisia held simultaneous elections on 6 May 2018. A general election, postponed since 2013, was finally taking place in Lebanon while Tunisia held its first local elections following Ben Ali's ouster. We watched the events as they unfolded, one in each country, to compare the role that media and journalism played. There were striking differences on display. Beirut was manifestly in election mood, with posters of prominent politicians everywhere on the city's buildings. Many carried the name of a local institution or businessman who had paid for them in the expectation that the show of support would pay off if the candidate was elected. Ambulating trucks with loudspeakers, music and slogans defied a formal prohibition of campaigning on the night before election day, rallying voters to the ballots. The media was also gearing up and sold its services to candidates at exorbitant prices. Tunis, by contrast, was downbeat. The electoral campaigning did not make big waves. Even though observers referred to the local elections as a milestone of democratic progress, only 35.6 per cent of registered voters took part in them (Wolf 2018). Rules and regulations were enforced, but the two biggest television channels, Nisma and al-Hiwar al-Tunisi, were strongly critical of the media regulator HAICA's instructions for coverage. In fact, they boycotted the entire event as an act of protest.

One year later, however, the stage was set for a much more heated election in which the media and journalism actually became a political issue. The presidency of the republic was the prize and the owner of Nisma, Nabil Karoui, was a frontrunner. The election campaign took a dramatic turn when

Karoui was detained on charges of tax evasion and money laundering. A spokeswoman for his party denounced what she described as 'a political arrest aimed at keeping Karoui out of the presidential race' (Amara 2019). The arrest had Tunisian journalists highly engaged and divided. As we shall see, both political and professional disagreements came to light. Eventually, Kais Saied won the election. His approach to the media could not have been more different than Karoui's, because he shunned Tunisia's private television channels during the campaign.

All the central topics we discuss in this book – journalism, democracy and media instrumentalisation – come together in elections. Elections are the ultimate barometer of democracy, and the media plays a crucial role in them. As Voltmer (2012: 232) argues,

> the link between effective democracy and the media becomes most obvious during elections, which can only be fair and free when oppositional voices have access to the media and when all citizens have the opportunity to learn about the alternatives at hand.

According to theory, journalism provides the critical, independent flow of information and the raw materials for public discussion that are required for a functioning democracy (Strömbäck 2005: 332).

Elections are also a prime time for media instrumentalisation, however. Politicians in hybrid regimes and transitional democracies engage in open-ended electoral competition and, since the possibility of winning – or the risk of losing – office is in the balance, the importance of influencing media coverage increases. The fact that the stakes are high makes it particularly difficult to preserve balanced media coverage. By the same token, doing so is especially important, because capture prevents the media from doing service to democracy.

In this chapter, we compare how Lebanon and Tunisia handled this challenge and how journalists engaged in the contests. We focus our discussion of Tunisia on the 2019 presidential election rather than the 2018 municipal elections because the former generated much debate about the media's political role. The levels of regulation the states imposed on the media in the two countries were worlds apart. Lebanese authorities showed little concern with media instrumentalisation and let media owners capitalise on their power tools. HAICA, on the other hand, took a strong stance against any political use of the media. This difference was reflected in the outcomes of the electoral contest. Lebanon's 2018 elections resulted in a perpetuation of the status quo and have been described as a 'triumph of the elites' (Deets and Skulte-Ouaiss 2021). Tunisia's 2019 election produced unforeseen change and brought the outsider Kais Saied to power. The questions we shall focus on are how the different levels of regulation affected journalistic coverage of the elections, and how journalists became contentious actors in the election process.

Media and Journalism in Lebanon's 2018 Parliamentary Elections

The 2018 competition for seats in the parliament of Lebanon was played out in a form that had been carefully designed and agreed upon by the country's political parties. Following a decade of difficult negotiations, dozens of drafts, and two extensions of the outgoing parliament's mandate, the parliament introduced a new electoral law in June 2017 (jfrant 2019). The making of the law had been delayed because the law-making body itself had been deadlocked. Mirroring the wider Middle Eastern stalemate after the 2011 Arab Uprising, the 8 and 14 March political alliances had quarrelled for years over the composition of cabinets and the nomination of a new president of the republic. The breakthrough came in October 2016, when the political forces agreed on General Aoun as president, a victory for Hizbullah. The new electoral law introduced a proportional representation system with constituencies reflecting sectarian demographics. Through this gerrymandering, the established political parties skewed the playing field to their advantage (El Kak 2019).

In contrast to their minute attention to the details of the boundaries of electoral districts, the same political forces cared little about media regulation. Whilst the new electoral law forbade candidates to engage in libel, slander and broadcasting susceptible to inflame religious tensions, it was 'vague in its definition of media outlets and the extent to which digital sources including social media fell under the law' (jfrant 2019: 18). The law gave all candidates the right to free airtime on the public broadcaster Tele Liban, but that did not count for much, since almost nobody watches that channel. What really mattered was access to the private television channels. Observers noted that 'unclear legal provisions regulating the coverage of candidates by private media opened the space for broadcasters to offer paid-for coverage of contestants across all kinds of programme formats, including news and political talk shows' (European Union Election Observation Mission 2018: 28). There was no ceiling on the amount of paid-for advertising and coverage.

Money talks

For media organisations and journalists, the elections offered a respite from otherwise downward trends in the advertising market and opportunities to make profits. Their services were strongly coveted. Several of our interviewees affirmed that paid-for coverage was common. For example, print media journalist Zayna remarked that 'you have articles written on demand' (L20, 9 May 2019). She observed that media organisations sold packages to the politicians that comprised exposure on different platforms. Television journalist Nasim confirmed that 'in the election period, the market for journalism blossoms, there is more money around' (L13, 30 January 2018). E-journalist Samir summed it up laconically: 'The electoral period is considered as a time when journalists do business' (L19, 9 May 2019).

By far the biggest beneficiaries were the owners of private television stations, who controlled the most sought-after publicity resource. The Lebanese Association for Democratic Elections conducted a survey on the prices of electoral advertising, and what they found was astounding. Participation in a primetime television show cost 100,000 USD on most stations. Outside of primetime, the price was 40,000 USD. If it was part of a package that included several appearances and exclusive interviews, the cost would run to the hundreds of thousands of dollars. The charge to cover a live campaign event was 45,000 USD. On most radio stations, the price was 10,000 USD for a half-hour episode (The Lebanese Association for Democratic Elections, 2018: 16). Paid-for coverage was seldom identified as such, in spite of legal requirements (European Union Election Observation Mission 2018).

The excessive price of media exposure put candidates from outside the establishment at a huge disadvantage. Encouraged by their strong showing in the 2016 Beirut municipality elections, civil society activists campaigned excitedly during the event. Eleven groups, comprising sixty-six candidates, came together in a coalition called Kulluna Watani (We Are All My Country) to wrest power from the traditional political parties (El Kak 2019). However, their election campaign coffers were small compared with the big players: Kulluna Watani's budget was 430,000 USD (Deets and Skulte-Ouaiss 2021: 178). The party received some advertising help from the channels al-Jadid, MTV and LBCI, which lowered and sometimes waived their fees for candidates from civil society lists. Still, its overall coverage rate among the political parties was only 5.8 per cent (Nader et al. 2018: 38).

We monitored all the news broadcasts on the television channels al-Manar, al-Jadid, al-Mustaqbal and OTV and selected programmes on other channels from 28 April to 4 May 2018. The coverage was highly partisan and the language combative. Journalists referred to the electoral campaign as 'the campaign struggle' and 'the war field' (MTV 2018). The broadcasts started with long editorial introductions in which the news anchor would criticise rivals to the channel's preferred candidate. The introductions were typically followed up by a news report about the multiple mistakes of the political opponents. Then journalists turned to interviewing people who were favourable to the supported candidate. The questions were often open invitations for praise, such as 'What do you think about [the Minister of Foreign Affairs and Emigrants] Jubran Basil's projects in Batroun?' (OTV 2018a) Much of the coverage was dedicated to 'popular meetings' between the candidate and his supporters. The reporters typically made a big point of the number of attendees and the people's reception of the candidate (al-Mustaqbal 2018a; al-Manar TV 2018b).

In terms of political messaging, the parties put emphasis on the threats posed by enemies. The Future Movement focused on the necessity of preserving Beirut as an Arab capital as opposed to a Persian outpost, alluding to Iran's influence in Lebanon through Hizbullah. The party accused Hizbullah of stealing Sunni votes (al-Mustaqbal 2018b). The Free Patriotic Movement highlighted the failure of security institutions in overcoming security threats such as areas that had fallen prey to drug traffickers. Jubran Basil accused rival candidates of being tools for regional and international powers and handing control over Lebanese resources to them (OTV 2018b). Hizbullah focused on several enemies: Israel, Saudi Arabia, and terrorist groups linked to ISIS and the war in Syria. Hasan Nasrallah said that Lebanon's integrity ideally should not depend on Hizbullah's military apparatus, but in practice, other institutions failed to provide security (al-Manar TV 2018a).

Journalists as candidates

Journalists were also running for office in the election. As is often the case in countries characterised by political parallelism (Mancini 2008), in Lebanon, the boundary between journalism and politics is blurred. Media actors take part in political life and commonly swap their professional role for that of a politician. Several Lebanese journalists have turned into prominent politicians over the years. One of them, Interior Minister Nuhad Mashnuq (2016–19), was a candidate for the Future Movement in the 2018 election. Mashnuq began his career as a journalist for the weekly edition of *al-Nahar* and later wrote for the newspaper *al-Safir*. He built a relationship of trust with ex-Prime Minister Rafik Hariri and became his political advisor. In 2009, he ran for parliament. Other journalists-turned-politicians include Rafik Hariri's confidant Basil al-Sab'a; Saad Hariri's ally 'Uqab Sahhar; Walid Jumblat's right-hand man Marwan Humayda; their opponent and the founder of the Arab Unification Party, Wiam Wahhab; and the Arab nationalist and pro-resistance politician Nasir Qandil.

'Here in the East', said the e-journalist Ahmad, 'the journalist is a political project.' He ironically commented on his own and other journalists' participation in the electoral contest. Ahmad joked that Lebanese politicians want to be journalists whereas journalists seek to become politicians:

> All our politicians want to write a book after they've governed, stolen and everything else; their last ambition is to write their own book. The journalist is the other way around, he starts with the book, but his ambition is to become a politician. (L27, 4 March 2019)

Ahmad explained the politicians' motive for becoming writers as an attempt to gain power in the last area where they do not possess it: 'the power over minds'. As for the journalists and their urge to join the world of politicians, he drew a parallel to sports:

> Like in the sports world, you strive to pass from the ranks of spectators to the ranks of players, inside the stadium. In politics, rather than watching the politicians from afar, you start sitting next to them. Journalism takes you to heights you would otherwise not have reached. (L27, 4 March 2019)

Journalism is widely seen as a prestigious profession in Lebanon and a social ladder to the elite. The television journalist Muʿizz shared Ahmad's impression that 'every journalist aspires to become a politician' (L10, 28 January 2018). For him, the explanation lay in the political sociology of the recruitment of the country's political elites. He reasoned that a political position in Lebanon is exceedingly difficult to obtain unless you are the offspring of a politician, a notable (*zaʿim*), or have a lot of money, like businessmen and doctors. Journalism opens a path through which ordinary people can access and potentially become a part of the elite. Muʿizz esteemed that these political ambitions are harmful for journalism because the journalists curry favours with the politically powerful to rise through the ranks: 'Because most journalists would like to be politicians in the future they have to put their journalism to the service of personal relations with the politicians' (L10, 28 January 2018).

However, in the 2018 election, journalists ran both with and against the established political parties. This bifurcation and the scale of journalists who presented their candidacy was new. Nasim commented on the commonness of journalist candidates in the elections: 'Today, all the election lists have a considerable share of journalists, comprising many of the stars who figure on the television screens. [. . .] The journalists are front-runners because they are well known and have their audiences' (L13, 30 January 2018). In Nasim's assessment, the parties put journalists on their lists because they attract attention from voters. An example of this was the familiar news anchor on MTV, Jessica Azar, who ran for the Lebanese Forces in the Greek Orthodox district of Northern Matn. Since her name was not at the top of the party's list, she was in practical terms campaigning for the less famous frontrunner, Eddie Abi al-Lama.

The most striking development in 2018 was that journalists ran on civil society lists or as independents, signalling opposition to the established political parties. Five female candidates illustrate this trend. Jumana Haddad is a journalist, feminist, professor, writer and poet who edits the cultural page at Al Nahar newspaper.[1] She ran in Beirut's first district on the Kulluna Watani list. Haddad was first announced to have won a seat, but according to

---

[1] She is also the founder of the quarterly women's magazine *Jasad* ('body') and a member of the board of advisors of MARCH Lebanon, a non-government organization that fights censorship and advocates for freedom of expression.

the official results, she lost by 431 votes (Fares 2018). She filed a complaint with the count-up to the Constitutional Council. Fadia Bazzi is a journalist at al-Jadid with a past in the Lebanese Communist Party. She ran in Bint Jubayl, South Lebanon, for a group called 'Citizens in a State' (*muwatinun wa muwatinat fi dawla*). Layal Bu Musa is another member of this group and an investigative researcher at al-Jadid known for her contributions to a programme that reports on corruption cases. She ran against Foreign Minister Jubran Basil in the Maronite district of Batrun. Ghada 'Aid is a talk show host on MTV who is also known for a television show on corruption (Beirut Today 2018). She competed for the Maronite seat in Shuf district for the Saba' party and the Kulluna Watani coalition, Finally, Paula Yaqubian, a former journalist at al-Mustaqbal, was a candidate in Beirut 1, also for Saba'. Garnering 2,500 votes, she became the only candidate on a civil society list to win a parliamentary seat (Atallah and Zoughaib 2019).

Female politicians lacked visibility in the media coverage of the election campaign. A study by the Maharat Foundation and Hivos documented the scope of this democratic problem. In newspapers, the overall share of press coverage for female candidates was about 5 per cent. When direct speech or the literal text of female candidates was monitored, this fell to 3.4 per cent (Nader et al. 2018: 7). On television, the picture was also bleak. Female candidates appeared as the first story on eleven occasions, as the main story on fifty-five occasions. The corresponding numbers for male politicians were 357 and 944. Men received about 84 per cent of the total television coverage, with women receiving the remaining 16 per cent (Nader et al. 2018: 11–12). Thus, the five candidates mentioned above faced a double challenge with regard to media exposure: being women and running on civil society lists. Being a journalist, though, was arguably an advantage in two respects. To varying degrees, their faces were already known to the public and the candidates knew people in the media that were willing to offer some help. The channels LBCI and al-Jadid in particular gave airtime to selected civil society actors without charging them.

Civil society's frustration

The gravitation of journalists toward civil society lists reflected a widespread frustration in society with the political status quo and a sense that the traditional parties were part and parcel of the problem. As illustrated by the 2015 You Stink protests, discussed in Chapter 5, people's patience with mismanagement and corruption had worn thin, and some Lebanese media professionals joined the critique of the elites in the confessional power-sharing system. In an interview with the Lebanese newspaper al-Nahar, Yaqubian expressed such sentiments and explained why she had decided to run on a civil society platform:

> I started getting more convinced that the current political class won't do anything to fix the problem [. . .]. We cannot stay in denial and work with the same people that brought this problem on us. Therefore, it made me want to join the opposition group, I looked for them and realised there weren't any, except for civil society. (Naoufal 2018)

New political initiatives had done well in the local elections in 2016. In the capital, a group of civil society activists known as Beirut Madinati (Beirut My City) had nearly won a majority in the city council. It had a cross-sectarian, civic profile and campaigned on the need to improve public services. This manifestly appealed to voters and demonstrated the potential impact of grassroots mobilisation for political change (Rizkallah 2016). However, in 2018, civil society actors failed to replicate their success and gain a tangible foothold in parliament. Except for Paula Yaqubian, no independent candidates were elected. The established political parties made a clean sweep, and Hizbullah and its allies won the majority. Moreover, the voter participation rate was disappointingly low. Only 49.7 per cent of 3.7 million eligible voters showed up at the polls (Atallah and Zoughaib 2019).

Internal disagreements and a shortage of coordination were part of the reason why civil society candidates failed. The Kulluna Watani coalition did not encompass all civil society forces and was internally fragmented (Deets and Skulte-Ouaiss 2021). The fundamental problem, however, was the unevenness of the election playing field (Levitsky and Way 2009). From the process of rewriting the electoral law to media access and the campaign resources of the contending parties, the competition was profoundly skewed in favour of the incumbents. As the female journalist Sahar, who ran on a civil society list, commented:

> Unfortunately, in Lebanon, those who give most money are the ones who get most votes. Those who promise people jobs are the ones who win the elections.

People have grown accustomed to trusting politicians who lie. It takes a lot of effort to make them trust in fair candidates. (L25, 20 October 2018)

Paula Yaqubian's experience in parliament after the election gave further evidence of the uphill battle facing candidates who defy the political mainstream. Yaqubian had previously worked for al-Mustaqbal and been close to Saad Hariri. In fact, she accompanied the prime minister on his dramatic visit to Saudi Arabia in November 2017 when he was forced to resign in a televised statement. The incident provoked an international uproar and provided the journalist with massive exposure six months before the election. Yaqubian acknowledged that her media visibility and connections facilitated her win in the elections. Nonetheless, as the sole civil society representative in parliament, she considered herself as 'representing those who don't have a voice and pay the price of segregation and the sectarian regime' (L26, 20 October 2018). To live up to people's expectations, she publicly denounced the political class. In television appearances and interviews in February and March 2019, she lambasted the pervasive corruption in Lebanese politics (al-Jadid 2019; Almarkazia 2019; Elnashra 2019). She even cited influential politicians by name, including Prime Minister Jubran Basil as well as Saad Hariri's election campaign manager, Nadir al-Hariri (al-Hashim 2019).

Yaqubian's accusations provoked a media storm against the newly elected MP. Both the Free Patriotic Movement and the Future block turned against her. Jubran Basil filed a court case against Yaqubian and sought to deprive her of her parliamentary immunity (Janoubia 2019). In a press conference on MTV, Yaqubian said, 'I have become the subject of a campaign that targets my private life, my son and my family [. . .] [following my media interventions], the gates of Hell were opened' (MTV Lebanon News 2019). The parties mobilised their electronic armies and Yaqubian lacked protection from a sectarian or political block. Thus, civil society actors' hope of attaining political change through participating in the 2018 elections was thwarted. As we shall see in Chapter 8, they took their agenda to the streets instead in November 2019.

Media and Journalism in Tunisia's 2019 Presidential Election

We now turn to Tunisia and a profoundly different regulatory approach to the media at election time. Whereas Lebanese politicians designed their own electoral playing field and did little to prevent political instrumentalisation of the media, Tunisia's elections were organised by the Independent High Authority for Elections (ISIE), an independent electoral commission established after the revolution. Media coverage was monitored jointly by the ISIE and the audiovisual regulating body HAICA. In the run-up to the 2019 presidential and parliamentary elections, the two organisations issued a joint decree on the rules of media coverage composed of forty-nine articles (HAICA 2019). It required media organisations to present detailed plans for fair and balanced coverage at least seven days before the start of the campaign periods and to publish these plans on their websites.

One of HAICA's key concerns was that time allotted to participants in political debates should be equal. In most Tunisian media, this rule had an eye-catching impact. During one of our visits to a radio station, an editor showed us a complicated software system for keeping track of how many seconds each politician could speak, calculated in relation to how many municipalities his/her party was represented in and how much time the party had received in previous debates in the same channel. In debates we observed on private television stations, such as Channel 9, the journalist was reduced to a timekeeper, letting each participant speak uninterrupted about his/her party's political programme for exactly two minutes, at which point the journalist pressed a red button in the studio and a buzzer signalled the end of that participant's intervention. It was scrupulously fair but made for excruciatingly boring television. Likewise, when the candidates 'debated' on the public broadcaster al-Wataniyya, the arbitration was left to the clock. Each candidate received a question and 90 seconds to answer it; at the 10-second mark, a timer started counting down. The candidates spoke without interruption but also without any real exchange of opinions.

Journalists and politicians we interviewed agreed that HAICA had a strong impact but held different views on whether this impact was enabling or disabling for journalism and political communication more generally. Journalists in public media (whether state-owned or confiscated media) tended to give a positive assessment. For example, Cathia, of al-Wataniyya, commented that 'HAICA is very important because it lifts the hand of the state away from the public media' (T19, 7 May 2018). She considered the independent media regulator as a safeguard against government meddling, giving journalists a freer hand to pursue the topics and angles they wanted.

Journalists in private media were less enthusiastic about HAICA, alleging that it showed more concern with punishing than regulating the media. It is tempting to attribute such misgivings to political motives, since journalists at several private media outlets support their owners' attempts to influence public opinion through the media. However, HAICA itself was suspected of having a political agenda even by journalists in public media. Musa, an editor at a state-owned newspaper, offered this critical assessment:

> HAICA has huge prerogatives and can make change by freeing media from government control. But it cannot play that role at the moment because it is the government's ally. This is a big threat against press freedom in Tunisia. (T27, 22 November 2018)

Others complained that HAICA tied the hands of journalists too much. A spokesperson for the Islamist party al-Nahda acknowledged the necessity of a strict media regulator in the political transition process but argued that HAICA's strictness emasculated public political debate. The regulator's rules for election coverage made it very difficult for journalists to present political debates in an interesting way, she claimed (T48, 7 May 2018).

A business mogul in prison

Not everyone abided by the ISIE and HAICA's rules for election coverage. Tunisia's most watched television channels, Nisma and al-Hiwar al-Tunisi, blatantly defied the requirements to not take political sides and to allocate equal airtime to all parties and candidates. The two stations have long-standing conflicts with HAICA, which considers them illegal broadcasters. HAICA insists that a media organisation should be free from political affiliations and not serve as an instrument of vested interests. The business mogul Karoui threw Nisma behind Beji Caïd Essebsi's bid for the presidency in 2014 and used the channel to prepare his own entry into politics. According to monitoring by the European Union's election observation mission, Nisma reserved 68 per cent of its airtime in the 2019 presidential election campaign for Karoui (EEAS 2020). Al-Hiwar al-Tunisi gave an extra push to the candidates 'Abd al-Karim al-Zabidi and Salim al-Riahi and negative press to Prime Minister Youssef Chahed. The owner Samy al-Fihri was facing prosecution over the illegal use of state television funds in connection with his production company Cactus Prod, under the old regime, and was eager to see Chahed lose the election. He personally travelled to France to interview the businessman-candidate al-Riahi who was living in self-imposed exile to evade a warrant for his arrest on corruption charges in Tunisia.

The election battle took an unexpected turn on 23 August 2019, when, returning from a campaign meeting in the city of Baja, Karoui and his brother Ghazi were detained by the police. The arrest inflamed the Tunisian media and the world of Tunisian journalism. Karoui had a large and loyal constituency, but also many critics in the media and beyond. Journalists both commended and condemned his detention. To begin with Karoui's critics, Bubakir bin 'Akasha, a journalist on Channel 9, posted the following statement on Facebook: 'There is no neutrality regarding the mafia' (bin 'Akasha 2019). The word 'mafia' recurred in other online articles, including a piece in the leading e-media Babnet ('Umrany 2019) that compared Karoui to Silvio Berlusconi and described Nisma as a 'state within the Tunisian state' and a 'media outlet outside the law'. Both Channel 9 and Babnet seemingly spoke for Prime Minister Youssef Chahed, himself a candidate in the presidential election. But criticism also came from journalists in politically neutral media. Najim, from the public broadcaster al-Wataniyya, judged that Karoui's showcasing of philanthropic activities, coupled with a blockbuster Turkish television series, gave him a political advantage that put Tunisia's democracy at risk:

> Everybody has been talking about the importance of equal opportunity in the presidential elections, but on this point I have something to say: Yes, it's good with equal opportunities, but we should pay attention to them at an earlier stage than during the actual elections – when you have a candidate that has been using his own TV channel to carpet-bomb the population with a political discourse designed to support his candidature. Then the candidates won't be starting from the same starting point in the contest. This candidate started his campaign three years ago, through philanthropic work and his influential TV channel that airs all these Turkish, dubbed soap operas that older people watch. Equal opportunity should be from the very beginning.
>   – You are saying that dubbed Turkish soap operas are used for a political purpose?

Yes, because there are commercial breaks during the screening where they cleverly insert things about charity work and so on. The women of my mother's generation, who watch these soap operas, were so aggrieved when Nabil Karoui was imprisoned, because they are so happy about him offering them these serials. There are people who voted for him just to have a guarantee that they will be able to continue watching these soap operas dubbed into Tunisian dialect. This use of the channel runs contrary to the regulations in the elections, that you are not allowed to employ a media organisation you own to help your campaign. (T34, 8 October 2019)

Najim found the electoral competition unfair because Karoui possessed a publicity machine that placed him ahead of the other candidates. To reuse a phrase from the discussion of Lebanon, above, he considered the electoral playing field uneven. Unsurprisingly, Karoui's supporters held a diametrically opposed view. From their vantage point, Karoui was detained at a strategically chosen time to prevent his election victory. They saw what happened as proof that the playing field was skewed against him. Journalists and commentators on Nisma TV worked day and night to defend their patron. The channel cancelled all its entertainment programmes, including Turkish soap operas, to give room for twenty-four-hour news updates about Karoui's arrest. This scale of coverage was perhaps not surprising, but the editorial tone was remarkably confrontational: Nisma openly accused Prime Minister Chahed of having ordered the arrest for political reasons, and the police of acting as his willing agents. Moreover, journalists and experts on its programmes, including lawyers, lambasted the Tunisian judiciary for being in the government's pockets. In a live stream on the night that the story broke, host Hassan Bilwa'r announced that Karoui had been 'kidnapped' by unknown forces (Nisma TV 2019b). The next day, the channel showed mobile camera footage of the detention under the headline 'Youssef Chahed's police kidnaps the presidential candidate Nabil Karoui' (Nisma TV 2019a). Guests on the talk show *Nas Nisma* referred to the government as 'Chahed's dictatorship'. Journalists on al-Hiwar al-Tunisi also criticised Karoui's detention, albeit in less sensationalist terms. They lent credibility to the claim that Chahed might have used the judiciary and police as his personal tools of power, pointing to the suspicious timing of the affair.

Polarisation and distrust

Karoui remained incarcerated and unable to campaign in person until 9 October, four days before the second round of the elections. He was banned from conducting media interviews, participating in television debates and directly communicating with voters (ataha 2020). Nonetheless, he won 15.58 per cent of the votes in the first round of the elections and qualified for the run-off. Nisma and its journalists were important contributors to this achievement. Along with Karoui's wife Salwa they became surrogates for his electoral campaign. One journalist on the frontline of the election battle was Muhammad Amin Matirawi. Defying Tunisian media culture and HAICA's expectations, he openly campaigned for Karoui in television interviews and Facebook posts. Matirawi reprimanded the judiciary and the security forces for their actions and changed his Facebook profile picture to a selfie with Karoui as a personal statement. The polarisation among journalists ran high on social media. Matirawi clashed with Bubakir bin 'Akasha, the host of Channel 9's presidential election programme *Sakin Kartaj* (literally translated as 'Living in [the Presidential Palace in] Carthage), who had compared Nabil Karoui to controversial Tunisian businessmen accused of corruption and criticised candidates who refused to take part in his programme. Matirawi took aim at bin 'Akasha in a vitriolic post on Facebook:

> The election candidates don't want to participate in Bubakir bin 'Akasha's program . . . because they are so vile, corrupt, and mafia, and they don't like to appear on a neutral platform . . . pee on them all, the most important is that Yousef Chahed is willing to appear and not afraid of strong and unexpected questions from our brother Bubakir, the symbol of professionalism and neutrality on the channel of 'Umar Junayyih, which receives millions without gaining a million and is the brother of the top candidate of the Tahya Tunis party in Sousse.
>
> Nabil must go to prison because he has a TV channel that HAICA must shut down . . . and Yousef does not have one but two TV channels, including the so-called 'national' TV [al-wataniyya] that Mufdi al-Masdi and his wife control. (al-Matirawi n.d.)

With posts like this, the pro-Karou Matirawi returned the accusation of media instrumentalisation against his opponents. Matirawi pointed to

Prime Minister Chahed and his communication advisor Mufdi al-Masdi and the fact that the brother of Channel 9 owner 'Umar Junayyih held a high position in Chahed's political party. The gloves were manifestly off. Journalists in al-Hiwar al-Tunisi contributed to the polemic as well. For example, Muhammed Bughallab, whom we introduced in Chapter 4, lashed out at journalists who sold their services to politicians, calling them prostitutes and 'bootlickers' (*quwwad*). To quote:

> It is ok that a journalist gives his opinion in an article or a TV or radio program, but when someone promotes himself by recommending, congratulating or denouncing a politician, that is not journalism, it is solicitation in the public space. He says 'hey Mister, look at me, I am on your side. I am all for you.' This is not the way respectable journalists behave. Excuse my language but those who want to lick asses and boots should do it in secret. Just like there are journalists who work in secret for politicians in the election campaign. (Babnet 2019b)

Bughallab also lashed out at journalists who declared support for Kais Saied on social media (Elhiwar Ettounsi 2019a). Channel 9 presenter Samir al-Wafi reacted angrily to him on Facebook, reminding the *chroniqueur* of all the times he had stood with politicians. 'What can we call all your interventions', al-Wafi asked heatedly, 'if not corruption?' (al-Wafi 2019).

An interview on *Sakin Kartaj* with al-Nahda's first-ever presidential candidate, 'Abd al-Fattah al-Muru, provoked a social media storm. One of the *chroniqueurs* on the programme confronted al-Muru with a fabricated clip that ostensibly showed him calling for an Islamic caliphate in Tunisia during a speech in Amman. Al-Muru, insisted that the video had been fabricated (Channel 9 2019). The following day, programme host Bubakir bin 'Akasha conceded Muru was right and offered his apologies. Ten days later, a satirical show on the al-Nahda-affiliated Zaytuna TV derided Tunisian journalists for being bought and co-opted. The host Ilyas al-Qarquri described the media's role during the election campaign as 'helping corrupted people come to power' (Babnet 2019f).

Against the backdrop of all these accusations, it is interesting to note that Kais Saied, who ultimately won the election, set himself apart from everyone else in his approach to the media. In fact, he refused to take part in television and radio shows – with the sole exception of the presidential debate on the public al-Wataniyya channel – or to give interviews to Tunisian journalists. Instead, he relied on a door-to-door and social media-based campaign organised by young activists (Boussen and Mbarki 2021). Saied's supporters mobilised bottom-up by creating a myriad of unofficial pages, including open and private Facebook groups. One of these was organised by the National Tunisian Youth Movement and had close to 300,000 followers (Zayat 2019).

Saied's choice to not have a relationship with the media was part of a larger project aimed at 'closing the gap between citizens and politics' that he called 'a new construction' (Brésillon 2019). Inspired by radical democracy ideals of equal access to the state and public services, he wanted to reduce the role of intermediaries between the government and the people (Wolf 2019). Saied was critical of political parties and preferred to organise his own 'movement' loosely. As president, he would also demonstrate his preference for face-to-face engagement with citizens. Hence, the media, by its very nature and name, stood in the way of Saied's political vision. More than anything, he was sceptical of the private media and the political and economic interests behind it. Saied's sidelining of the private media continued after he was elected to office. For example, when he gave his first media interview, a hundred days into his presidency, he refused to let the private media attend (Business News 2020). Similarly, on the occasion of his 23 October 2019 investiture ceremony, no representatives of the journalist syndicate, the Tunisian Federation of Newspaper Directors or HAICA were invited (Sarra 2019).

The leading private media held a grudge against Saied from the start. Nisma's coverage was naturally biased, since the channel had backed his opponent in the run-off to the presidential race. However, Al-Hiwar al-Tunisi's campaign against Saied was in fact more bitter. Along with Channel 9, these private television stations attacked him for his social-conservative views on gender equality, homosexuality and the death penalty, portraying him as a hidden supporter of al-Nahda. They warned that his win would lead Tunisia back into the troubles it experienced between 2011 and 2014, when the 'Troika' coalition governed.[2] The channels fed the tensions between secular

---

[2] The Troika was a coalition government led by Hamadi al-Jibali (al-Nahda), al-Munsif al-Marzuqi (CPR), and Mustafa Ibn al-Ja'far (Ettakatol).

and Islamist segments of society that the politicians had toned down during the 2015–19 grand coalition between al-Nahda, Nida Tunis and other parties.

The *chroniqueurs* of al-Hiwar al-Tunisi took the lead in this media-driven polarisation. On 23 September 2019, the high-profile journalists Maya al-Qusuri, Muhammad Bughallab and Lutfi al-'Amari commented on the news that a man had stabbed a security officer to death and injured a soldier in Bizerte. The three interpreted the episode as an ominous sign of 'the return of ISIS' to Tunisia. They drew a line between this development and the government project of Kais Saied. Bughallab described Saied's project as an attempt to move power from the periphery to the centre, as local revolutionary councils had done in 2011 (Babnet 2019c). Al-'Amari raised his voice in theatrical fashion, exhorting civil society and the Tunisian people to block the road for terrorists so that they did not end up in the Carthage palace (Babnet 2019a).

The *chroniqueurs* did not limit their anti-Saied campaign to the candidate himself. They also criticised his supporters and the people who voted for him. Al-'Amari reasoned that Saied's voters should carry the responsibility and be blamed if the country fell into the hands of extremists and terrorists. In a post on Instagram, al-Qusuri ridiculed the idea that Saied was a revolutionary figure, clean and progressive. Only the ignorant and uncultivated could make that claim, she stated (Arabesque 2019). Bughallab mocked a rural woman who, in an election day interview, explained why she had cast her vote for Saied. 'After the election of Saied', he commented, 'I expect her handcart will be transformed into a D-MAX [Pickup 4x4]' (Babnet 2019d).

Backlash for journalists

Al-Hiwar al-Tunisi was out of sync with the Tunisian people in its appraisal of Saied. The election results showed a resounding victory for the candidate the channel had ardently sought to discredit. Saied outclassed Karoui in the second round, gaining 72.7 per cent of the ballots (ataha 2020). He had won the voters' trust despite – or perhaps because of – the three main private television channels working against him. He managed to turn the media establishment's opposition to him into a political asset. In reaction to the election results, al-'Amari compared Tunisia to Iran and Sudan, saying: 'We are now in a state that has fallen under the [Muslim] Brothers' rule' (al-Hiwar al-Tunisi 2019). However, the list of political forces that had sided with Saied went far beyond al-Nahda and included traditional opponents of the brotherhood. such as socialists, social democrats and Arab nationalists.

Saied's supporters were profoundly upset with the private television stations and their journalists. After the first election round, activists called on Tunisians to boycott al-Hiwar al-Tunisi. As a consequence, the channel lost more than 1.5 million followers on Facebook (Maghrebvoices 2019). On the day of the run-off, reporters from al-Hiwar al-Tunisi and other channels were physically attacked in the streets. Programme host Myriam Bulqadi and the above-mentioned *chroniqueurs* also received death threats on Facebook (al-Masdar 2019). At this point, journalists from across the political spectrum came to the defence of their colleagues at al-Hiwar al-Tunisi. The journalists' syndicate (SNJT) condemned the use of violence, and fifteen human rights organisations as well as HAICA and the Union of Tunisian Workers published declarations of support (Babnet 2019e). Kais Saied himself also pleaded with people to respect and not attack Tunisian journalists (Shams FM 2019).

The journalists who had criticised Saied were not the only victims of the anger in the air. Other members of the profession felt threatened because they were associated with politicised journalists. At a roundtable for journalists we organised in January 2020, a reporter shared her experience of reporting from the main street of Tunis on the day Saied was declared the winner of the election. She explained that she perceived the situation as intimidating:

> Nasima: I was in avenue Habib Bourguiba on the day of election results of Kais Saied. We were filming the victory of Kais Said and all, while our colleagues of al-Hiwar al-Tunisi who were prevented from . . .
> 'Usman: Attacked.
> Nasima: Exactly, attacked, and prevented from filming. We were also prevented from filming. We were morally attacked, not to say physically attacked. And were prevented from filming because they thought that we were al-Hiwar al-Tunisi. So I published about this the next day, because I felt very insulted. They were around me chanting 'Maya, oh Maya' and whatever about 'Bughallab'. They were really, really violent, even their discourse. They would look at me, they gave me this look that was very insulting. So, on the next day I published an article stating that we are field journalists and we

have nothing to do with the commentators you see on TV, and who are promoting some politicians or creating very precise political discourse in favour of certain people. I said that we are people working in the field, while they are commentators on TV sets. It means that they should not be regarded as journalists in the same way we are, because it's us who are paying the price for all of this. (Roundtable, Tunis, 26 January 2020)

Nasima's story is cause for concern for Tunisian journalists. It illustrates how damaging the consequences are for the profession when the public perceives that the media and key journalists are being used to promote specific political agendas. The crowd on Avenue Habib Bourguiba made little distinction between Nasima and the journalists of al-Hiwar al-Tunisi. As this dedicated journalist expressed it, she felt that she was 'morally attacked'. She reacted by writing an article where she separated herself as a correspondent from the *chroniqueurs*, in the hopes that this would save her reputation. However, losing trust is easier than building it and people may not see the difference between one journalist and another: the more so when social media distortion becomes part of the equation. In our roundtable, Nasima explained that the article she wrote was later manipulated on digital platforms. Taken together, media instrumentalisation and fake news made it very difficult for her to preserve her integrity.

Conclusion

Elections are the cornerstone of democracies, and therefore they also tend to bring the tensions produced by media instrumentalisation to a head. Where people are relatively free to vote for candidates for national assemblies, manipulating public discourse becomes crucial for unpopular elites bent on maintaining or assuming the reins of power. This desire was evident in both Lebanon and Tunisia during the elections in 2018 and 2019. Entire media organisations and well-known journalists openly acted as mouthpieces for candidates, to the extent that their involvement became a contentious issue in and of itself. On the other side, we found journalists that sided with civil society activists and their wish to reform the whole system, and reporters who were dismayed by the lack of objective reporting and analysis. That said, apart from the impulse to instrumentalise the media and the controversies it leads to, Lebanon and Tunisia are in many ways contrasting cases. Lebanon's election was engineered by the elites to assure authoritarian survival and produced no political change. The state made only half-hearted attempts to limit the political use of the media, and journalists unabashedly took part in the political competition. Tunisia's elections took place in a much more regulated environment. They were free and fair and resulted in the rise of a adamant critic of the establishment to the apex of state power. The Independent High Authority for Audiovisual Communication made ardent efforts to regulate the media and prevent the instrumentalisation of journalism. Plainly speaking, these differences showed why Lebanon was considered a hybrid regime whereas Tunisia counted as a democracy at the time. Civil society's mobilisation for change by peaceful means was frustrated in Lebanon whereas the young activists who fought for Kais Saied's election victory in Tunisia achieved their goal. This last contrast is important, because it meant that the political system in Tunisia provided a safety valve to channel ordinary people's frustration: the possibility of voting unpopular leaders out of office. In Lebanon, the system provided no such safety valve, and frustration had to find other outlets. That was exactly what happened in 2019, when thousands of Lebanese poured into the streets to protest against the entire political establishment. In addition to the streets, the media acted as an outlet of frustration, and the latent tension between instrumentalised and critical journalists sprang into full bloom. It is to this milestone in Lebanese media history that we turn in the next chapter.

8

PROTESTS AND DISRUPTIVE JOURNALISM

From 17 October 2019 until well into 2020, Lebanon witnessed massive popular protests that shook the country's political system to its core. The protests were precipitated by the government's plans to impose taxes on IP telephony, gasoline and tobacco, but the underlying issues were corruption, deteriorating living standards and a profound sense of political alienation. In a matter of days, the protests spread across the country and the protesters' slogans expanded to become a denunciation of the entire political system and the elite, irrespective of religious affiliation. Demonstrators closed some of the main roads to and from Beirut and brandished placards reading: 'All of them means all of them' (thus condemning the whole political establishment regardless of religious identity) and 'Down with sectarian rule'. Ordinary Lebanese across the country realised the extent of hardship and misery among their fellow citizens: Tripoli, a neglected city north of Beirut that was formerly notorious as a hotbed of militant Salafism, was bestowed with the honorary title 'bride of the revolution' on account of the vast, dignified demonstrations by its marginalised populace. Hundreds of thousands of people from all of the religious communities in Lebanon participated in the demonstrations, demanding the resignation of the entire government and a major overhaul of the political system (The Economist 2019). Despite the government's heavy-handed response, including beatings, tear gas, arrests and deployment of the army, the protests continued with remarkable force through 2019 and for much of 2020. They caused a protracted political crisis that included the resignation of an entire cabinet and some of the top bureaucrats in the country. Most importantly, however, the force and duration of the protests showed the shocking disconnect between ordinary Lebanese and the leaders who were supposed to represent them, but in reality, ruled them without accountability.

The '17 October Revolution', as demonstrators called it, was a watershed event in Lebanon's recent history. In a brief but incisive analysis, Marwan Kraidy (2019) has compared the 2019 protests with the previously most recent mass mobilisation of the Lebanese streets: the 2005 demonstrations against the assassination of Prime Minister Rafiq Hariri and the Syrian military presence in Lebanon. Kraidy notes that in 2005, 'feuding sectarian leaders' organised the protests, paid advertising executives to brand the demonstrations and employed their loyal and powerful media to full effect. In 2019, by contrast, the protests were genuinely popular and directed against the whole establishment: 'The breathtaking corruption of politicians [. . .] trumped sectarian loyalties and turned the entire ruling class into the target of protest', writes Kraidy. Traditional media, which the elites used to great effect in 2005, were still powerful, but they had been partly overtaken by social media in an 'information sphere that [was] diverse but fragmented and volatile'.

As the protests continued with undiminished vigour, the elites scrambled to keep up with the situation and turn it to their advantage. Sunni Prime Minister Saad Hariri stepped down in an attempt to deflect criticism from himself and channel it towards the dominant force in the government (the alliance between Christian president Aoun, Hizbullah and the AMAL movement led by Speaker of Parliament Nabih Berri). Hizbullah leader Hasan Nasrallah replaced the yellow Hizbullah flag with the Lebanese flag in his televised appeals to the people, trying to signal solidarity with the nation. Such machinations were to little avail, however; the popular anger did not abate. Predictably, the naked power of the regime soon replaced the attempts at deflecting criticism, as security forces and thugs attacked demonstrators and tried to scare people off the streets.

Through all this, traditional and new media alike played a very important role, as Kraidy alludes to in the quote above. Journalists and ordinary citizens would probably agree that 'if during the start of the uprising there had been no media [coverage] we wouldn't have seen an uprising like this – it wouldn't have lasted for more than two or three days' (L39, 31 January 2020). A major change upset the whole media community in Lebanon and had implications for politics–media relations: several media outlets and individual journalists assumed a new, critical attitude against all the political elites, irrespective of sectarian identity, and independent media organisations experienced a boost.

New Fault Lines in the Established Media

In parallel with the struggles in the streets, the media and individual journalists fought over the narrative about the protests. The different approaches taken by the main television channels were clear from the first editorial introductions to the evening news on 18 October, the day after the demonstrations started.[1] Acknowledging the deep-felt frustration on the street, none of the channels criticised the protesters, but they explained the demonstrations in very different terms. On one side were OTV, NBN and al-Manar, channels loyal to the alliance between President Aoun, Speaker of Parliament Berri and Hizbullah. Al-Manar's news presenter started the broadcast by acknowledging the suffering of ordinary Lebanese, but in the next breath warned against the cynicism of alleged, unnamed conflict entrepreneurs. The protests were 'a cry of pain – even if some reckless gamblers (*muqamirun*) try to appropriate it [. . .]'. The presenter then criticised Prime Minister Hariri, a long-time adversary of Hizbullah, for not stepping up to the task of engaging with the protesters' demands, but rather giving himself a three-day deadline to decide whether he would continue or step down. She contrasted the fecklessness of Hariri with the alleged honesty and decisiveness of Minister of Foreign Affairs Jubran Basil (who belonged to President Aoun's movement) and Hizbullah's secretary general, Hasan Nasrallah. In this way, al-Manar tried simultaneously to align with the protesters and pin the blame for the troubles on the Sunni elite. Meanwhile, OTV took an even blunter tone: 'We are with the people. It could not be otherwise, based on our media profile and our position towards the nation, for we are part of this people to begin with.' Having thus cast itself as the champion of all Lebanese, the channel proceeded to hail President Aoun

---

[1] The following quotations and summaries are taken from transcripts of all the television channels' evening news hours, which are published daily on several Lebanese websites (e.g. Lebanese Forces 2019).

for standing up to the post-civil war elites and trying to create a new and better state. In contrast to these efforts, according to OTV, the opponents of the Hizbullah-Aoun alliance tried to impede progress at every turn.

Viewers of MTV and LBCI were exposed to a very different picture. MTV made the exceptional choice not to air an evening newscast at all; instead, it provided continuous live coverage from the protests throughout the evening, reporting from within the throng of people who took to the streets. LBCI focused on analysing the reactions to the protests from the various elite factions. It concluded that the way the elites dealt with the demonstrations would decide whether the demonstrations represented a window of opportunity or the last outpost before a popular explosion. In sharp contrast to al-Manar and OTV, neither MTV nor LBCI took it upon themselves to commend or defend *any* of the elite factions. Instead, they concentrated on relaying what was going on in the streets or trying to make sense of the political implications of the demonstrations from a standpoint outside of sectarian rivalries.

This contrast only deepened in the days and weeks that followed. Thus, on 3 November, OTV spread the claim that the protesters blocking Lebanon's roads were supporters of the Lebanese Forces, the Sunni Muslim Future Movement and Druze leader Kamal Jumblatt. The channel juxtaposed this picture with the words of President Aoun, who days before had told a cheering crowd, 'I love you all, meaning all of you' (an appropriation of the protesters' anti-sectarian slogan 'all of them means all of them'). In other words, for OTV Aoun preached a message of national unity, while those who continued to demonstrate against the political elite were saboteurs belonging to specific political factions. LBCI, on the other hand, continued to refrain from partisanship and presented an analysis of the political machinations taking place after Hariri had resigned from his position of prime minister on 29 October. The channel's critical attitude toward the political establishment was apparent in its summary of the scant progress made by the politicians: 'On the one hand, political meetings; on the other, the street.' MTV was less restrained. It hailed the 'revolutionary Lebanese' while describing the elite's political meetings as 'naked manoeuvring'.

More sharp-edged criticism of the elites was also apparent in the established print media. For example, Muhammad Zabib, a financial journalist for the traditionally pro-Hizbullah newspaper *al-Akhbar*, wrote a series of articles on corruption and Lebanon's financial crisis in which he argued, among other things, that Lebanon's richest had drained the Central Bank of US dollars, thereby preventing the state from subsidising medicine and bread for ordinary people (Zabib 2019). Zabib forcefully criticised the government (of which Hizbullah was part) and denounced the 'oligarchy' stealing the country's riches from the population (Reporters Without Borders 2020). *L'Orient-Le Jour* provided detailed coverage of the protest movement, from a social media campaign to stop paying taxes to the demonstrations in the street (El-Hage 2019b).

As several of the agenda-setting media outlets started allowing more critical coverage, the journalists working for them also experienced an increased sense of professional solidarity across political divides as well as a feeling that the power balance between the media and top politicians had tilted towards the former. Several journalists who covered the demonstrations on the ground were at times abused or harassed by either demonstrators or security personnel, depending on the orientation of the media house they worked for. Fellow journalists would then intervene and protect them, despite their differences of opinion. Such reports were all the more striking when compared with interviews we conducted before the demonstrations, in which journalists lamented the lack of professional solidarity. Mayisa covered the events on the streets extensively for al-Jadid channel and fondly remembered the mutual professional sympathy:

> When we were in the middle of tear gas grenades, the OTV reporter was giving me onions and I was carrying her microphone. And I defended her when the protestors were annoying her, as al-Jadid would be closer to the demonstrators at that time. So yes, I was able to speak with them and make them leave her. We sort of became like one family on the ground, we became friends and we became much closer to each other. (L42, 31 January 2020)

Investigative reporters started noticing a very different attitude from politicians who had previously ignored them. Jalal, who worked as an investigative reporter for al-Jadid, reflected that normally politicians had the advantage over journalists, to the extent that they did not even worry about serious allegations of corruption: 'Yes, it's me, I grabbed 2 million USD from the state coffers. What are you going to do about it?' However, after the demonstrations rocked the country, he only needed to send a single message and they would call back instantly. 'Now they want to explain and clarify [. . .]. The general social mood is changed to the advantage of the journalist' (L38, 31 January 2020).

It is important to note that the real changes journalists experienced did not erase the economic and political imperatives governing the major television channels in Lebanon. This resulted in what one journalist called 'schizophrenic' editorial policies (L40, 31 January 2020). A channel such as LBCI would try to reconcile honest reporting with editorial policies designed to avoid clashes with important funders or political actors, making the news anchor in the studio appear at odds with the reporter calling in live from the demonstrations on the evening news. When al-Jadid hosted an interview with Minister of Foreign Affairs Jubran Basil, many regarded this as an attempt to reconcile with him and polish his image. Activists accused al-Jadid of opposing the revolution and launched a social media campaign to boycott the interview. It seemed that the television stations were testing their audience to see how they would respond. Media organisations did not change fundamentally because of the uprisings; they allowed their journalists to adopt opposing positions to accommodate popular feelings whilst remaining loyal to their financial backers. They were not immune to the pressures of powerful people who wanted them to avoid certain terms, such as intifada and revolution, substituting for them the more neutral, less dramatic 'movement' (*hirak*). One of our informants also claimed that even channels that ostensibly supported the uprising would not turn away a government minister who offered to pay 100,000 USD for a sympathetic interview on the channel (L34, 22 January 2020).

Nevertheless, there was a clear difference between these media and the really pro-government media, who stuck to their guns and did not attempt to accommodate different voices. During the first weeks of the protests, politicians were either avoiding or being boycotted by the media and some prominent journalists effortlessly assumed the role of 'trumpets'. For example, Ibrahim al-Amin, the editor-in-chief of *al-Akhbar*, published a five-minute video on the newspaper's homepage addressing the people only four days after the uprising. He rejected the slogan all of them means all of them whose rhetorical force was 'every single one of the elites is corrupt', and accused the protestors of being part of the problem (al-Akhbar 2019). Al-Amin voiced what many politicians were reluctant to say at the time and was one of many journalists who replaced politicians in media appearances at a time when they were not present to speak for themselves.

As the great divide between the major television channels became apparent to demonstrators, reporters from the pro-government media were sometimes harassed or even attacked. Their independent colleagues were dismayed by such threats to the profession but could understand why they occurred: 'I am against attacking or harming any journalist but when people chant against them, this is a result of how [their] media organisation was transformed to barricades [for the politicians]' (L22, 4 February 2020). The uprising was a catalyst for media change: the fault lines ran less between elite factions than between the entire elite and the people. The system of instrumentalised political parallelism in part broke down and opened the eyes of many Lebanese journalists to new professional vistas.

Digital independence

Of course, some journalists had already taken independent action at this point. In Chapter 5, we briefly mentioned Khalid Saghiyah as an example of journalistic 'change agents' who placed journalism in the service of democratisation. For these journalists, the digital revolution was a boon that served them very well in the cataclysmic months of late 2019 and early 2020. Setting up a digital, edited newspaper is relatively inexpensive and Lebanon's media laws have not kept pace with technological developments, so there were few impediments to starting digital news sites. As we mentioned in Chapter 5, Saghiyah joined the news site Megaphone soon after its launch in 2017. Megaphone defines itself as an independent media platform that 'produces explainer multimedia content covering local news', publishing 'analytical and critical content' (Megaphone 2020). Saghiyah and others made the most of the unprecedented opportunity afforded by the 2019–20 protests. Megaphone published intensively on the politics of the demonstrations from the very start, and their coverage made no pretence of neutrality. For example, an analysis piece by Saghiyah on 28 October was headlined 'Why do we hate the pact?' (The word 'pact' referred to the tacit agreements between the elites.) Saghiyah started the piece by stating that 'the one word that best describes what is referred to as "the pact" is *greed*'. Then he distinguished three kinds of greed (for power, money and control) pinning them to Jubran Basil (FPM), Saad Hariri (Future Movement) and Hasan Nasrallah (Hizbullah), respectively – the three most prominent public persons in Lebanon, all from different sectarian groups. The article concluded with the rhetorical question: 'Is it possible to meet any demand without limiting these three kinds of greed, which are the backbone of what is called "the pact"?' Between 18 October and 31 December 2019, Saghiyah published twenty articles on the protests on Megaphone, discussing the virtues of the 'revolution' and roundly condemning leading politicians by name. The website also carried dozens of critical articles by other journalists during the same period.

Although Megaphone was among the most critical voices in Lebanon, it was not at all unique. Digital news outlets offered a new kind of freedom and independence to many journalists. Whether these journalists were too critical for the taste of established media organisations, or too community-oriented to be interesting for national media outlets, they found a haven in digital news sites. For example, Daraj.com, an independent, high quality digital news site was founded by the prominent journalists Hazim Amin, Diana Muqallid and 'Aliya Ibrahim, who were all disillusioned with the instrumentalisation of traditional media in Lebanon. It draws on a wide professional network in Lebanon and beyond, covering the whole Middle East region with critical reporting and commentary. Daraj was quick to produce videos on the demonstrations in Lebanon and post them on its YouTube channel. It sided with the protesters and directed vehement criticism against Hizbullah, in particular (Daraj Media 2019). On the community-oriented end was Yasour.org, a news site and portal for the city of Tyre (*Sur* in Arabic) and its environs, including a network of correspondents in the Lebanese diaspora around the world. Yasour reported neutrally on all kinds of events in the Tyre area, big and small, without discernible bias towards any of the sectarian groups, and was one of the top news sites in Lebanon when we worked on this book. Such news sites are cheap to set up and operate and production is simple. Yasour stayed true to its community-centred profile throughout the protests, reporting on both the latest protest events and the speeches from political leaders without advocating for one or the other.

Social media

While professionally edited digital news were important contributors to the media landscape of the uprising, the real digital protagonist was social media. For many Lebanese, and certainly the activists who took to the streets, Twitter, Facebook, YouTube, WhatsApp groups and Instagram were the most important sources of information. Many activists transformed their Facebook pages into 'revolutionary media', sharing amateur video clips from demonstrations and other incidents that quickly reached thousands more viewers. Lebanese revolutionaries also covered the various debates, teach-ins and artistic gatherings; provided deeper analysis of micro- and macro-level developments; and – perhaps most importantly – created structures for disseminating critical and time-sensitive information on national as well as local levels (Lteif 2020). Obviously, the role and dynamics of social media in times of upheaval is a vast topic requiring a book of its own. Our ambition here is limited to analysing how social media affected professional journalism. Social media had two main functions for Lebanese journalists, over and above being sources of information. First, social media provided journalists with an opportunity to intervene personally in public debate, something that proved to be contentious and amplified the conflict between journalists who were 'trumpets' for the various elite factions and those who were critics of the whole system. Second, social media facilitated a kind of symbiosis between activists and journalists by which new information was shared and mutual respect grew.

Let us start with social media as an arena for personal intervention in the public sphere. Twitter and Facebook offer journalists great opportunities to communicate with the public. Each day, most Lebanese citizens browse their smartphones or computers and read or listen to the news without having to wait for their daily television broadcast or newspapers. To stay up to date on political news, many subscribe to social media updates by famous politicians and well-known journalists, some of whom have hundreds of thousands of followers on Twitter.

Journalists use social media to share videos, quotes or news about incidents, adding their own comments. When sharing a news link, they often write in simple language, using the Lebanese dialect instead of formal Arabic. Snappy comments are delivered in an often sarcastic tone. Friends as well as followers respond to posts they like by sharing and spreading the content further, commenting on it and engaging in debate, or simply expressing emotions towards it. In this way, social media use for journalists in Lebanon is closely related to their job and no clear demarcation lines between the private and the public persona exist. This phenomenon was apparent well before the 17 October uprising. For example, the well-known journalist Diana Muqallid posted an outraged tweet when Hizbullah activist Jamil al-Sayyid was elected to parliament in 2018. Al-Sayyid is controversial because he cooperated with the Syrian occupation of Lebanon until 2005 and was imprisoned for four years under suspicion of aiding in the assassination of former Prime Minister Rafik Hariri in 2005. Muqallid, who had close to 100,000 followers on Twitter, commented on his candidacy with the following tweet: 'Hizbullah will nominate [for the parliamentary elections] Jamil al-Sayyid, a man who dirtied his hands in the security sector, in politics, journalism and conspiracies in the 1990s. Worse is to come . . .' (Figure 8.1).

Her tweet was retweeted by other famous journalists who also enjoy very high numbers of followers. The social media ecology thus allowed journalists to reach both their colleagues and many ordinary Lebanese very quickly, augmenting their independence and political influence.

When the uprising started, journalists were very active on Twitter. To some extent, Twitter served merely as an extended arm of their public comments in established media. For example, Lana Mudawwar, a journalist at the

Figure 8.1 Diana Muqallid tweet, 15 February 2018

pro-Hizbullah media organisation Mayadin, tweeted on 21 October that 'this movement [*hirak*], with the people who participate in it and all the things that accompanies it, no longer represents us' (Mudawwar 2019). Mudawwar's comment was unsurprising, since Hizbullah had failed in its early attempt to align with the protesters and instead become one of the main targets of the demonstrations, along with all the other elites. From then on, Hizbullah officials as well as journalists who were loyal supporters or sympathisers tried to discredit the protesters. Mudawwar, of course, positioned herself firmly as a 'trumpet' for Hizbullah. But other journalists who ostensibly supported the protests whole-heartedly were also accused of being trumpets. Jessica Azar, one of the famous television profiles at MTV, enthusiastically tweeted, four days after the first demonstrations:

> What is happening in Lebanon broke all the barriers. It shook all the political parties, movements and leaders and broke the blind sectarian loyalty. Our basic demand as a new generation and young people of Lebanon must be the dismantling of sectarianism and political allotments. (Azar 2019)

Her post received a raft of replies, many of which were severely critical. They sarcastically commented that Azar's plea to end sectarianism rang hollow, considering the fact that she had recently stood as a parliamentary candidate for the Lebanese Forces, a movement that is very much part of the sectarian system in Lebanon.

Such partisan use of social media was not the most striking feature of the digital media landscape during the uprising, however. What was new was that many journalists used Facebook and Twitter to publicly support the demonstrators in ways that went beyond the editorial lines of their media organisation (in the case of media sympathetic to the protests), or even made a clean break with the editorial line (in the case of media that tried to walk a neutral line or were critical of the protest movement). Social media thus became the prime public arena for individual journalists to show that the uprising had changed their professional and moral priorities. In other words: social media was a bellwether of a new and rebellious spirit in Lebanese journalism that awoke because of the uprising. One high-profile journalist whose support of the demonstrations went further than her media organisation was prepared to accept was Dima Sadiq. At the start of the uprising, Sadiq worked as a news anchor and reporter at LBCI, which, as we have seen above, was regarded as sympathetic to the uprising. The LBCI leadership, however, took care to accommodate journalists with opposing views of the protests, and they had to navigate the tense sectarian climate to stay in business. Sadiq was one of the best-known news anchors and reporters at LBCI. She quickly proved to be personally heavily invested in the demonstrations and posted live reports from the streets on her personal Facebook page, in addition to her reporting for LBCI. More importantly, not only did she cover the events of the uprising, but she also participated openly in blocking roads, such as the Ring Bridge. In late November 2019 she was attacked by Hizbullah and AMAL supporters, who stole her mobile phone. Then the LBCI management denied Sadiq airtime, ostensibly because of an administrative error she had committed. The real reason was that she had publicly expressed her support for the revolution through her personal Twitter account and directly accused high government officials of corruption. She was no longer allowed to anchor the news and her tweets were subjected to censorship by the LBCI administration. Sadiq reacted by resigning from LBCI, and her resignation letter, posted on Facebook, is worth quoting in full because it shows so well what kinds of changes the revolution wrought in the relationships between journalists, media organisations and the political elite (Figure 8.2).

Dima Sadek
26. november 2019

بيان استقالة .
هو بالنسبة لي زمن ثورة . و في الثورة لا سقف للحريات . هي فرصة لنسمي الأشياء بأسمائها ، لنسمي المرتكبين بأسمائهم ، وأن نقول لا بأعلى صوت . منذ ثلاث أسابيع ، أبعدت عن هواء المؤسسة التي أعمل فيها ، بسبب خطأ اداري . تم الاعتذار علنا عن الخطأ ، و تلقيت عقوبتي بمسؤولية تامة . الا ان الإدارة لم تحدد مدى و شكل هذه العقوبة . فبقيت مبعدة عن الهواء دون أسباب مقنعة . بعدها التقيت مع السيد بيار الضاهر الذي شرح لي ان المشكلة ليست فقط الخطأ الإداري ، و إنما أيضا طبيعة تغريداتي ، و تحديدا التي تطال بعبدا ، و المعلومات التي سربتها عن قصر بعبدا (والتي لم يتمكن احد من نفيها) ، طالبا ايقافها مع الوعد بعودتي . الا ان هذه العودة اقتصرت على قراءة الأخبار مع إبعادي التام عن البرامج السياسية و وضع تغريداتي تحت الرقابة. و هو ما اعترضت عليه . ثم جاءت حادثة سرقة هاتفي على الرينغ حيث كانت ردة فعل المؤسسة ايقافي مجددا عن الهواء دون ادنى الاطمئنان علي. و عليه، أجد نفسي على يقين ان سبب الاستبعاد هو سياسي،و هو ما لن اقبل به لا في زمن الثورة و لا غير زمن ، مع التأكيد ان الإدارة أبلغتني التمسك بي مع توقيفي مؤقتا عن الهواء . و عليه أعلن استقالتي من المؤسسة اللبنانية للإرسال . و للحديث تتمة . شكرا.

Figure 8.2 Dima Sadiq's resignation letter on Facebook

Resignation statement

It is a revolutionary time for my part, and in a revolution, there is no limit to freedom. It is an opportunity to call things by their true name, to call out the criminals [lit. perpetrators] by their name, and to shout 'no' at the top of our lungs. For three weeks I have been kept off the air of the organisation I work for because of an administrative mistake. The mistake has been apologised for explicitly and I took my punishment with full responsibility. However, the management did not specify how long this punishment would last and what form it would take, and so I remained off air without there being convincing reasons for it. Then I met with Mr. Pierre Dahir [the owner and manager of LBCI], who told me that the problem was not only the administrative mistake, but also the nature of my tweets – particularly those that criticise Baʻbda [the presidential palace] and the [leaked] information I spread about it (information nobody has been able to refute). He asked that I stopped it, promising me a return to the airwaves. However, I would be limited to reading out the news, being barred from any political programme, and my tweets would be placed under censorship. I protested against this. Then came the incident where my phone was stolen on the Ring road, and where the reaction of my organisation was to take me off air again, without offering me any reassurance. And so I find myself convinced that the reason for marginalising me is a political one. This is something I will not accept in a time of revolution, nor, indeed, at any other time, despite the management informing me that they will retain me, with a temporary banishment from the airwaves. Based on this, I announce my resignation from the Lebanese Broadcasting Corporation. There is more to be said at a later time.

Some of Sadiq's colleagues in other media organisations used social media to openly criticise the political affiliations of their employers. For example, Sami Kulayb was a pillar of the controversial channel al-Mayadin from its start in 2012. True to its political affiliation with its Syrian and Iranian backers, the channel adopted a negative editorial stance on the uprising. On 22 November, Kulayb tweeted that 'in line with my ideas, convictions and conscience, I resigned today from al-Mayadin, wishing it continued prosperity and success' (Kulayb 2019). He followed up by expressing his frustration that 'everything is adaptable' in Lebanon. The next day, he was seen among protesters on the streets of Beirut, posing for pictures with them. His colleague Lina Zahr al-Din, a news presenter with the channel, followed suit, using Facebook to reach the public. First, she posted a sharp rebuke to those who were blocking al-Jadid's reporters from gaining access to the southern suburbs of Beirut, an area controlled by Hizbullah. 'No matter whether we agree or disagree with the politics of this or that channel, it is our professional and moral duty to reject practices of this kind', Zahr al-Din wrote on 21 November, prioritising her own professional ethos over the political affiliation of her television employer. Just days later she posted news of her resignation on Facebook. The post, pictured in Figure 8.3, reads: 'Considering the historical moment we are living in, I feel obliged to resign from al-Mayadin, wishing continuity for it and for the people a better future. May God grant success' (Yassine 2019).

The tweets and Facebook posts by Sadiq, Kulayb and Zahr al-Din occasioned long threads of comments and replies, as did many of the social media interventions made by independent-minded journalists during the uprising. More to the point, the large following of some of these journalists (at the time of their postings, Sadiq had 735,000 followers on Twitter, and Kulayb

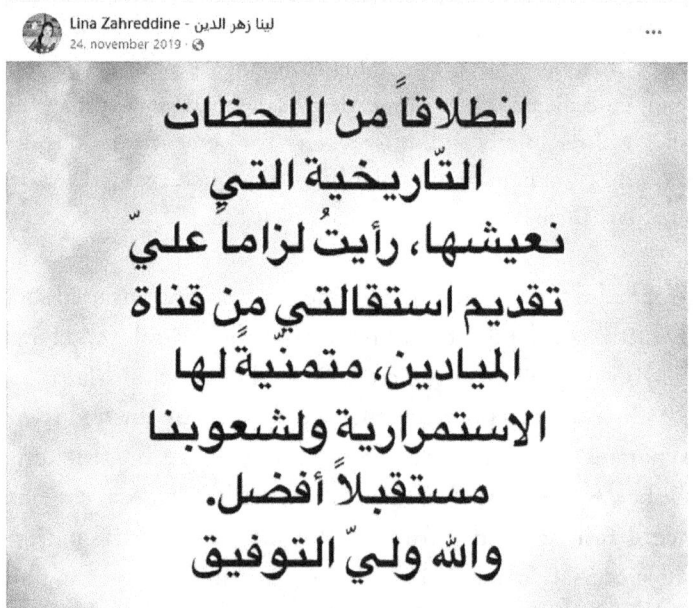

Figure 8.3 Lina Zahr al-Din's resignation letter on Facebook

had 323,000) ensured that even if they lost their jobs, they did not lose their voice. Both Sadiq and Kulayb continued to comment on the uprising; and a year after her resignation from LBCI, Sadiq was offered her own programme at the pro-uprising channel MTV, while Sami Kulayb had started his own news site, The Game of Nations. In this way, social media made it possible for some journalists to defy the instrumentalised parallelism governing the media in Lebanon, and to openly side with the people against the elite.

But social media was more than an arena for journalists to intervene personally in the public sphere. Twitter and Facebook were used in ways that created a symbiosis between protesters and sympathetic journalists, not unlike what was seen during the mass demonstrations of the Arab uprisings in 2011. Many demonstrators converted their Facebook pages or created new ones that served as amateur news sites featuring running coverage of events, such as Akhbar al-Saha (Public Square News). Reporters and television studios made use of the news and footage posted to these sites, and in addition, individual journalists could be alerted to new videos or incidents through WhatsApp groups they were part of or via tweets they received. This information enabled journalists to stay on top of unfolding events:

> I started to have my own reporters [. . .] As a reporter myself, I have gained a huge network of amazing people. The moment a road is blocked they will send me the video before anyone else. When there are clashes, I receive the video and they tell me what is going on. They will also let me know if there is a piece of information regarding a meeting, an event for a political party . . . (L40, 31 January 2020)

For their part, the journalists who roamed the streets reporting on the goings-on could warn demonstrators about imminent crackdowns or other trouble through their Twitter accounts and WhatsApp groups. This was an important asset for the demonstrators, since journalists often have tens or even hundreds of thousands of followers, making them highly effective for mobilisation purposes:

> I may tell [the demonstrators] 'be careful, there is a checkpoint for the police there, make sure you have your ID, or take that shortcut to evade them' [. . .]. [Sometimes] I have cut the live broadcast, pretending that I have a technical problem, and I would call someone inside and tell them 'leave now, I just saw

[the security forces or thugs] coming from this or that road.' Then I called the TV studio back, telling them I had momentarily lost the connection . . . (L40, 31 January 2020)

The daily presence of journalists among the demonstrators, the stream of supportive social media posts by journalists, and the way they sometimes used social media to help and warn protesters all contributed to a sense of togetherness. More than once, a reporter would suddenly get a kiss on the cheek from a passing activist just as she or he was starting a live television report from a demonstration.

Disruptive journalism

Journalism critical of the whole political and media system had become visible in the years leading up to 2019, specifically during the You Stink protests and the 2018 elections, which we looked at in Chapters 5 and 7. However, the uprising in October 2019 was the real catalyst that caused Lebanese journalists' simmering discontent with media–politics relations to boil over. While the You Stink incident in 2015 activated the latent conflict between people and elite for a limited time in some media and among some journalists, the scale and intensity of reporting and commentary sympathetic to the grassroots protests in 2019 were unprecedented. The usual, horizontal conflict between different elites virtually disappeared in the media coverage, and the logic of the vertical conflict between ordinary people and the elite replaced it and imposed itself even on media outlets that were loyal to the system and tried to avoid it. The journalists themselves claimed that the media were divided along new lines: instead of the horizontal inter-elite conflicts, journalists now sided with or against what they called a social 'revolution', sometimes at the risk of being fired by their media employers (Surprenant 2019). Some established outlets – notably MTV – transitioned fully into becoming critical of the entire system, while many journalists who worked for outlets that did *not* make that transition challenged the editorial line, and even quit. It was not only news celebrities like Dima Sadiq and Sami Kulayb who lost their jobs. At *al-Akhbar* alone, five journalists resigned before February 2020 because their personal convictions clashed with the editorial line of the newspaper, the most important in Lebanon. The new electronic media we described above, independent from the existing sectarian divisions, became a haven for some of these rebellious journalists.

However, challenging the elites by defying the logic of clientelism could be dangerous. The many journalists who gave sympathetic coverage to the uprising reported live from the demonstrations at considerable physical risk. Several were attacked and subjected to systematic harassment campaigns. MTV's reporter Nawal Birri was spat on, kicked, and had her camera smashed early in the uprising by Hizbullah and AMAL supporters who were angry about her support for the protests. On the night of 24 October, they chased her into a building while reporting, and she had to be escorted out by security forces (Mroue 2019). Muhammad Zabib, who specialised in corruption coverage for *al-Akhbar*, was attacked by three individuals in a carpark on 12 February 2020 and had to be hospitalised for his injuries. Journalists who happened to be Shi'a Muslims but were critical towards Hizbullah and AMAL faced some of the worst harassment, since they were regarded as traitors to their religious community, according to the sectarian logic. This was true of Nawal Birri, but even more so of her colleague Maryam Sayf al-Din. Sayf al-Din was a journalist with the progressive electronic newspaper *Nida al-Watan* (roughly, 'The National Herald'), and her entire family lived in a house in Burj al-Barajnah, a suburb of Beirut controlled by Hizbullah. When Hizbullah-affiliated thugs vandalised her parents' house and physically assaulted her father and brothers because of her critical reporting, she quit her job, but the harassment continued (Topalian 2021).

Others who were attacked struck back on social media and continued their critical reporting (El-Hage 2019a; Reporters Without Borders 2020; SKEyes 2019; Topalian 2021). A tweet by Muhammad Zabib the day after he was attacked is characteristic of these journalists' spirit of defiance. Above a facsimile of an official document detailing bank transactions in Lebanon for 2018–19, Zabib wrote:

هذه الاوليغارشية ليست نهّابة فقط بل غبية جدا. هل يعتقدون حقا اننا سنخاف ونستسلم؟
امعنوا النظر في الجدول. وتعرّفوا على من يسرقنا.
طبقة الـ 1% مسؤولة عن 98% من سحوبات الودائع. صادروا اجورنا ومدخراتنا. ليسحبوا 15.3 مليار دولار في العام الماضي وحده
احبكم/ن حبا جما.
#تسقط_الاوليغارشية

This oligarchy are not just thieves, they're very stupid, too. Do they really think that we will be frightened and surrender? Examine this table and get to know who is stealing from us. The 1% community is responsible for 98% of the deposit withdrawals. They confiscated our wages and savings to withdraw 15.3 billion USD last year alone.
I love you all dearly.
#Let the oligarchy fall. (Zabib 2020)

The violence and harassment against journalists were a clear sign that the elites feared critical journalism. With good reason: journalism during the uprising indeed proved disruptive. Disruption may range from a disturbance that interrupts politics as usual to a complete altering or even destruction of political structures. The uprising itself was disruptive in the sense that it brought down a government and threw Lebanon into a political crisis that is still ongoing at the time of writing, the fall of 2021. The way journalists covered and commented on the uprising disrupted the political communication strategy of the elites, which was premised on empty praise of national unity and keeping people occupied with the intrigues and games of sectarian leaders, instead of focusing on the fundamental problems besetting Lebanon. So even though neither the political system nor the system of instrumentalised political parallelism entirely collapsed after the 2019 'revolution', the uprising proved to be a watershed moment for the media. The political communication of the elites was disrupted in three ways.

First, in positioning themselves alongside the people in a vertical axis of conflict between grassroots and political elite, journalists changed their professional practices. For years, the news in Lebanon has been focused on the sayings and doings of the sectarian leaders, with reporters converging on the palaces and villas where the powerful call their press conferences. The beginnings of change in the media were visible with the You Stink protests in 2015 but came to full fruition during the uprising. The politicians who formerly occupied the limelight were completely sidelined – for the first couple of weeks, most media were not interested at all in hearing what they had to say, concentrating instead on ordinary citizens. A previously deferential attitude was replaced by combative, critical reporting:

> The revolution broke so many relationships and created distance between [journalists and politicians], and courage started to surface. Now I can look a politician in the eye and ask him the questions that ordinary people would ask. Journalists have more courage dealing with politicians. There has been a divorce, the distance between the two has increased. [. . .] Personally, when Hasan Diyab was announced to form [a caretaker] government, I asked him an embarrassing question. I told him 'No one on the streets trusts you, the state is bankrupt [. . .] So how can Hasan Diyab represent the uprising?' (L40, 31 January 2020)

This critical, even dismissive attitude towards politicians was accompanied by a renewed interest in the plight of ordinary Lebanese and the regions beyond Beirut. Many major media outlets shifted their focus from reporting on the doings of prominent politicians to reporting on ordinary people, whether this meant reporting from the ongoing demonstrations or visiting poor families in Tripoli who were struggling to survive amidst a deepening economic crisis. As we have described in earlier chapters, some of the best-known journalists in Lebanon have been very close to leading politicians. Such relationships stand in stark contrast to the dismissal of politicians by a prominent television journalist who became famous for his sympathetic coverage of the demonstrations in Tripoli: 'I separated myself from [the politicians]. They mean nothing to me; they are boring' (L35, 28 January 2020). Others talked enthusiastically about their reporting on poverty, pollution and the school system in the north and south of the country – marginalised issues in marginalised regions of Lebanon. In a situation in which ordinary Lebanese were feeling the impact of intense political alienation and an economic crisis, this turn towards people-focused journalism was a breath of fresh air. It was also an eye-opener for some of the journalists we talked to. Knowing that the country was full of struggling people was one thing; experiencing it first-hand was something else. Reporters described it as a 'discovery' to see the slums and poor neighbourhoods that were the massive social consequences of Lebanon's derailed economy, the more so as they were used to seeing the opulence of the elite. The full and unflattering picture of Lebanon was unknown to most because of

> the centralised media system and the subordination of the press. [. . .] Lebanon is always portrayed as the country of all freedoms, the country of

beauty, the mountain and the sea, the place for economic growth, while all the facts point in the other direction. (L34, 22 January 2020)

Second, the alternative and independent digital media, as well as the rebellious behaviour of individual journalists, constituted a turn toward what Silvio Waisbord calls 'civic advocacy journalism': newsmaking that seeks to promote social change while adhering to standard reporting practices (Waisbord 2009: 378). The entrepreneurs in news outlets such as Daraj and Megaphone replaced the traditional advocacy for an elite faction with advocacy for ordinary people. Breaking with the system of instrumentalised political parallelism and aligning with the people against the elite on a vertical axis of conflict was fraught with difficulties. Some journalists clearly crossed the boundary between professional journalism and political activism. Consider the following tweet:

بكرا كلنا فارشين الطرقات و قاعدين ! #المجد_لاقفالها

Tomorrow we will all spread out on the roads and stage a sit-in! #Glory_to closing them (Sadiq 2019)

This is an activist rallying cry, but it was written by the journalist Dima Sadiq while she was reporting on the uprising for LBCI. As we have seen, Sadiq was eventually obliged to leave LBCI, and even colleagues sympathetic to her cause could understand why. As Rahma, a reporter for the pro-uprising channel MTV, commented:

This is not her role, especially when she is a reporter on the ground. If you are a reporter on the ground, you must be neutral. You can't go down and say I am against you or I am with you. The role of a journalist is very critical and very hard. You can have your political opinions, but you can't show it in public. (L36, 28 January 2020)

Yet this was exactly what many journalists did. Sadiq is an extreme example, but many others publicly and repeatedly voiced their support for the demonstrations and their criticism of the political class. Consequently, they laid themselves open to the charge that they were just as much 'trumpets' as anyone else: 'trumpets of strife', an epithet customarily pinned to people accused of threatening the stability of Lebanon. The truth of the matter is that it was extremely difficult to remain neutral since the uprising was directed against a political system in which most media are embedded. Even more important, journalists felt they had a moral obligation to protect ordinary people who were violently attacked by the elite when they voiced their frustration and anger. At the risk of exhausting the musical metaphor, one could say that journalists acted as trumpets of warning for the protesters, rather than trumpets of strife. Jalal, a journalist at al-Jadid, said that their teams had to stay on air because they knew that the moment they turned off the cameras, the demonstrators would be attacked by the security apparatus or thugs. His riposte to those who accused the media of going beyond their professional remit was that someone had to protect ordinary people when the police and security agencies failed their professional duty (L38, 31 January 2020).

The third media change we want to highlight took place on the organisational level, when journalists from several different media organisations established a new, independent professional union. In Tunisia, the Journalist Syndicate has played an important political role for decades, resisting the Ben Ali autocracy and, after the 2011 revolution, safeguarding the freedom and security of journalists. In contrast, the two Lebanese press unions (one for publishers/editors and one for journalists) have failed to play any meaningful role. Our interviewees dismissed them as corrupt personal networks whose leaders did not care about the journalistic profession at all. The General Secretary of the Union of Journalists, 'Awni al-Ka'ki, involuntarily confirmed this assessment in January 2020. The day after security forces attacked journalists covering anti-bank demonstrations in Beirut, hospitalising one of them, al-Ka'ki stood alongside the Director for Internal Security at a press conference, praising the security forces and assuring the audience that 'there is not a single Lebanese journalist or cameraman who does not support the state'. For good measure, he condemned the demonstrations against the banks as vandalism (Lebanese National News Agency 2020). The journalists he was supposed to represent were outraged. As one commentator in *al-Akhbar* wrote the day after the incident, it was a 'shameful' (*muʿib*) performance (al-Akhbar, 2020). Rula, one of the most experienced and well-known journalists in Beirut, was incensed:

> They don't even know the ABC of this profession. In what capacity do you issue a statement defending banks!? Just do the minimum and shut up! Your role as a journalist is critique, you should monitor those institutions, you should defend journalism and give it space, not defend the bankers which have a primary responsibility for the economic crisis that we are experiencing. (L22, 20 October 2018)

The tipping point had been reached for many journalists well before al-Kaʿki's undignified performance, and they had taken the initiative to establish an independent union for journalists. In its founding statement, the group wrote that the new union was a 'part of the popular uprising [aiming] to bring down the system and replace it with a secular system based on social justice and liberty' (Alternative Journalist Union 2019). They took a clear stand against advocacy journalism on behalf of the elites, accusing the existing professional institutions of being mere 'postal boxes' for powerful politicians and their propagandists. The new union was hailed by many journalists as a manifestation that the 'atmosphere of comfort that the old system enjoyed had changed' (L38, 31 January 2020). Another journalist described it as a weapon in Lebanese journalists' 'conflict with the general reality of the profession' (L34, 22 January 2020).

In summary, the 2019 uprising catalysed three changes among Lebanon's journalists. They turned their attention away from elite squabbles and self-congratulatory press conferences to focus on ordinary people. This change was accompanied by a turn towards civic advocacy journalism as a professional ethos, whereby journalists and civil rights activists supported each other's work, sharing a common aim to dismantle sectarianism and hold officials accountable. In the media sector, that aim was manifested in the establishment of a new, alternative union which explicitly identified with the aims of the '17 October revolution', as they called it. These changes amounted to a journalism that disrupted the media system and shook the entire political order – not bringing them down but putting a huge spanner in the works of the elite's political communication. The politically affiliated media organisations survived and, to be sure, many journalists never wavered in their support for one specific movement or sectarian leader. However, those media professionals who supported the uprising succeeded in showing both that media pluralism and freedom were a sham and that an alternative existed.

* * *

Our cut-off point for interviews and other primary data was February 2020, five months into the uprising. The depressing events in Lebanon that followed underlined why so many Lebanese took to the streets in October 2019. On 4 August 2020, 2,750 tons of improperly stored ammonium nitrate exploded in the port of Beirut, killing 190 people, injuring 9,000 and laying waste to large parts of the city. It was the worst catastrophe ever to befall Lebanon, even including the civil war years. It was soon shown that the explosion was a result of corruption, incompetence and mismanagement among the top bureaucrats and politicians responsible for the port. However, nobody knew exactly why or how it came to happen, since the political elites stonewalled or sabotaged all attempts at holding the responsible officials to account. The rubble from the explosion was barely cleared from Beirut's streets when another, less violent but even deeper crisis erupted: Lebanon's economy, long kept on life support by the central bank, finally collapsed. Inflation ran wild, dollar reserves disappeared, pharmacies ran out of medicines and the electrical grid collapsed, leaving people reliant on aggregates that ran on expensive fuel. At the time of writing, it is estimated that three quarters of Lebanese live below the poverty line, and Lebanon's politicians seem unable or unwilling to address the crisis. In short, after October 2019, the Lebanese had more and more reasons to revolt against the sectarian elites that run the country. Paradoxically, the continuous state of crisis exhausted ordinary people so that quiet despair replaced mass protests. There is a limit to how long any protest cycle can last, and the 2019–20 demonstrations eventually lost momentum, without having led to changes in the political system.

However, in the media, journalists and activists succeeded in disrupting the system of instrumentalised political parallelism which has for so long supported the corrupt sectarian order. They openly sided with the people rather than an elite faction and thus exposed the existing 'pluralist' media landscape as just that: a make-believe pluralism, a fig leaf that hid how the entire elite exploited the system at the cost of ordinary people by drawing their attention to carefully calibrated conflicts between the factions running the country. And their efforts bore lasting fruit. In August 2020, several independent media outlets, media watchdogs and other civil society organisations came together to establish a coalition to defend freedom of expression in Lebanon. The alternative union of journalists elected a new board in July 2021, thus consolidating the organisation. The prominent journalists who raised their voices against the system in 2019–20 continued to do so afterwards. As Dima Sadiq put it during a political talk show on the independent media channel Sarde in August, 2021: 'We are orienting our hopes about the solutions towards the wrong place. This political class can't generate any solution anymore [. . .]. The solution is elsewhere. The solution is through us' (Sarde After Dinner 2021). This newfound confidence in their strength vis-à-vis the political class may well have been the biggest change in Lebanese journalism after 2019.

9

CONCLUSION

This book began with intellectual curiosity regarding the consequences of media pluralism and manipulation for Arab journalism and democracy. During the six years (2015–20) on which we centred our empirical investigation, Tunisia and Lebanon had freer media environments than most other countries in their region. In that sense, we may consider them test cases of what media–politics relations could look like if more Arab states broke out of the authoritarian mould. The freedom to speak one's mind is not a trivial advance in a part of the world where politics is too often held prisoner by fear and repression. But freedom of expression is also not a guarantee for keeping politicians in check and preserving democratic progress. As we have seen, the journalists who provide the raw material of news are liable to become the objects of instrumentalisation. When this occurs, they are far from constituting a fourth estate, instead serving as amplifiers and agents of the decision-makers.

Summary of Findings

As laid out in the Introduction, three questions guided our investigation. We would now like to sum up the answers we found and discuss lessons learned for studies of the Middle East, media and communication and comparative politics. Our first working question was why media instrumentalisation has accompanied press freedom in Tunisia and Lebanon. By combining different sources and foregrounding the experiences of journalists, we have provided a thick description (Geertz 2008) spanning different levels of analysis.

Let us break our observations into explanations at the macro, meso and micro levels. At the macro level, the state of the economy, the political institutions and the regulatory environment all have important consequences for media capture. For Tunisia and Lebanon, the combination of strained economies and fragile institutions has made the media vulnerable to political meddling. On the one hand, a constant shortage of funds makes media organisations and journalist increasingly dependent upon the holders of capital; on the other, the uncertainty of the political situation incites contenders for power to invest in loyal supporters in the media realm. In terms of regulation, the response of the Tunisian state has been far more robust than that of its Lebanese counterpart, and to some extent effectual in tying politicians' hands. However, even in Tunisia, some prominent television channels have refused to comply with HAICA directives.

At the meso level, media ownership structures, business–politics connections and aspects of the political culture have deepened the impact of media instrumentalisation. In Lebanon, a preponderance of politically affiliated media coupled with confession-based power sharing have given sectarian leaders huge influence over media outlets and made it challenging for journalists to form a counterweight to the political class. In Tunisia, the mainstream media belong to businessmen who maintain deep ties with political actors without declaring their biases and interests, and sometimes interfere in editorial decisions. Both Tunisian and Lebanese politicians are especially eager to influence the public debate during election campaigns. Since competition for votes is the name of the political game in both countries, a strong media presence is coveted. The presence of a 'culture of informality', which Zielonka (2015) tied to instrumentalisation in Eastern Europe, is also a factor in the Arab region. Both the ways in which Tunisian and Lebanese politicians have been accustomed to building support in society through clientelism and their habit of exercising politics behind closed doors, via backroom deals, reveal a tradition of the informal exercise of power. By paying or threatening journalists or entire media organisations so that they provide favourable media coverage, political actors have found another way to run political affairs outside of formal democratic channels.

At the micro level, the journalistic environment is fragmented because of cleavages in society, historical legacies such as the civil war in Lebanon and authoritarianism in Tunisia, and a lack of autonomy from politics. In the absence of strong professional norms and a shared identity and solidarity, journalists are easily co-opted and divided. They also lack effective protection from pressure by politicians and media owners, whether such pressures are economic (e.g. being denied access to employment), information-based (e.g. defamation campaigns) or security-related (e.g. intimidation). Particularly in Lebanon, journalists run the risk of physical attack at the hands of thugs and security forces. Journalists can also be brought to trial under vague criminal law statutes. On the other hand, some journalists wilfully choose co-optation because of the advantages it brings, such as access to centrally placed sources of information, material benefits or even plain envelopes stuffed with money, since corruption is a widespread problem as well. Whatever the price, instrumentalisation works as a mutually beneficial arrangement between the patron and his or her 'trumpet'.

Our second question was how journalists deal with media instrumentalisation and react when key democratic assets are at stake. There are three main ways for journalists to relate to media capture. The first, as mentioned, is to embrace instrumentalisation and become the voice of a party, organisation, politician or plausibly also a foreign country. We have seen indications of such intimate relations throughout the book, and especially in Lebanon where the polarised nature of media and politics combined with a culture for a 'journalism of views' manifests in alliances between journalists and politicians that are tight and often openly displayed. Tunisia has its share of 'trumpets' as well, but they tend to keep their political allegiances to themselves because society and most media professionals expect the media to be neutral. We have described how the upper echelon of media commentators, the *chroniqueurs*, have acted as journalist-entrepreneurs, making good money by 'shopping around' among the private broadcasters. The second way to deal with the system is to keep a distance from political actors to preserve one's professional reputation, all the while avoiding direct confrontations with decision-makers. Although we have focused on media capture in this book, it is important to stress that journalists can still exercise their profession in Tunisia and Lebanon without selling services to politicians. Doing so conforms to widely shared professional ideals and may be a source of peer recognition.

The third option is to openly defy both the instrumentalisation of the media and the political actors behind it. We have used the term 'change agents' to describe journalists who take this approach as they challenge elite domination over media and politics. In Lebanon, criticism of the system became more widespread during the years we studied. An early indication of this trend was the 2018 parliamentary election in which a growing number of journalists stood as candidates on civil society lists. More journalists turned to activism after the 2019 protests and their condemnation of the elites also became more uncompromising. In Tunisia, the 2011 revolution infused the profession with a new generation of 'change agents' who think of journalism as a means to deepen the transition to democracy. The most explicitly activist journalists are found outside the mainstream, on digital media platforms. However, we also noted system-critical opinions in interviews with journalists from state-owned newspapers, private radio stations and the public broadcaster al-Wataniyya.

Just as there is wide variation in journalists' preparedness to take on decision-makers, their reactions in situations where key democratic assets are at stake also vary widely, from genuflecting to the authorities to principled protest. Our case study of Tunisian media commentary after the 2015 Bardo attack showed journalists failing to defend fundamental civil liberties at a sensitive time in the country's democratic transition. Leading commentators called for strengthening the authority of the state and above all the executive office, paving the way for then President Essebsi's authoritarian drift. In Chapter 7, we analysed how Lebanese journalists positioned themselves in parliamentary elections engineered to perpetuate incumbent domination. We found a striking split between journalists playing the elites' game and those mobilising for a political renewal. In Tunisia, the 2019 elections saw journalists campaigning for rival presidential candidates, leading to a spike in polarisation. The large private television stations ran a campaign against Kais Saied, who had the majority of voters behind him, provoking popular anger with Tunisian media and journalism.

In situations where citizens demonstrate against authorities, the reactions of journalists are also strikingly diverse. In Lebanon, since the 2015 You Stink protests, the tendency has been for one part of the journalistic corps to lend credence to the popular demands, whilst another part seeks to delegitimise them. This was clearly the case in 2019, when journalists from the three private broadcasters MTV, LBCI and al-Jadid portrayed the 'revolution' in a positive light whereas OTV, NBN and al-Manar framed it as a threat and conspiracy. Journalistic engagement went beyond editorial lines on several occasions. For example, we noted Dima Sadiq's active participation in the uprising and her subsequent revolt when LBCI tried to limit her agency. Other journalists quit their jobs with pro-regime media outlets because they could not stomach the vilification of the protest movement.

Journalists in Tunisia also disagree in their appraisal of and involvement in popular protests. As we saw towards the end of Chapter 6, the tendency among some to put security first led them to denounce popular protests over living costs in 2018, despite the fact that both protesters and journalists themselves were victims of police brutality at the time. Notwithstanding such disagreements over the interpretations of protests, Tunisian journalists have shown considerable will to mobilise when their own professional interests are at stake. The presence of a strong union is crucial in this respect. The SNJT formulates, and unites a good portion of Tunisia's journalists behind, shared professional demands. On important occasions, it also takes to the street. A recent example of such journalist collective action occurred in 2020 in response to a parliamentary bill for reform of the media sector defended by the salafi-dominated Karama coalition, al-Nahda and Nabil Karoui's party Qalb Tunis. The bill proposed changes in HAICA's status that would liberalise the access to broadcasting licenses and ease the day-to-day regulation of the media's activities (HAICA 2020). According to the supporters of the decree-law, removing state restrictions was a necessary step to increase the freedom of expression. Many journalists reacted strongly against the bill and argued that it would have the exact opposite effect. From their vantage point, media regulation was a way to preserve the freedom of expression and one of the main achievements of the revolution. The SNJT organised campaigns on social media, online meetings to explain the impact of the reforms, and held sit-ins behind the parliament and the presidential palace. It invited other syndicates, like the national labour union, and civil society organisations to take part in the protests. On the day of voting on the bill, 20 October 2020, concerned journalists showed up behind the parliament in big numbers.

Political Implications

Our third working question concerned the political implications of media instrumentalisation and journalist responses to it. If we take a bird's eye view of the findings summarised above, one observation stands out. Throughout the book, we have observed tensions in journalistic attitudes and practices. In fact, they constantly point in opposite directions along a democracy autocracy continuum. As a reminder, we began the discussion in Chapter 1 with the observation that the combination of media pluralism and instrumentalisation creates tensions for journalists in their everyday work. They have considerable freedom to speak, but in fact will often speak for someone else. In Chapter 2, we explained the reasons for a lack of media and journalistic independence, situating instrumentalisation in the context of hybrid politics. Chapter 3 observed that journalists are vulnerable to political pressures because of their working conditions, but equally that they hold grudges against this state of affairs. Chapter 4 analysed Tunisian journalism after the revolution and the contrast between those who rode the wave of media capture and the journalists who actively resisted it. Chapter 5 compared change agents to 'trumpets' in the Lebanese media context, arguing that a system of instrumentalised political parallelism is prone to instability. Chapter 6 discussed journalist responses to the terrorist attack against the Bardo Museum, finding in-group variation there as well. Whereas some commentators blamed democracy and the revolution for the terrorism problem in Tunisia, others continued to stress the value of civil liberties. Chapter 7 showed that journalists may pursue opposing agendas in elections, with some selling themselves to the highest bidder and others confronting the political class. Finally, Chapter 8 documented the schism in Lebanese journalism provoked by the 2019–20 protests.

These findings bring us back to our conceptual starting point and the relevance of hybridity for making sense of the relationship between Arab journalism and politics. Rather than premising our analysis on an assumed, teleological struggle for democracy, we have made a case for studying journalistic practices in context to reassess journalism's political role. Journalism in Tunisia and Lebanon is a complex terrain where competing political (and personal) interests and agendas meet. It cannot be reduced to either a 'democratising force' or, to paraphrase Chomsky, a 'manufacturer of consent' (Herman and Chomsky 2010).

Journalism is better thought of as a part of what makes politics in Tunisia and Lebanon hybrid. That is, it pulls both ways on the struggle for democracy. On the one hand, journalism is part of the communication system that keeps the elites in both countries in power. We have many indications that journalists are co-opted and used for purposes that undermine democratic rule. On the other hand, journalism serves as a channel for resistance to abuse and mobilisation for accountability. We noticed a strong normative commitment to professional journalism in our interviews and a widespread opinion that instrumentalisation is wrong. Moreover, we found signs that journalists are able to act independently of their masters. This will and ability to defy the powers that be make journalism in hybrid political contexts a potentially disruptive force.

Media instrumentalisation is not the end of journalistic aspiration, and the ideal of free and independent journalism continues to motivate individuals to fight back. Herein lies the impetus for change in journalism in the Middle East. We have observed that journalists may resist political pressures and mobilise against the instrumentalising elites. The foremost illustration is the role they played in Lebanon in the 2019–20 revolt against the pervasive corruption in that country. A large number of influential media professionals successfully disrupted the political machinery of sectarianism by siding with the protesters against the elites. Individual journalists and entire media outlets contributed to energising popular mobilisation rather than dampening it, as was the aim of the sectarian leaders.

Lessons Learned

This study has takeaways for debates in Middle Eastern studies, media and communication and comparative politics. The area-specific question is what media pluralism entails for the Arab region. As we pointed out in the introduction, the existing literature revolves around the prospect of democratisation and takes a principally negative view of the contribution of the media and journalism to this goal (Cavatorta and Mekki 2021). Marc Lynch (2015) has gone as far as asserting that the media 'trashed the transitions'. One of the main arguments used to support this claim is the presence of widespread media instrumentalisation. However, judging by our findings in this book, there is a risk of misinterpreting and overestimating the impact of media capture. The consequences of elite domination over the media ought to be checked against developments at the micro level. Having done so in two countries, we have discovered that the elites' power to control political communication is limited, despite strong instrumentalisation of the media. Avenues of resistance to authoritarianism exist inside the structures of media co-optation, and media professionals can take advantage of them. Independent-minded journalists find ways of undermining the communication strategies of the elites. To fully appreciate the media role in Arab politics, one needs to factor in this resistance.

A related lesson applies to media and communication studies. The principal prism for observing media–politics relations has become the media systems framework, which looks for structural differences between countries to explain variations in outcomes. Without questioning its merits and contributions to the discipline over the past decades, it is worth reflecting on its inherent limitations. The keyword here is change, which a system-oriented framework by its very nature is ill-equipped to explain. Following the trendsetting work of Hallin and Mancini (2004; 2011), the analytical aim of the media systems framework is to identify and compare stable features of media-politics relations across countries, beginning with the established democracies of the West. By contrast, in the context of fragile institutions and volatile politics, the challenge is ultimately to make sense of transformations. To illustrate with our country cases, there is every indication that the nature of journalism–politics relations in Tunisia and Lebanon is shifting. In Tunisia, the process began in 2011 and is still unfolding, whereas in Lebanon, the 2019–20 revolt marked a watershed. Because of these changes, journalism as a political force is emergent rather than a given. Journalists in both countries think differently of their role in society and assert themselves more confidently vis-à-vis politicians than they did before. True, they remain in a difficult situation and are vulnerable to media capture. However, their understandings of, and responses to, instrumentalisation evolve alongside changes in the political context. To capture such developments and clarify their origin points, studying the nature of the system is not enough. In this book, we have focused on processes and incidents where the relations between politics, media organisations and journalists were moulded and re-moulded as a result of choices made by the different actors.

The picture that emerges is of a media sector characterised by multidimensional hybridity. The interviews we have cited show that different and sometimes contradictory ideas about journalism's political role and its professional norms coexist in mainstream media – even within one and the same media organisation. Some journalists are happy to be 'trumpets' for an elite group; others believe in a detached, critical media; yet others see themselves as champions of 'the people' against the elite. When important events occur, whether elections or national emergencies such as the Bardo terror attack and the 2019 uprising in Lebanon, the friction between the professional and political ideologies intensifies and some journalists break with the whole media system, as we have seen in Lebanon. Technological hybridity feeds into this friction. Expensive legacy media – television and newspapers – are challenged by the flexible and appealing format of new media collectives, such as Nawaat and Inkyfada in Tunisia, and Daraj, Megaphone and various community news sites in Lebanon. Influential journalists use social media platforms such as Facebook and Twitter to voice their personal opinions free from the constraints of the editorial room, with problematic implications for professional norms and practices. As a result, those who pull the political strings face a more unpredictable and complex media landscape that is harder to manipulate. However, journalists and ordinary citizens must also live with a great deal of informational uncertainty.

The notion of hybridity is also important to comparative politics. Our findings imply that fresh attention should be given to the interrelations between journalism and hybrid politics. The scholarship on hybrid regimes has traditionally taken a top-down perspective that focuses on media manipulation by politicians and magnates, overlooking bottom-up responses that constrain the available options for elites. To the extent that journalism is deemed relevant at all to debates about why regimes are caught in a 'grey zone' between democracy and autocracy, it is treated as a passive subject. In this book, we have foregrounded the agency of Lebanese and Tunisian journalists, analysing how they navigate vis-à-vis politicians in the space that is available to them. Through strategies such as playing the relations game, exploiting internal contradictions in the system and connecting with popular grievances, they gain wiggle room for their professional and personal ambitions. The structure of these opportunities varies from country to country.

Whatever the political setting, however, journalists adapt and search for possibilities to act. Again, this is an argument for investigating journalism empirically in contexts where media pluralism and political manipulation come together. By producing more knowledge about how journalists relate with hybrid politics, we can gain new insights about what drives and inhibits political change.

The political role of journalism in Tunisia and Lebanon is ambiguous. A journalism geared toward preserving the power of the incumbents coexists with a journalism that defies the communication strategies of the elites. The presence of co-opted journalists is a brake on the development towards full democracy. At the same time, indomitable critical voices counteract the drift towards full authoritarian rule. Journalism under pluralism and media instrumentalisation is thus an amalgamation of different forces, producing an equilibrium of sorts. Ultimately, its net effect may be to perpetuate hybrid politics, as we argued above. The ability of the elites to maintain control over media and journalism differs strongly between countries and shifts over time. Looking at our two cases, Lebanon is where the elites lost this ability, and a reminder that clientelist power arrangements may be fragile. The irony is that the strategies used to control journalism in Lebanon added fuel to the revolt that eventually struck the political class. Media instrumentalisation provokes resistance and is a source of latent tension, which in the long run can burst free.

APPENDIX 1
INTERVIEWS: LEBANON

Number	Pseudonym	Date
L1	Dina	27 May 2016
L2	Adam	27 May 2016
L3	'Umar	28 May 2016
L4	Isma'il	30 May 2016
L5	Mustafa	30 May 2016
L6	Ayub	31 May 2016
L7	Nawal	1 June 2016
L8	Kamal	27 January 2018
L9	Raghib	27 January 2018
L10	Mu'izz	28 January 2018
L11	Halim	29 January 2018
L12	Anas	30 January 2018
L13	Nasim	30 January 2018
L14	Taha	31 January 2018
L15	Nasim (bis)	3 May 2018
L16	Yakhlif	4 May 2018
L17	Assi	7 May 2018
L18	Karim	9 May 2018
L19	Samir	9 May 2018

L20	Zayn	9 May 2018
L21	Julia	30 May 2018
L22	Rula	20 October 2018
L23	Aysar	20 October 2018
L24	Dalida	20 October 2018
L25	Sahar	20 October 2018
L26	Layla	20 October 2018
L27	Ahmad	4 March 2019
L28	Munir	5 March 2019
L29	Jamal	6 March 2019
L30	Shafiq	7 March 2019
L31	Faris	7 March 2019
L32	Yusuf	7 March 2019
L33	Amna	8 March 2019
L34	Joe	22 January 2020
L35	Muqaddim	28 January 2020
L36	Rahma	28 January 2020
L37	Sawsan	28 January 2020
L38	Jalil	31 January 2020
L39	Sahar	31 January 2020
L40	Latif	31 January 2020
L41	Amira	4 February 2020
L42	Maysa	31 January 2020

Interviews with non-journalists, Lebanon

L43	Lutfi	1 June 2016
L44	Yahya	3 May 2018
L45	Milawi	3 May 2018
L46	Mukrim	20 October 2018
L47	Nidal	6 March 2019
L48	Samih	1 February 2020

APPENDIX 2
INTERVIEWS: TUNISIA

Number	Pseudonym	Date
T1	Lunis	5 April 2016
T2	Mirna	6 April 2016
T3	Murad	7 April 2016
T4	Habiba	8 April 2016
T5	Shawqi	8 April 2016
T6	Sami	6 March 2018
T7	Mahraz	6 March 2018
T8	Rihab	7 March 2018
T9	Sadiq	8 March 2018
T10	Badir	8 March 2018
T11	Usama	9 March 2018
T12	Marwan	9 March 2018
T13	Wasim	9 March 2018
T14	Bilal	10 March 2018
T15	Nawfal	3 May 2018
T16	Na'im	3 May 2018
T17	Luqman	4 May 2018
T18	Sa'd	4 May 2018
T19	Katya	7 May 2018

T20	Brahim	7 May 2018
T21	Lubna	19 November 2018
T22	Raqim	20 November 2018
T23	Yaman	20 November 2018
T24	Lamin	21 November 2018
T25	Shahira	21 November 2018
T26	Nadim	22 November 2018
T27	Musa	22 November 2018
T28	Khaldun	17 June 2019
T29	Asmar	17 June 2019
T30	Muhammad	17 June 2019
T31	Khayra	18 June 2019
T32	Maymun	18 June 2019
T33	Anais	19 June 2019
T34	Najim	8 October 2019
T35	Muhsin	8 October 2019
T36	Fakhriya	9 October 2019
T37	Rafiq	10 October 2019
T38	Mu'tasim	10 October 2019
T39	Aghilas	10 October 2019

Interviews with non-journalists, Tunisia

T40	Zakariya	6 April 2016
T41	Mirbah	6 March 2018
T42	Samira	7 March 2018
T43	Dunya	8 March 2018
T44	Fahid	3 May 2018
T45	Jalil	4 May 2018
T46	Kahina	4 May 2018
T47	Hisham	7 May 2018
T48	Muna	7 May 2018
T49	Warda	19 November 2019

BIBLIOGRAPHY

Abu-Rish, Z. (2016), 'Garbage politics', Jadaliyya, http://www.jadaliyya.com/pages/index/24713/garbage-politics.

Akasha, Bu Bakir bin (2019), 'لا حياد مع المافيا' (There Is No Neutrality Regarding the Mafia), Facebook [blog], 25 September 2019, https://www.facebook.com/benakecha.boubaker/posts/1072584402945364.

al-Akhbar (21 October 2019), من غرفة التحرير | إبراهيم الأمين (From the Editorial Office: Ibrahim al-Amin), https://www.youtube.com/watch?v=8WCDkaQbDRw.

al-Akhbar (17 January 2020), ''Awni al-Ka'ki—[Syndicate] president for whom?', al-Akhbar, https://al-akhbar.com/Media_Tv/282641.

Alexander, C. (2016), *Tunisia: From Stability to Revolution in the Maghreb*, Routledge.

al-Hashim, N. (3 May 2019), ليلة سقوط بولا يعقوبيان؟ (The night of Paula Ya'qubian's downfall?), almodon; المدن, https://www.almodon.com/media/2019/3/5/يعقوبيان-ليلة-سقوط-بولا

al-Hiwar al-Tunisi (17 October 2019), لطفي العماري: تونس تحت شر الإخوان المسلمين (Lutfi al-'Amari: 'Tunisia is under the thumb of the Muslim Brothers'), https://www.facebook.com/watch/?v=404241990499137.

al-Jadid (22 February 2019), الشعب يعرف أن المسؤولين يسرقونه لكن الانتخابات تبقى تجديدا للزعيم: يعقوبيان (Ya'qubian: the public knows that the leaders are stealing from them, nevertheless the elections remain a renewed term for the leader), AlJadeed.tv, https://www.aljadeed.tv/arabic.

al-Jurayjiri, R. and al-Shaluhi, C. (2017), «التلفزيونية: إشكالية التغيير في ظلّ المنظومة الطائفية الحراك المدني» في نشرات الأخبار (The civil movement in the TV news casts: the problem of change in the shadow of the sectarian system), in N. al-Qadiri 'Isa (ed.), *Arab Media: Betting on Change in the Shadow of Transformations* [in Arabic], Center for Arab Unity Studies, pp. 227–50.

al-Manar TV (3 May 2018a), مقدمة نشرة الأخبار الرئيسية (Introduction to prime time news), https://www.almanar.com.lb/3730879.

al-Manar TV (5 May 2018b), نشرة الإنتخابات النيابية (Lebanese elections news), https://program.almanar.com.lb/episode/13561.

Almarkazia (3 April 2019), المركزية - يعقوبيان: الجميع فاسدون (Almarkazia - Yaʿqubian: everyone is corrupt), المركزية, https://www.almarkazia.com/ar/news/show/106803.

al-Masdar (17 October 2019), اعلاميّة بقناة الحوار التونسي تتعرّض الى التهديد بالقتل.. وهذه التفاصيل (Media figure in al-Hiwar al-Tunisi receives death threat ... and these are the details), المصدر تونس, https://ar.webmanagercenter.com/2019/10/17/276463/اعلاميّة-بقناة-الحوار-التونسي-تتعرّض

al-Matirawi, A. (n.d.), [Facebook post (subsequently deleted)], https://www.facebook.com/emine.Matirawi/posts/2564514293610932 (accessed 23 October 2019).

al-Mustaqbal (27 April 2018a), طرابلس بعشرات الآلاف من كبارها وصغارها تستقبل الحريري (Tens of thousands of Tripolitanians, young and old, welcome al-Hariri), https://www.youtube.com/watch?v=dCUkGBd6Fms.

al-Mustaqbal (30 April 2018b), المشنوق: بيروت عربية ولا مكان لولاية الفقيه في لبنان (al-Mashnuq: Beirut is Arab and there is no room for the guardianship of the jurist [Iran's political system] in Lebanon), https://www.youtube.com/watch?v=8PGkJamMdM8

al-Nahar (15 September 2018), حديث سالم زهران عن الكويت يتفاعل: القضاء يتحرك والقناعي يرد (The consequences of Salem Zahran's talk about Kuwait: the judiciary takes action and al-Qana'i responds), Annahar.Com, https://www.annahar.com/arabic/article/861832-حديث-سالم-زهران-عن-الكويت-يتفاعل-القضاء-يتحرك-والقناعي-يرد

Alnajjar, G. and Selvik, K. (2015), 'Kuwait: the politics of crisis', in *Oil States in the New Middle East*, Routledge, pp. 105–24.

al-Saʿid, al-S. (2017), المانفستو: النداء الأخير الى الباي الكبير (The Manifesto: The Last Call to the Great Bey), Sotumedia.

Alternative Journalist Union (8 November 2019), 'Founding statement: towards an alternative journalism syndicate', The Alternative Journalist Union, https://nakababadila.com/9/.

al-Wafi, S. (13 October 2019), [Facebook post], https://www.facebook.com/samelwafi/posts/2577473509038419.

Amara, T. (23 August 2019), 'Tunisian police arrest presidential candidate Karoui on tax evasion charges', Reuters, https://www.reuters.com/article/us-tunisia-election-karoui-idUSKCN1VD22F.

Amara, T. (18 April 2021), 'Tunisian president draws security powers into dispute with PM', Reuters, https://www.reuters.com/world/tunisian-president-draws-security-powers-into-dispute-with-pm-2021-04-18/.

Amos, D. (2010), *Confusion, Contradiction and Irony: The Iraqi Media in 2010*, Joan Shorenstien Center on the Press, Politics and Public Policy Discussion Paper Series D-58, John F. Kennedy School of Government, Harvard University, http://nrs.harvard.edu/urn-3:HUL.InstRepos:4421401.

Arabesque (2019), مايا القصوري: جاهل من يعتبر قيس سعيد ثوري و تقدمي و نظيف اليد (Maya al-Qusuri: whoever considers Kais Saied revolutionary and progressive and clean-handed is ignorant), arabesque.tn, https://www.arabesque.tn/ar/article/57650/ايا-القصوري-جاهل-من-يعتبر-قيس-سعيد-ثوري-و-تقدمي-و-نظيف-اليد.

Arsenault, A. and Castells, M. (2008), 'Switching power: Rupert Murdoch and the global business of media politics: a sociological analysis', *International Sociology*, 23(4), 488–513.

Article 19 (29 April 2021), 'Tunisia: civil society welcomes moves to strengthen independent public media', ARTICLE 19, https://www.article19.org/resources/tunisia-tunisian-and-foreign-ngos-welcome-withdrawal-of-controversial-nomination-of-director-of-tunisias-national-news-agency-and-support-tunisians-right-to-independent-public-media/.

ataha (13 August 2020), *Tunisia International Election Observation Mission Final Report* [Text], https://www.ndi.org/publications/tunisia-international-election-observation-mission-final-report.

Atallah, S. and Zoughaib, S. (2019), 'A snapshot of parliamentary election results', Lebanese Center for Policy Studies, p. 34, https://www.lcps-lebanon.org/articles/details/2246/a-snapshot-of-parliamentary-election-results.

Ayalon, A. (1995), *The Press in the Arab Middle East: A History*, Oxford University Press.

Azar, J. (21 October 2019, October 21), [Tweet]. @i. https://twitter.com/i/web/status/1186316636418117632.

Babnet (10 January 2019a), وماجول: الارهاب سيدخل قرطاج وباردو بالانتخابات وانتم تحكيو عالحياد؟؟ العماري في حالة ذعر ... يناشد الطبوبي (al-'Amari in a state of horror ... appeals to al-Tabubi and Majul: terrorism is entering Carthage and Bardo in the elections and you are speaking about impartiality??), Babnet, https://www.babnet.net/rttdetail-190156.asp.

Babnet (9 May 2019b), يمارسون المراودة للمرشحين ويهزو في القفة ويخدمو في السر حملات انتخابية بوغلاب: صحفيون (Bughallab: journalists flatter candidates and pat them on their backs, and secretly serve election campaigns), Babnet, https://www.babnet.net/rttdetail-188550.asp.

Babnet (24 September 2019c), ومشروعهم يتقاطع مع اليسار الفوضوي وقيس سعيّد ثمرة هذا التقاطع بوغلاب: الدواعش رجعوا يقعدوا في القهاوي (Bughallab: ISIS's members have returned to the coffee shops, their project intersects with the anarchic left and Kais Saied is the fruition of this intersection), Babnet, https://www.babnet.net/rttdetail-189681.asp.

Babnet (16 October 2019d), غلاب على النساء الريفيات والكريطة تهكم ودخلنا في مرحلة تقزيم كل شيء "مراد الزغيدي: "ماقاله محمد بو (Murad al-Zughaydi: 'What Muhammad Bughallab said about rural women and the handcart is mockery, and we have entered the stage in which everything is downgraded'), Babnet, https://www.babnet.net/rttdetail-191067.asp.

Babnet (October 21 2019e), عدد من صحافيين والمُعلّقين على الأخبار بقنوات إذاعيّة وتلفزيّة خاصّة 15 منظمة حقوقية، تحذر من التحريض والاعتداءات على (15 human rights organizations warn against incitement and violations against a number of journalists and (news) commentators on private radio stations and tv-channels), Babnet, https://www.babnet.net/cadredetail-191350.asp.

Babnet (9 November 2019f), ومأجور، اعلاميون صبايحية فرنسا ..وقناة القروي تبيّض الفساد والفاسدين القرقوري: اعلامنا فاسد (al-Qarquri: our media is bribed and corrupt, and the journalists are France's mercenaries . . . and al-Karoui's channel whitewash corruption and the corrupt), Babnet, https://www.babnet.net/rttdetail-188900.asp.

Baker, C. E. (2006), *Media Concentration and Democracy: Why Ownership Matters*, Cambridge University Press.

Barata, J. (2013), 'Tunisian media under the authoritarian structure of Ben Ali's regime and after', in *National Broadcasting and State Policy in Arab Countries*, Springer, pp. 117–30.

Beirut Today (30 April 2018), 'An interview with parliamentary candidate: Ghada Eid', Beirut Today, https://beirut-today.com/2018/04/30/interview-parliamentary-candidate-ghada-eid/.

bin 'Ukasha, B. B. (25 September 2019), لا حياد مع المافيا (There is no neutrality regarding the mafia), Facebook, https://www.facebook.com/benakecha.boubaker/posts/1072584402945364.

Blanford, N. (1 September 2015), 'Lebanon's garbage crisis: can activists move beyond trash to politics?', *Christian Science Monitor*, https://www.csmonitor.com/World/Middle-East/2015/0901/Lebanon-s-garbage-crisis-Can-activists-move-beyond-trash-to-politics.

Bobin, F. (25 January 2018), 'Le consensus politique tunisien, étouffoir des idéaux de la révolution de jasmin', Le Monde.fr, http://www.lemonde.fr/afrique/article/2018/01/25/le-consensus-politique-tunisien-etouffoir-des-ideaux-de-la-revolution-de-jasmin_5247125_3212.html.

Bobin, F. and Haddad, M. (29 January 2018), 'En Tunisie, les anciens bénalistes passent de l'ombre à la lumière', Le Monde.fr, https://www.lemonde.fr/afrique/article/2018/01/29/en-tunisie-les-anciens-benalistes-passent-de-l-ombre-a-la-lumiere_5248856_3212.html.

Boubekeur, A. (2015), 'Islamists, secularists and old regime elites in Tunisia: bargained competition', *Mediterranean Politics*, 21(1), 1–21.

Boukhars, A. (2017), 'The fragility of elite settlements in Tunisia', *African Security Review*, 26(3), 257–70.

Boussen, Z. and Mbarki, M. I. (2021), 'Tunisian youth and political life: from stagnation to revival?', Arab Reform Initiative, https://www.arab-reform.net/publication/tunisian-youth-and-political-life-from-stagnation-to-revival/.

Bracciale, R. and Martella, A. (2017), 'Define the populist political communication style: the case of Italian political leaders on Twitter', *Information, Communication and Society*, 20(9), 1310–29.

Brésillon, T. (6 November 2019), 'Tunisia. For President Kais Saied, democracy can be a new idea', *Orient* XXI, https://orientxxi.info/magazine/tunisia-for-president-kais-saied-democracy-can-be-a-new-idea,3402.

Brooten, L., McElhone, J. M. and Venkiteswaran, G. (2019), *Myanmar Media in Transition: Legacies, Challenges and Change*. ISEAS-Yusof Ishak Institute.

Business News (30 January 2020), 'Les médias privés écartés de l'interview de Kaïs Saïed', www.businessnews.com.tn, https://www.businessnews.com.tn/les-medias-prives-ecartes-de-linterview-de-kais-saied,520,94899,3.

Business News (18 May 2020), 'La Fédération générale de l'information appelle au boycott d'Al Karama', www.businessnews.com.tn, https://www.businessnews.com.tn/la-federation-generale-de-linformation-appelle-au-boycott-dal-karama,520,98635,3.

Camaj, L. (2016), 'Between a rock and a hard place: consequences of media clientelism for journalist–politician power relationships in the Western Balkans', *Global Media and Communication*, 12(3), 229–46.

Carothers, T. (2002), 'The end of the transition paradigm', *Journal of Democracy*, 13(1), 5–21.

Cavatorta, F. and Mekki, N. (2021), 'How can we agree on anything in this environment? Tunisian media, transition and elite compromises: a view from parliament', *International Journal of Press/Politics*, 26(4), 822–41.

Chadwick, A. (2017), *The Hybrid Media System: Politics and Power*, Oxford University Press.

Channel 9 (30 August 2019), عبد الفتاح مورو: الفيديو هذا مفبرك ('Abd al-Fattah Muru: 'This video is fabricated'), https://www.facebook.com/watch/?v=713779922427533.

Chouikha, L. (2015), *La difficile transformation des médias*, Editions Finzi.
CNN Arabic (11 January 2018), 'الجمعة.. وهندة الشناوي ل سي.ن.ن: "تعودنا على شيطنة الاحتجاجات" فاش نستناو؟' في تونس ('What are we waiting for?' in Tunisia on Friday . . . and Hinda al-Shinawy to CNN: we are used to the demonization of protests), CNN Arabic, https://arabic.cnn.com/middle-east/2018/01/11/tunisia-protests-henda-chennaoui.
Collier, D. and Levitsky S. (1997), 'Democracy with adjectives: conceptual innovation in comparative research', *World Politics*, 49(3), 430–51.
Committee to Protect Journalists (March 2015), 'Journalists assaulted in Lebanon amid violent protests', Committee to Protect Journalists, https://cpj.org/2015/08/journalists-assaulted-in-lebanon-amid-violent-prot.php.
Constitution de la République Tunisienne (2015), L'Imprimerie Officielle de la République Tunisienne, https://lib.ohchr.org/HRBodies/UPR/Documents/Session27/TN/6Annexe4Constitution_fr.pdf.
Corstange, D. (2016), *The Price of a Vote in the Middle East: Clientelism and Communal Politics in Lebanon and Yemen*, Cambridge University Press.
Coşkun, G. B. (2020), 'Media capture strategies in new authoritarian states: the case of Turkey', *Publizistik*, 1–18.
Cottle, S. (2006a), 'Mediatized rituals: beyond manufacturing consent', *Media, Culture and Society*, 28(3), 411–32.
Cottle, S. (2006b), *Mediatized Conflicts: Understanding Media and Conflicts in the Contemporary World*, Open University Press.
Dajani, N. (2019), *The Media in Lebanon: Fragmentation and Conflict in the Middle East*, I. B. Tauris.
Daraj Media (29 October 2019), 'كلن يعني كلن' (All of them means all of them), https://www.youtube.com/watch?v=pesfWCryueA.
D'Arma, A. (2015), *Media and Politics in Contemporary Italy: From Berlusconi to Grillo*, Lexington Books.
Davis, A. (2019), *Political Communication: A New Introduction for Crisis Times*, Polity Press.
Deets, S. and Skulte-Ouaiss, J. (2021), 'Breaking into a consociational system: civic parties in Lebanon's 2018 parliamentary election', Ethnopolitics, 20(2), 157–85.
Dobreva, A., Pfetsch, B. and Voltmer, K. (2011), 'Trust and mistrust on 'yellow brick road'. Political communication culture in post-communist Bulgaria', in B. Dobek-Ostrowska and M. Glowacki (eds), *Making Democracy in 20 Years: Media and Politics in Central and Eastern Europe*, Wydawnictwo Uniwersytetu Wroclawskiego.

Dot-Pouillard, N. (2012), '"Résistance" et/ou "révolution": un dilemme libanais face à la crise syrienne', https://halshs.archives-ouvertes.fr/halshs-00658796/.

Diamond, L. (2002), 'Elections without democracy: thinking about hybrid regimes', *Journal of Democracy*, 13(2), 21–35.

Diamond, L. J. and Plattner, M. F. (eds) (2001), *The Global Divergence of Democracies*, Johns Hopkins University Press.

Diamond, L. and Whittington, Z. (2019), 'Social Media', in C. W. Haerpfer, P. Bernhagen, C. Welzel and R. F. Inglehart (eds), *Democratization*, 2nd edn, Oxford University Press, pp. 253–66.

Dragomir, M. (2018), 'Control the money, control the media: how government uses funding to keep media in line', *Journalism*, 19(8), 1131–48.

EEAS (European External Action Service) (23 January 2020), 'Elections présidentielle et législatives 2019 en Tunisie: la mission d'observation électorale de l'UE présente son rapport final avec 27 recommandations pour le renforcement des scrutins futurs', EEAS – European External Action Service – European Commission, https://eeas.europa.eu/delegations/tunisia/73380/elections-présidentielle-et-législatives-2019-entunisie-la-mission-d'observation-électorale_en.

Eickelman, D. F. (2004), 'The Middle East's democracy deficit and the expanding public sphere', in S. Munshi and P. van der Veer (eds), *Media, War and Terrorism: Responses from the Middle East and Asia*, Routledge, pp. 61–73.

El-Hage, A.-M. (12 December 2019a), 'Paula Nawfal à "L'OLJ ": "J'avais beau crier que je suis journaliste, il continuait à me frapper ', *L'Orient-Le Jour*, https://www.lorientlejour.com/article/1198292/paula-nawfal-a-lolj-javais-beau-crier-que-je-suis-journaliste-il-continuait-a-me-frapper-.html.

El-Hage, A.-M. (14 December 2019b), '"Nous ne paierons pas ! ": Des contestataires appellent à la désobéissance fiscale', *L'Orient-Le Jour*, https://www.lorientlejour.com/article/1198609/-nous-ne-paierons-pas-des-contestataires-appellent-a-la-desobeissance-fiscale.html.

El-Husseini, R. (2004), 'Lebanon: building political dynasties', in V. Perthes (ed.), *Arab Elites: Negotiating the Politics of Change*, Lynne Rienner Publishers, pp. 239–66.

El Issawi, F. (2012), *Tunisian Media in Transition*, Carnegie Endowment for International Peace, http://carnegieendowment.org/2012/07/10/tunisian-media-in-transition.

El Issawi, F. (2016), *Arab National Media and Political Change*, Palgrave Macmillan.

El Issawi F. (2020), 'Egyptian journalists and the struggle for change following the 2011 uprising: the ambiguous journalistic agency between change and conformity', *International Communication Gazette*, 82(7), 628–45.

El Issawi, F. (2021), 'Media pluralism and democratic consolidation: a recipe for success?', *International Journal of Press/Politics*, 26(4), 861–81.

El Kak, N. (2019), *A Path for Political Change in Lebanon? Lessons and Narratives from the 2018 Elections*, Arab Reform Initiative.

El Khazen, F. (2020), *The Breakdown of the State in Lebanon, 1967–1976*, Bloomsbury Publishing.

El-Nawawy, M. and Khamis, S. (2016), *Egyptian Revolution 2.0: Political Blogging, Civic Engagement, and Citizen Journalism*, Springer.

El-nawawy, M., Iskandar, A. and Farag, A. I. (2002), *Al Jazeera: How the Free Arab News Network Scooped the World and Changed the Middle East*, Basic Books.

El-Richani, S. (2016), *The Lebanese Media: Anatomy of a System in Perpetual Crisis*, Palgrave Macmillan.

Elhiwar Ettounsi (14 October 2019), [TV] 'Presidentielle Aujourdhui Episode 02 13-10-2019 Partie 02', https://www.youtube.com/watch?v=NyI9S2Tg3iU.

Elmasry, M. H. (2012), 'Producing news in Mubarak's Egypt: an analysis of Egyptian newspaper production during the late Hosni Mubarak era', *Journal of Arab and Muslim Media Research*, 4(2–3), 121–44.

Elmasry, M. H., Basiony, D. M. and Elkamel, S. F. (2014), 'Egyptian journalistic professionalism in the context of revolution: comparing survey results from before and after the January 25, 2011 uprising', *International Journal of Communication*, 8, 23.

Elnashra (28 February 2019), الفساد يحاربون الفساد وأحزاب السلطة وظفت 5000 شخص قبل الانتخابات يعقوبيان: أرباب (Yaʿqubian: the lords of corruption are fighting corruption and the parties in power employed 5000 people before the elections), Elnashra News, http://www.elnashra.com/news/show/1288438/يعقوبيان-أرباب-الفساد-يحاربون-الفساد-وأحزاب-السلط.html.

Engesser, S., Ernst, N. Esser, F. and Büchel, F. (2017), 'Populism and social media: how politicians spread a fragmented ideology', *Information, Communication and Society*, 20(8), 1109–26.

Entman, R. M. (2007), 'Framing bias: media in the distribution of power', *Journal of Communication*, 57(1), 163–73.

Etzioni, A. (2005), *How Patriotic is the Patriot Act?: Freedom Versus Security in the Age of Terrorism*, Routledge.

Evron, Y. (2013), *War and Intervention in Lebanon (Routledge Revivals): The Israeli-Syrian Deterrence Dialogue*, Routledge.

European Union Election Observation Mission (2018), *Lebanon: Final Report—Parliamentary Elections 2018*, European Union, https://eeas.europa.eu/sites/eeas/files/final_report_eu_eom_lebanon_2018_english_17_july_2018.pdf.

Fandy, M. (2007), *(Un)civil War of Words: Media and Politics in the Arab World*, Greenwood Publishing Group.

Fares, E. (7 May 2018), 'Kollouna Watani's Joumana Haddad and Paula Yacoubian are now parliament members', A Separate State of Mind, https://stateofmind13.com/2018/05/07/kollouna-watanis-joumana-haddad-paula-yacoubian-are-now-parliament-members/.

Farmanfarmaian, R. (ed.). (2020). *Media and Politics in the Southern Mediterranean: Communicating Power in Transition after 2011*, Routledge.

Fawaz, M. (2013), 'The Role of The Media in a Precarious Plural Democracy: The Case of Lebanon', unpublished PhD dissertation, Georgia State University, http://scholarworks.gsu.edu/cgi/viewcontent.cgi?article=1045andcontext=communication_diss.

Figenschou, T. U. (2013), *Al Jazeera and the Global Media Landscape: The South is Talking Back*, Routledge.

Fishman, M. (1988), *Manufacturing the News*, University of Texas Press.

Fisk, R. (2001), *Pity the Nation: Lebanon at War*, Oxford University Press, USA.

Fox, E. and Waisbord, S. (2009), *Latin Politics, Global Media*, University of Texas Press.

France24 (25 April 2019), 'Tunisie: saisie des équipements d'une importante télévision privée', France 24, https://www.france24.com/fr/20190425-tunisie-saisie-equipements-dune-importante-television-privee.

Gade, T. (2018), 'The reconfiguration of clientelism and the failure of vote buying in Lebanon', in L. Ruiz de Elvira, C. L. Schwarz and I. Weipert-Fenner (eds), *Clientelism and Patronage in the Middle East and North Africa: Networks of Dependency*, ch. 6, p. 100.

Gade, T. and Moussa, N. (2017), 'The Lebanese army after the Syrian crisis: alienating the Sunni community?', in A. J. Knudsen and T. Gade (eds), *Civil-Military Relations in Lebanon: Conflict, Cohesion and Confessionalism in a Divided Society*, Cham: Springer, pp. 23–49.

Gans, H. J. (2004), *Deciding what's News: A Study of CBS Evening News, NBC Nightly News, Newsweek, and Time*, Northwestern University Press.

Geertz, Clifford (2008), *Thick Description: Toward an Interpretive Theory of Culture*, Routledge.

Gellner, E. and Waterbury, J. (1977), *Patrons and Clients in Mediterranean Societies*, Gerald Duckworth and Company.

Geukjian, O. (2016), *Lebanon after the Syrian Withdrawal: External Intervention, Power-sharing and Political Instability*, Taylor and Francis.

Ghosn, F. and Khoury, A. (2011), 'Lebanon after the civil war: peace or the illusion of peace?', *Middle East Journal*, 65(3), 381–97.

Gitlin, T. (2003), *The Whole World is Watching: Mass Media in the Making and Unmaking of the New Left*, University of California Press.

Gobe, É. (2018), 'La Tunisie en 2017: impotence de l'état et tentations autoritaires', *L'Année du Maghreb*, 19, 235–56, https://doi.org/10.4000/anneemaghreb.4305.

Günay, C. and Sommavilla, F. (2020), 'Tunisia's democratization at risk', *Mediterranean Politics*, 25(5), 673–81.

Guerrero, M. A. (2014), 'The "Captured Liberal" model of media systems in Latin America', in M. A. Guerrero and M. Márquez-Ramírez, *Media Systems and Communication Policies in Latin America*, Springer, pp. 43–65.

Guerrero, M. A. and Márquez-Ramírez, M. (2014), *Media Systems and Communication Policies in Latin America*, Springer.

Hadith al-Sa'a (Talk of the Hour) (4 December 2015), al-Manar.

Hafez, K. (2002), 'Journalism ethics revisited: a comparison of ethics codes in Europe, North Africa, the Middle East, and Muslim Asia', *Political Communication*, 19(2), 225–50.

Hafez, K. (2008), *Arab Media: Power and Weakness*, Continuum.

HAICA (n.d.), About HAICA (in Arabic) (accessed 19 April 2020), https://haica.tn/عن-الهيئة/التقديم/

والهيئة العليا المستقلة للاتصال السمعي والبصري مؤرخ في 21 أوت 2019 ,(HAICA (21 August 2019 قرار مشترك بين الهيئة العليا المستقلة للانتخابات | A joint agreement between The Independent High Authority for Elections, and The Independent High Authority for Audiovisual Communication on 21 August 2019, https://haica.tn/ar/المستقلة-قرار-مشترك-بين-الهيئة-العليا

HAICA (2020), "مستقبل قانون الاتصال السمعي البصري في تونس": (The Future of the Audiovisual Law in Tunisia)", HAICA [blog], 12 October 2020, https://haica.tn/ar/مستقبل-قانون-الاتصال-السمعي-البصري-في/.

Hallin, D. C. and Papathanassopoulos, S. (2002), 'Political clientelism and the media: Southern Europe and Latin America in comparative perspective', *Media, Culture and Society*, 24(2), 175–95.

Hallin, D. C. and Mancini, P. (2004), 'Comparing media systems: three models of media and politics', Cambridge University Press.

Hallin, D. C., Mellado, C. and Mancini, P. (2021), 'The concept of hybridity in journalism studies', *International Journal of Press/Politics*, published online September 30, 2021.

Hamdy, N. (2009), 'Arab citizen journalism in action: challenging mainstream media, authorities and media laws', *Westminster Papers in Communication and Culture*, 6(1).

Hammami, S. (2017), دراسة الميديا في السياق الانتقالي: الميديا التونسية نموذجاً (The media in a transitional context: the Tunisian case), in N. al-Qadiri 'Isa (ed.),

الإعلام العربي ورهانات التغيير في ظل التحولات (The Arab Media: Betting on Changes under Transformation), Centre for Arab Unity Studies, pp. 45–65.

Hamzeh, A. (2001), 'Clientalism, Lebanon: roots and trends', *Middle Eastern Studies*, 37(3), 167–78.

Hanitzsch, T. (2007), 'Deconstructing journalism culture: toward a universal theory', *Communication Theory*, 17(4), 367–85.

Hanitzsch, T., Hanusch, F. and Lauerer, C. (2016), 'Setting the agenda, influencing public opinion, and advocating for social change', *Journalism Studies*, 17(1), 1–20.

Hanitzsch, T., Hanusch, F., Mellado, C., Anikina, M., Berganza, R., Cangoz, I., Coman, M., Hamada, B., Elena Hernández, M. and Karadjov, C. D. (2011), 'Mapping journalism cultures across nations: a comparative study of 18 countries', *Journalism Studies*, 12(3), 273–93.

Hanitzsch, T., Hanusch, F., Ramaprasad, J. and De Beer, A. S. (2019), *Worlds of Journalism: Journalistic Cultures around the Globe*, Columbia University Press.

Hanusch, F. (2019), 'Journalistic roles and everyday life: an empirical account of lifestyle journalists' professional views', *Journalism Studies*, 20(2), 193–211.

Hanusch, F. and Hanitzsch, T. (2017), 'Comparing journalistic cultures across nations', *Journalism Studies*, 18(5), 525–35.

Harik, I. F. (1965), 'The "Iqṭā'" system in Lebanon: a comparative political view', *Middle East Journal*, 19(4), 405–21.

Haugbølle, R. H. (2013), 'Rethinking the role of the media in the Tunisian uprising', in N. Gana (ed.), *The Making of the Tunisian Revolution: Contexts, Architects, Prospects*, Edinburgh University Press.

Haugbølle, R. H. and Cavatorta, F. (2012), '"Vive la grande famille des médias tunisiens": media reform, authoritarian resilience and societal responses in Tunisia', *Journal of North African Studies*, 17(1), 97–112.

Hawi, Z. (2 December 2015), اكرم الضيافة عند ... 'النصرة' اسألوا حسين خريس (al-Nusra's hospitality . . . Ask Husayn Khurays!), al-Akhbar, https://al-akhbar.com/Media_Tv/91.

Herman, E. S. and Chomsky, N. (2010), *Manufacturing Consent: The Political Economy of the Mass Media*, Random House.

Herrero, L. C., Humprecht, E., Engesser, S., Brüggemann, M. L. and Büchel, F. (2017), 'Rethinking Hallin and Mancini beyond the West: an analysis of media systems in Central and Eastern Europe', *International Journal of Communication*, 11(0), 27.

Hess, S. and Kalb, M. (2003), *The Media and the War on Terrorism*, Brookings Institution Press.

Hibou, B. (2011), *The Force of Obedience*, Polity.

Hizawi, A. al-Karim (2017), رهانات الإصلاح في تونس بعد الثورة: مكاسب الحرية وإكراهاتها (The stakes of reform in Tunisia after the revolution: its gains and constraints), in N. al-Qadiri 'Isa (ed.), الإعلام العربي ورهانات التغيير في ظل التحولات (The Arab Media: Betting on Changes under Transformation), Centre for Arab Unity Studies, pp. 135–40.

Høigilt, J. and Selvik, K. (2020), 'Introduction', *International Communication Gazette*, 82(7), 591–3, https://doi.org/10.1177/1748048519897486.

Hourani, A. (1968), 'Ottoman reform and the politics of notables', in W. R. Polk and R. L. Chambers (eds), *Beginnings of Modernization in the Middle East in the Nineteenth Century*, University of Chicago Press.

Howard, P. N. and Hussain, M. M. (2013), *Democracy's Fourth Wave?: Digital Media and the Arab Spring*, Oxford University Press.

Hroub, K. (ed.) (2012), *Religious Broadcasting in the Middle East*, Hurst.

Hughes, S. and Lawson, C. (2005), 'The barriers to media opening in Latin America', *Political Communication*, 22(1), 9–25.

Human Rights Watch (2019), *There is a Price to Pay: The Criminalization of Peaceful Speech in Lebanon*, Human Rights Watch.

Inkyfada (2017), Panama Papers, Inkyfada, https://inkyfada.com/fr/dossier/panama-papers/.

Inkyfada (2020), Who we are, Inkyfada, https://inkyfada.com/ar/من-نحن/.

International Crisis Group (10 May 2017), 'La transition bloquée: corruption et régionalisme en Tunisie', Crisis Group, https://www.crisisgroup.org/fr/middle-east-north-africa/north-africa/tunisia/177-blocked-transition-corruption-and-regionalism-tunisia.

International Crisis Group (26 March 2019), 'Décentralisation en Tunisie: consolider la démocratie sans affaiblir l'Etat', Crisis Group, https://www.crisisgroup.org/fr/middle-east-north-africa/north-africa/tunisia/198-decentralisation-en-tunisie-consolider-la-democratie-sans-affaiblir-letat.

IPSI (n.d.), IPSI - Historique, Institut de Presse et Des Sciences de l'Information, http://www.ipsi.rnu.tn/fra/pages/104/Loi-de-cr%C3%A9ation (accessed 11 April 2020).

Isakhan, B. (2008), 'The post-Saddam Iraqi media: reporting the democratic developments of 2005', *Global Media Journal*, 7(13).

Jakli, L., Fish, S. M. and Wittenberg, J. (2019), 'A decade of democratic decline and stagnation', in C. W. Haerpfer, P. Bernhagen, C. Welzel and R. F. Inglehart (eds), *Democratization*, 2nd edn, Oxford University Press, pp. 267–82.

Janoubia (3 September 2019), باسيل رأس حربة السلطة لإسقاط حصانة يعقوبيان (Bassil—The authorities' spearhead to end Yaʿqubian's impunity), جنوبية. https://janoubia.com/2019/03/09/باسيل-رأس-حربة-السلطة-لإسقاط-حصانة-يعق/.

Jelassi, M. Y. (3 May 2021), حرية الصحافة في تونس: تحت السيطرة ؟ (Press Freedom in Tunisia: Under Control?), Nawaat, https://nawaat.org/2021/05/03/؟-تحت-السيطرة-حرية-الصحافة-في-تونس/.

Jeune Afrique (2 February 2018), 'Tunisie: "journée de colère" des journalistes après des menaces', Jeune Afrique, https://www.jeuneafrique.com/527037/politique/tunisie-journee-de-colere-des-journalistes-apres-des-menaces/.

Jeune Afrique (28 May 2019), 'Tunisie: Nabil Karoui candidat à l'élection présidentielle – Jeune Afrique', Jeune Afrique, https://www.jeuneafrique.com/780841/politique/tunisie-nabil-karoui-candidat-a-lelection-presidentielle/.

jfrant (24 June 2019), *NDI Lebanon 2018 Parliamentary Elections International Observation Mission Final Report* [Text], National Democratic Institute, https://www.ndi.org/publications/ndi-lebanon-2018-parliamentary-elections-international-observation-mission-final-report.

Joffé, G. (2014), 'Government–media relations in Tunisia: a paradigm shift in the culture of governance?', *Journal of North African Studies*, 19(5), 615–38.

Johnson, M. (1986), *Class and Client in Beirut: The Sunni Muslim Community and the Lebanese State, 1840–1985*, Political Studies of the Middle East vol. 28, Ithaca Press.

Jones, M. O. (2020), *Political Repression in Bahrain*, Cambridge University Press.

Kapitalis (6 November 2019), 'Mohamed Boughalleb limogé du bureau de presse et de communication de la Cité de la culture', Kapitalis, http://kapitalis.com/tunisie/2019/11/06/mohamed-boughalleb-limoge-du-bureau-de-presse-et-de-communication-de-la-cite-de-la-culture/.

Kapitalis (13 April 2021), اقتحام قوات الأمن لوكالة تونس افريقيا للأنباء سابقة خطيرة في الشأن الاعلامي النقابة الوطنية للصحفيين تعتبر (The SNJT regards the security forces' attack on on TAP as a dangerous precedent in the media sphere), Kapitalis, http://www.kapitalis.com/anbaa-tounes/2021/04/13/اقتحا-تعتبر-النقابة-الوطنية-للصحفيين/.

Kaya, R. and Çakmur, B. (2010), 'Politics and the mass media in Turkey', *Turkish Studies*, 11(4), 521–37.

Kellner, D. (2015), *Media Spectacle and the Crisis of Democracy: Terrorism, War, and Election Battles*, Routledge.

Kellner, D. (2016), *American Nightmare: Donald Trump, Media Spectacle, and Authoritarian Populism*, Springer.

Khalaf, S. (1977), 'Changing forms of political patronage in Lebanon', in E. Gellner and J. Waterbury (eds), *Patrons and Clients in Mediterranean Societies*, Duckworth, pp. 185–205.

Khalaf, S. (2002), *Civil and Uncivil Violence in Lebanon: A history of the Internationalization of Communal Conflict*, Columbia University Press.

Khalil, J. and Kraidy, M. M. (2009), *Arab Television Industries*, British Film Institute.

Khamis, S. and Vaughn, K. (2011), 'Cyberactivism in the Egyptian revolution: how civic engagement and citizen journalism tilted the balance', *Arab Media and Society*, 14(3), 1–25.

Kim, H. S. and Hama-Saeed, M. (2008), 'Emerging media in peril', *Journalism Studies*, 9(4), 578–94.

Kraidy, M. M. (2011), 'The rise of transnational media systems. Implications of pan-Arab media for comparative research', in D. C. Hallin and P. Mancini (eds), *Comparing Media Systems Beyond the Western World*, Cambridge University Press.

Kraidy, M. M. (2016), 'Trashing the sectarian system? Lebanon's "You Stink" movement and the making of affective publics', *Communication and the Public*.

Kraidy, M. M. (2019), 'The Lebanese rise up against a failed system', *Current History*, 118(812), 361–3.

Krämer, B. (2014), 'Media populism: a conceptual clarification and some theses on its effects', *Communication Theory*, 24(1), 42–60.

Kulayb, S. (22 April 2015), صحافيون لا أبواق (Journalists, not trumpets), Facebook, https://www.facebook.com/samikleib/posts/426064467518587/.

Kulayb, S. (22 November 2019), Tweet 22 November 2019 [Tweet], @samykleyb, https://twitter.com/samykleyb/status/1197860259588722691.

Lazkani, S. (9 March 2021), 'Even this former Aounist is criticizing Lebanese politicians' uselessness'. The961, https://www.the961.com/aounist-criticizing-govt-uselessness/.

LBCI (23 August 2015), 'In live on air during her coverage of 'You stink': LBC's reporter is assaulted (in Arabic)', LBCI, https://www.youtube.com/watch?v=WIJq9esyrIs.

Lebanese Association for Democratic Elections (2018), التمهيدي لمراقبة الانتخابات النيابية تقرير الثاني (The second preliminary report for the parliamentary election observation), LADE, https://docs.google.com/gview?embedded=trueandurl=http://www.lade.org.lb/getattachment/041167a8-c606-4446-bcae-8eccf29ab0f6/تقرير-الثاني-التمهيدي-لمراقبة-الانتخابات-النيابية.aspx.

Lebanese Forces (18 October 2019), مقدمات نشرات الأخبار المسائية ليوم الجمعة 18/10/2019 (Introductions to the evening news, Friday 18 October 2019), Lebanese Forces Official Website, https://www.lebanese-forces.com/2019/10/18/news-intros-81/.

Lebanese National News Agency, (17 January 2020), 'Uthman in press conference: I apologize for what happened to journalists . . .', Lebanese National News Agency, http://nna-leb.gov.lb/ar/show-news/457130/.

Leenders, R. (2012), *Spoils of Truce: Corruption and State-Building in Postwar Lebanon*, Cornell University Press.

Lefèvre, R. (2017), 'The roots of growing social unrest in Tunisia', *Journal of North African Studies*, 22(4), 505–10.

Le Livre noir des 'journalistes amis' en Tunisie sous Ben Ali (5 December 2013), Le Monde.fr, https://www.lemonde.fr/international/article/2013/12/05/le-livre-noir-des-journalistes-amis-sous-ben-ali_3525709_3210.html.

Levitsky, S. and Way, L. A. (2009), 'Why democracy needs a level playing field', *Journal of Democracy*, 21(1), 57–68.

Levitsky, S. and Way, L. A. (2010), *Competitive Authoritarianism: Hybrid Regimes After the Cold War*, Cambridge University Press.

Lewis, S. C. and Reese, S. D. (2009), 'What is the war on terror? Framing through the eyes of journalists - Seth C. Lewis, Stephen D. Reese', *Journalism and Mass Communication Quarterly*, 86(1), 85–102.

Lijphart, A. (1969), Consociational democracy', *World Politics*, 21(2), 207–25.

L'Obs (5 February 2000), 'Conseils amicaux', L'Obs, https://www.nouvelobs.com/opinions/00004084.EDI0001/conseils-amicaux.html.

L'Orient-Le Jour (12 February 2018), 'Jean Aziz, conseiller en communication de Michel Aoun, aurait démissionné', L'Orient-Le Jour, https://www.lorientlejour.com/article/1099555/demission-de-jean-aziz-conseiller-en-communication-de-michel-aoun.html.

Lteif, D. (1 July 2020), 'The Lebanon revolution takes on the media: a resource on alternative news outlets', Jadaliyya - جدلية. https://www.jadaliyya.com/Details/40379.

Lustick, I. (1979), 'Stability in deeply divided societies: consociationalism versus control', *World Politics*, 31(3), 325–44.

Lutterbeck, D. (2015), 'Tool of rule: the Tunisian police under Ben Ali', *Journal of North African Studies*, 20(5), 813–31.

Lynch, M. (2006), *Voices of the New Arab Public: Iraq, Al-Jazeera, and Middle East Politics Today*, Columbia University Press.

Lynch, M. (2015), 'How the media trashed the transitions', *Journal of Democracy*, 26(4), 90–99.

Maboudi, T. (2020), 'Reconstituting Tunisia: participation, deliberation, and the content of constitution', *Political Research Quarterly*, 73(4), 774–89.

Mabweazara, H. M., Muneri, C. T. and Ndlovu, F. (2020), 'News "Media Capture", relations of patronage and clientelist practices in sub-Saharan Africa: an interpretive qualitative analysis', *Journalism Studies*, 21(15), 2154–75.

McChesney, R. W. (1999), *Rich Media, Poor Democracy: Communication Politics in Dubious Times*, New Press.

McCombs, M. (2018), *Setting the Agenda: Mass Media and Public Opinion*, John Wiley and Sons.

McElhone, J. M. (2017), 'The state, the military, and the market: capture in the new Burmese media landscape', in A. Schiffrin (ed.), *In the Service of Power: Media Capture and the Threat to Democracy*, Center for International Media Assistance, p. 59.

McKnight, D. (2010), 'Rupert Murdoch's News Corporation: a media institution with a mission', *Historical Journal of Film, Radio and Television*, 30(3), 303–16.

McNair, B. (1998), *The Sociology of Journalism*, Oxford University Press.

Maghrebvoices (19 September 2019), ‏بسبب قيس سعيد.. قناة تونسية تخسر 1.5 مليون متابع!‏ (Tunisian TV-channel loses 1.5 million viewers because of Kais Saied) [Maghrebvoices.com], https://www.maghrebvoices.com/2019/09/19/تخسر-15-مليون-متابع-بسبب-قيس-سعيد-قناة-تونسية

Maharat Foundation (2019), *Maharat Foundation Report on the Occasion of World Press Freedom Day*, Maharat Foundation, http://www.maharatfoundation.org.

Mancini, P. (2008), 'Party–Press Parallelism', in *The International Encyclopedia of Communication*.

Mancini, P. (2012), 'Instrumentalization of the media vs. political parallelism', *Chinese Journal of Communication*, 5(3), 262–80.

Mancini, P. (2018), '"Assassination campaigns": corruption scandals and news media instrumentalization', *International Journal of Communication* 12, 3067–86.

Mazzoleni, G. (2014), 'Mediatization and political populism', in F. Esser and J. Strömbäck (eds), *Mediatization of Politics*, Springer, pp. 42–56.

Media Ownership Monitor (2019), 'Media Ownership Monitor—Tunisia', Media Ownership Monitor, http://tunisia.mom-rsf.org/en/.

Megaphone (2020), 'About page – Megaphone, https://megaphone.news/about/.

Melki, J. (2008), 'Television news and the state in Lebanon', unpublished doctoral dissertation, University of Maryland.

Melki, J. (2009), Journalism and media studies in Lebanon, *Journalism Studies*, 10(5), 672–90.

Melki, J. P. and Mallat, S. E. (2016), Block her entry, keep her down and push her out, *Journalism Studies*, 17(1), 57–79.

Mellado, C. (2020a), 'Theorizing journalistic roles', in *Beyond Journalistic Norms: Role Performance and News in Comparative Perspective*, Routledge, pp. 22–45.

Mellado, C. (ed.) (2020b), *Beyond Journalistic Norms: Role Performance and News in Comparative Perspective*, Routledge.

Mellado, C., Hellmueller, L. and Donsbach, W. (2016), *Journalistic Role Performance: Concepts, Contexts, and Methods*, Taylor and Francis.

Mellado, C., Hellmueller, L., Márquez-Ramírez, M., Humanes, M. L., Sparks, C., Stepinska, A., Pasti, S., Schielicke, A.-M., Tandoc, E., and Wang, H. (2017), 'The hybridization of journalistic cultures: a comparative study of journalistic role performance', *Journal of Communication*, 67(6), 944–67.

Mellor, N. (2005), *The Making of Arab News*, Rowman and Littlefield Publishers.

Mellor, N. (2007), *Modern Arab Journalism: Problems and Prospects*, Edinburgh University Press.

Mellor, N. (2009), 'Strategies for autonomy', *Journalism Studies*, 10(3), 307–21.

Merkel, W. (2004), 'Embedded and defective democracies', *Democratization*, 11(5), 33–58.

Meyen, M. and Riesmeyer, C. (2012), 'Service providers, sentinels, and traders: journalists' role perceptions in the early twenty-first century', *Journalism Studies*, 13(3), 386–401.

Morlino, L. (2009), 'Are there hybrid regimes? Or are they just an optical illusion?', *European Political Science Review*, 1(2), 273–96.

Middle East Monitor (20 June 2017), 'Tunisia arrests TV host on corruption charges', Middle East Monitor, https://www.middleeastmonitor.com/20170620-tunisia-arrests-tv-host-on-corruption-charges/.

Miladi, N. (2021), 'Tunisia: the transformative media landscape after the revolution', in C. Richter and C. Kozman (eds), *Arab Media Systems*, Open Book Publishers, pp. 267–83.

Miles, H. (2010), *Al Jazeera: How Arab TV News Challenged the World*, Hachette UK.

Ministry of the Interior - Tunisia (16 January 2018), في برنامج 24-7 على قناة الحوار التونسي (الناطق الرسمي لوزارة الداخلية العميد خليفة الشيباني The spokesman for the Ministry of the Interior, colonel Khalifa al-Sahybani, on the 24/7 show), https://www.youtube.com/watch?v=x7DSRUaAVlI.

Mroue, B. (8 December 2019), 'Lebanon's journalists suffer abuse, threats covering unrest', HuffPost, https://www.huffpost.com/entry/lebanon-journalists-protests_n_5ded4fe4e4b07f6835b49d89.

MTV (3 May 2018), Prime Time News—03/05/2018—المقدمة, https://www.youtube.com/watch?v=ZpFMDO_Y7WU.

MTV Lebanon News (18 March 2019), مؤتمر صحافي ليعقوبيان—تكشف خلاله وثائق متعلقة بملفات الفساد (Press conference with Yacoubian in which she reveals documents relating to cases of corruption), https://www.youtube.com/watch?v=YOuY9EZocu8.

Mudawwar (21 October 2019), Tweet 21 October 2019 [Tweet], @MedawarLana, https://twitter.com/MedawarLana/status/1186317120738676736.

Mungiu-Pippidi, A. (2012), 'Freedom without impartiality. The vicious circle of media capture', in P. Gross and K. Jakubowicz (eds), *Media Transformations in the Post-Communist World: Eastern Europe's Tortured Path to Change*, pp. 49–66.

Nacos, B. (2016), *Mass-Mediated Terrorism: Mainstream and Digital Media in Terrorism and Counterterrorism*, 3rd edn, Rowman and Littlefield Publishers.

Nader, D. J., Mikhael, M. T. and Sadaka, D. G. (n.d.), *Women in Lebanon's 2018 Legislative Elections*, 119.

Najem, T. (2012), *Lebanon: The Politics of a Penetrated Society*, Routledge.

Naoufal, P. (13 September 2018), 'NAYA | QandA with Paula Yacoubian: a maverick out to shake up the parliament - Paula Naoufal', An-Nahar, https://en.annahar.com/article/860401-naya--qa-with-paula-yacoubian-a-maverick-out-to-shake-up-the-parliament.

Nawaat (9 January 2018a), فاش نستناو: حراك احتجاجي يُجابه بقمع بوليسي (The Answer to the Protest Movement is Repression by the Police), https://www.youtube.com/watch?v=wp_dTHJgiMw.

Nawaat (12 January 2018b), مسيرة فاش نستناو: رغم الشيطنة والإيقافات الحملة مستمرّة (What Are We Waiting for March: Despite Vilification and Arrests the Campaign Continues), https://www.youtube.com/watch?v=f0WE852BGjQ.

Nawaat (2020), 'À propos de Nawaat', Nawaat, http://nawaat.org/.

Nichols, J. (2005), *Tragedy and Farce: How the American Media Sell Wars, Spin Elections, and Destroy Democracy*, New Press.

Nisma TV (11 January 2018), هات الصحيح (Give me the right), 11 January 2018, https://www.youtube.com/watch?v=OR7K2cG1Q2U.

Nisma TV (23 August 2019a), (لحظة اختطاف نبيل القروي (فيديو (The moment Nabil Karoui was kidnapped [video]), https://www.nessma.tv/ar/أخبار-وطنية/actu/157648/لحظة-اختطاف-نبيل-القروي-فيديو

Nisma TV (23 August 2019b), متابعة خاصة لعملية إيقاف نبيل القروي (Breaking news: the apprehension of Nabil Karoui), https://www.nessma.tv/ar/video/-أهم-الفيديوهات/26312/القروي-نبيل-إيقاف-لعملية-خاصة-متابعة

Nötzold, K. (2009), *Defining the Nation?: Lebanese Television and Political Elites (1990–2005)*, Frank and Timme.

Nouira, H. (6 September 2017), 'Le président Béji Caïd Essebsi à Assahafa et à La Presse: "Le système politique actuel ne peut assurer le développement et la stabilité du pays"',. La Presse de Tunisie, https://www.turess.com/fr/lapresse/135783.

Örnebring, H. (2012), 'Clientelism, elites, and the media in Central and Eastern Europe', *International Journal of Press/Politics*, 17(4), 497–515.

OTV (3 May 2018a), Prime time news 3 May 2018, https://www.youtube.com/watch?v=3xjxUTmmjHw.

OTV (4 May 2018b), Prime time news 4 May 2018, https://www.youtube.com/watch?v=5UYZXC070OI.

Perkins, K. (2014), *A History of Modern Tunisia*, Cambridge University Press.

Peters, C. and Broersma, M. J. (2013), *Rethinking Journalism: Trust and Participation in a Transformed News Landscape*, Routledge.

Peters, C. and Broersma, M. (2017), *Rethinking Journalism Again: Societal Role and Public Relevance in a Digital Age*, Taylor and Francis.

Picard, E. (2016), *Liban-Syrie, intimes étrangers: Un siècle d'interactions sociopolitiques*, Éditions Actes Sud.

Pintak, L. (2011), *The New Arab Journalist: Mission and Identity in a Time of Turmoil*, I. B. Tauris.

Pintak, L. and Ginges, J. (2008), 'The mission of Arab journalism: creating change in a time of turmoil', *International Journal of Press/Politics*, 13(3), 193–227.

Rabah, A. (6 October 2016), 'The Sects' security apparatuses: the arrest of al-Taras as example [in Arabic] [News]', almodon, https://www.almodon.com/politics/2016/10/6/أجهزة-الطوائف-الأمنية-نموذج-توقيف-الطراس

Ramaprasad, J. and Hamdy, N. N. (2006), 'Functions of Egyptian journalists: perceived importance and actual performance', *International Communication Gazette*, 68(2), 167–85.

Reich, Z. and Hanitzsch, T. (2013), Determinants of journalists' professional autonomy: individual and national level factors matter more than organizational ones, *Mass Communication and Society*, 16(1), 133–56.

Reporters Without Borders (14 February 2020), 'Another journalist attacked in Beirut | Reporters without borders', Reporters Without Borders, https://rsf.org/en/news/another-journalist-attacked-beirut.

Reporters Without Borders (2020a), 2020 World Press Freedom Index, RSF, https://rsf.org/en/ranking/2020.

Reporters Without Borders (2020b), 'Lebanon: highly politicized media, free speech under attack', Reporters Without Borders, https://rsf.org/en/lebanon.

Richter, C. and Kozman, C. (eds) (2021), *Arab Media Systems*, Open Book Publishers, https://doi.org/10.11647/OBP.0238.

Rizkallah, A. (11 May 2016), 'Beirut's election was surprisingly competitive. Could it shake up Lebanese politics?', *Washington Post*, https://www.washingtonpost.com/news/monkey-cage/wp/2016/05/11/beiruts-election-was-surprisingly-competitive-could-it-shake-up-lebanese-politics/.

Roudakova, N. (2008), 'Media—political clientelism: lessons from anthropology', *Media, Culture and Society*, 30(1), 41–59.

Roudakova, N. (2009), 'Journalism as "prostitution": understanding Russia's reactions to Anna Politkovskaya's murder', *Political Communication*, 26(4), 412–29.

Roudakova, N. (2017), *Losing Pravda: Ethics and The Press in Post-Truth Russia*, Cambridge University Press.

Rugh, W. A. (2004), *Arab Mass Media: Newspapers, Radio, and Television in Arab Politics*, Praeger.

Ryabinska, N. (2014), 'Media capture in post-communist Ukraine: actors, methods, and conditions', *Problems of Post-Communism*, 61(2), 46–60.

Sadiq (28 October 2019), Tweet 28 October 2019 [Tweet], @dimasadek, https://twitter.com/dimasadek/status/1188606143008006149.

Saghiyah, K. (16 June 2011), الممانعة والثورة (Revolt and revolution), al-Akhbar, https://al-akhbar.com/Opinion/90117.

Sakr, N. (2005), The changing dynamics of Arab journalism, in H. de Burgh (ed.), *Making Journalists: Diverse Models, Global Issues*, Routledge, pp. 142–56.

Sakr, N. (2007), *Arab Television Today*, I. B. Tauris.

Sakr, N. (2013), *Transformations in Egyptian Journalism*, Bloomsbury Publishing.

Sakr, N., Skovgaard-Petersen, J. and Della Ratta, D. (2015), Arab Media Moguls, I. B. Tauris.

Salamé, G. (1994), 'Small is pluralistic: democracy as an instrument of civil peace', in G. Salamé (ed.), *Democracy without Democrats*, I. B. Tauris, pp. 84–111.

Salem, N. (1984), *Habib Bourguiba, Islam and the Creation of Tunisia*, Croom Helm.

Salibi, K. (1990), *A House of Many Mansions: The History of Lebanon Reconsidered*, University of California Press.

Salloukh, B. F. (2017), 'The Syrian war: spillover effects on Lebanon', *Middle East Policy*, 24(1), 62–78.

Salloukh, B., Barakat, R., Al-Habbal, J. S., Khattab, L. W. and Mikaelian, S. (2015), *The Politics of Sectarianism in Postwar Lebanon*, Pluto Press.

Samir Kassir Foundation and Reporters Without Borders (2018), 'Media Ownership Monitor—Lebanon', Media Ownership Monitor, http://lebanon.mom-rsf.org/en/media/.

Sarde After Dinner (1 August 2021), 'DIMA SADEK: One year after the blast, make your voice heard | Sarde (after dinner) [Podcast #48]', Sarde, https://www.youtube.com/watch?app=desktopandv=dTGoKsOFDAQandt=2257sandfbclid=IwAR0PwYEBxoAuZjGVuPcBKNRMU7Wla7bbQmndfA2BxAb4yYzi35HY9CbeQ5E.

Sarra, A. (25 October 2019), 'Présidentielle 2019: A l'investiture de Kaïs Saïed, tous sauf les médias!', Webmanagercenter, https://www.webmanagercenter.com/2019/10/25/440398/presidentielle-2019-a-linvestiture-de-kais-saied-tous-sauf-les-medias/.

Schedler, A. (2002), 'The menu of manipulation', *Journal of Democracy*, 13(2), 36–50.

Schedler, A. (2013), *The Politics of Uncertainty: Sustaining and Subverting Electoral Authoritarianism*, Oxford University Press.

Schiffrin, A. (2017), *In the Service of Power: Media Capture and the Threat to Democracy*, Center for International Media Assistance, Washington, DC.

Schiffrin, A. (2018), Introduction to Special Issue on media capture.

Schudson, M. (1989), 'The sociology of news production', *Media, Culture and Society*, 11(3), 263–82.

Schudson, M. (2003), *The Sociology of News*, Norton New York.

Selvik, K. (2011a), Elite Rivalry in a Semi-democracy: The Kuwaiti Press Scene, *Middle Eastern Studies*, 47(3), 477–96.

Selvik, K. (2011b), 'Mediemakt og politisk krise i Kuwait', *Babylon - Nordisktidsskrift for Midtøstenstudier*, 9(1), 46–57.

Selvik, K. and Høigilt, J. (2021), 'Journalism under instrumentalized political parallelism', *Journalism Studies*, 22(5), 653–69.

Shams FM (18 October 2019), قيس سعيد يدعو إلى احترام الإعلاميين وعدم التعرّض لأحد (Kais Saied calls for respect for journalists and to avoid harming anyone), Shemsfm, https://www.shemsfm.net/amp/ar/الأخبار_أخبار-تونس_الأخبار-الوطنية/233619/قيس-سعيد-يدعو-مجدداـإلى-احترام-الإعلاميين-والمؤسسات-الإعلامي-ة-وعدم-التعر-ض-لأحد.

Siebert, F., Siebert, F. T., Peterson, T. B., Peterson, T. and Schramm, W. (1956), *Four Theories of the Press: The Authoritarian, Libertarian, Social Responsibility, and Soviet Communist Concepts of what the Press Should Be and Do*, University of Illinois Press.

Singer, J. (2017), 'The journalist as entrepreneur', in C. Peters and M. Broersma (eds), *Rethinking Journalism Again: Societal Role and Public Relevance in a Digital Age*, Taylor and Francis, pp. 131–45.

SKEyes (18 November 2019), 'The phone numbers of five journalists in al-Jadeed publicized to harass and abuse them; the campaign against Dima Sadiq continues [NGO]', SKeyes Center for Media and Cultural Freedom, https://www.skeyesmedia.org/ar/News/News/18-11-2019/8142.

SNJT (2019), التقرير السنوي لواقع الحريات الصحفية في تونس (Annual report on the reality of press freedom in Tunisia), Syndicat National des Journalistes Tunisiens, snjt.org/wp-content/uploads/2019/05/1-التقرير-السنوي.pdf

SNJT (3 May 2021), *The 2021 Report on Press Freedom*, National Syndicate of Tunisian Journalists, http://snjt.org/2021/05/03/التقرير-الحري/

Stenslie, S. and Selvik, K. (2019), 'Elite survival and the Arab Spring: the cases of Tunisia and Egypt', in Elites and People: Challenges to Democracy, *Comparative Social Research*, Emerald Publishing Limited, 34, 17–34.

Stetka, V. (2010), 'Between a rock and a hard place? Market concentration, local ownership and media autonomy in the Czech Republic', *International Journal of Communication*, 4(2010), 865–85.

Stetka, V. (2012), 'From multinationals to business tycoons: media ownership and journalistic autonomy in Central and Eastern Europe', *International Journal of Press/Politics*, 17(4), 433–56.

Strömbäck, J. (2005), 'In search of a standard: four models of democracy and their normative implications for journalism', *Journalism Studies*, 6(3), 331–45.

Surprenant, A. (5 December 2019), 'Lebanon protests are dividing the country's struggling media', Al Arabiya English, https://english.alarabiya.net/en/media/print/2019/12/05/Lebanon-protests-are-dividing-the-country-s-struggling-media.html.

Tansel, C. B. (2018), 'Authoritarian neoliberalism and democratic backsliding in Turkey: beyond the narratives of progress', *South European Society and Politics*, 23(2), 197–217.

The Economist (24 October 2019), 'A surge of public anger sends Lebanon's politicians reeling', *The Economist*, https://www.economist.com/middle-east-and-africa/2019/10/24/a-surge-of-public-anger-sends-lebanons-politicians-reeling.

The Guardian (25 July 2015), 'Tunisia adopts tougher counter-terrorism law in wake of attacks', *The Guardian*, http://www.theguardian.com/world/2015/jul/25/tunisia-adopts-tougher-counter-terrorism-law-in-wake-of-attacks.

Topalian, N. (8 June 2021), 'Lebanese journalist speaks out about Hizbullah's ongoing threats, assaults', al-Mashareq, https://almashareq.com/en_GB/articles/cnmi_am/features/2021/06/08/feature-03.

Traboulsi, F. (2012), *A History of Modern Lebanon*. Pluto Press.

Transparency International (2020), *Corruptions Perceptions Index 2019 for Tunisia*, Transparency.Org, https://www.transparency.org/en/cpi/2019/tun.

Tripp, C. (2015), *Battlefields of the Republic: The Struggle for Public Space in Tunisia*, LSE, http://www.lse.ac.uk/middleEastCentre/publications/Paper-Series/2015/BattlefieldsofRepublic.aspx.

Tucker, J. A., Theocharis, Y., Roberts, M. E. and Barberá, P. (2017), 'From liberation to turmoil: social media and democracy', *Journal of Democracy*, 28(4), 46–59.

Tunisian Republic Presidential Office (2013), منظومة الدعاية تحت حكم بن علي (The System of Propaganda under Ben Ali), https://issuu.com/babnettunisie/docs/kitabasoued.

Tunisie numérique (2 November 2018), 'Tunisie: Samir El Wafi attérit à la chaîne Attessia', Tunisie Numerique, https://www.tunisienumerique.com/tunisie-samir-el-wafi-atterit-a-la-chaine-attessia/.

'umrany, T. (30 August 2019), "ماكينة الدمغجة الإعلامية" في ليلة السكاكين الطويلة على قناة التاسعة، هكذا أوقف مورو! (This is how Muru put an end to the 'demagogic media machine' on the Night of the Long Knives, on Channel 9!), Babnet, https://www.babnet.net/festivaldetail-188185.asp.

Voltmer, K. (2012), 'How far can media systems travel', in D. C. Hallin, P. Mancini (eds), *Comparing Media Systems beyond the Western World*, Cambridge University Press, 224–45.

Voltmer, K. (2013), *The Media in Transitional Democracies*, Polity.

Voltmer, K. (2015), 'Converging and Diverging Pathways of Media Transformation', in J. Zielonka (ed.), *Media and Politics in New Democracies: Europe in a Comparative Perspective*, Oxford University Press, p. 217–30.

Voltmer, K. and Rawnsley, G. (2009), 'The media', in C. W. Haerpfer, P. Bernhagen, R. F. Inglehart and C. Welzel (eds), *Democratization*, Oxford University Press, pp. 234–48.

Voltmer, K., Selvik, K. and Høigilt, J. (2021), 'Hybrid media and hybrid politics: contesting informational uncertainty in Lebanon and Tunisia', *International Journal of Press/Politics*, 26(4), 842–860.

Wahl-Jorgensen, K. (2017), 'Is there a "postmodern turn" in journalism?', in C. Peters and M. Broersma (eds), *Rethinking Journalism Again: Societal Role and Public Relevance in a Digital Age*, Routledge, pp. 97–112.

Wahl-Jorgensen, K. (2018), 'Media coverage of shifting emotional regimes: Donald Trump's angry populism', *Media, Culture and Society*, 40(5), 766–78.

Waisbord, S. (2009), 'Advocacy journalism in a global context', *The Handbook of Journalism Studies*, 371–85.

Waisbord, S. (2014), *Media Sociology: A Reappraisal*, John Wiley and Sons.

Waisbord, S. (2016), 'Professionalism, journalistic role performance, and situated ethics beyond the West', in C. Mellado, L. Hellmueller and W. Donsbach (eds), *Journalistic Role Performance: Concepts, Contexts, and Methods*, Routledge, ch. 10, 171 references.

Watania 1 (11 January 2018), دقيقة 75 (75 minutes), https://www.youtube.com/watch?v=ZiYExtZh5Zc.

Webb, E. (2014), *Media in Egypt and Tunisia: From Control to Transition?*, Springer.

Weimann, G. and Winn, C. (1994), *The Theater of Terror: Mass Media and International Terrorism*, Longman.

Witschge, T. and Nygren, G. (2009), 'Journalistic work: a profession under pressure?', *Journal of Media Business Studies*, 6(1), 37–59.

Wolf, A. (2017), *Political Islam in Tunisia*, C. Hurst and Company Publishers.

Wolf, A. (2018), 'Former RCD officials stage a comeback in municipal elections in Tunisia', *Journal of North African Studies*, 23(4), 551–6.

Wolf, A. (2019), 'In search of "consensus": the crisis of party politics in Tunisia', *Journal of North African Studies*, 24(6), 883–6.

Wolfsfeld, G., Segev, E. and Sheafer, T. (2013), 'Social media and the Arab Spring: politics comes first', *International Journal of Press/Politics*, 18(2), 115–37.

Wollenberg, A. and Pack, J. (2013), Rebels with a pen: observations on the newly emerging media landscape in Libya', *Journal of North African Studies*, 18(2), 191–210.

World Press Freedom Index 2010 (20 April 2016), RSF, https://rsf.org/en/world-press-freedom-index-2010.

Yassine, H. (25 November 2019), 'Lebanese journalists just resigned from al-Mayadeen TV', The961, https://www.the961.com/lebanese-journalists-just-resigned-from-al-mayadeen-tv/.

Yerkes, S. and ben Yahmed, Z. (2019), *Tunisia's Political System: From Stagnation to Competition*, Carnegie Endowment for International Peace.

Yerkes, S. and Muasher, M. (2017), *Tunisia's Corruption Contagion: A Transition at Risk*, Carnegie Endowment for International Peace.

Yıldırım, K., Baruh, L. and Çarkoğlu, A. (2020), 'Dynamics of campaign reporting and press-party parallelism: rise of competitive authoritarianism and the media system in Turkey', *Political Communication*, 1–24.

Zabib, M. (10 November 2019), 'The interests of the oligarchy first [in Arabic], al-Akhbar, https://al-akhbar.com/Capital/277748.

Zabib, M. (13 February 2020), Tweet 13 February 2020 [Tweet], @mzbeeb, https://twitter.com/mzbeeb/status/1227884291125805056.

Zayani, M. and Sahraoui, S. (2017), *The Culture of Al Jazeera: Inside an Arab Media Giant*, McFarland.

Zayat, I. (19 September 2019), 'The many faces of Kais Saied', Thearabweekly, https://thearabweekly.com/many-faces-kais-saied.

Zelizer, B. (1993), Journalists as interpretive communities, *Critical Studies in Media Communication*, 10(3), 219–37.

Zelizer, B. (2004), *Taking Journalism Seriously: News and the Academy*, Sage Publications.

Zelizer, B. (2013), 'On the shelf life of democracy in journalism scholarship', *Journalism*, 14(4), 459–73.

Zielonka, J. (2015), 'Introduction: fragile democracy, volatile politics, and the quest for a free media, in J. Zielonka (ed.), *Media and Politics in New Democracies: Europe in a Comparative Perspective*, Oxford University Press, pp. 1–25.

Zielonka, J. (ed.) (2015), *Media and Politics in New Democracies: Europe in a Comparative Perspective*, Oxford University Press.

INDEX

Abu Fadil, Joseph, 94–5
Adam (Lebanese journalist), 44–5, 48
Ahmad (Lebanese journalist), 139
'Aid, Ghada, 141
Algeria, 50
'Ali, Mundhir Bilhajj, 123
AMAL movement, 156, 166, 171
al-Amari, Lutfi, 118–19, 120, 122, 124, 125, 127, 151
Amin, Hazim, 162
al-Amin, Ibrahim, 95, 160–1
Anais (Tunisian reporter), 77
Aoun, Michel, 28, 39, 94, 136, 157–8
Arab Spring, 1, 7
al-Asad, Bashar, 28
'Asi (Lebanese radio host), 64
Azar, Jessica, 140, 165
Aziz, Jean, 94

Bahrain, 7
Bakasini, Georges, 94

Basil, Jubran, 95, 138, 141, 143, 157, 160, 162
al-Bawsala (NGO), 60, 68
Bazzi, Fadia, 141
Beirut, 47
  attack on journalists (2020), 175–6
  elections: 2016, 137–8; 2018, 134, 140–1, 167–8
  explosion (August 2020), 177
  post-civil war, 48–9
  protests (2015), 53, 108–10, 155, 170
Beirut Madinati (activists), 142
Ben Ali, Zinedine, 2, 17, 28, 34, 43, 49, 51, 67, 70, 75, 115, 127, 128, 130
Ben Ali family, 36
Berlusconi, Silvio, 9
Bghuri, Naji, 130
Bilal (Tunisian journalist), 71, 130–1
Biltayyib, Nur al-Din, 121
Bil'umi, Hamza, 118, 120

Bilwaʻr, Hassan, 147
bin ʻAkasha, Bubakr, 146, 148, 149
bin Brik, Tawfiq, 50
bin Hamida, Sufiyan, 119, 120, 126
bin Husayn, Tahar, 41
bin Salim, Usama, 41
bin Salman, Muhammad, 89
bin Sidrin, Siham, 123
Birri, Nawal, 109, 171
Bourgiba, Habib, 28
Brahim (Tunisian journalist), 48
Broersma, M. J., 12
Bu Musa, Layal, 141
Bughallab, Muhammad, 85, 123, 149, 151
Bughuri, Naji, 88–9
Bulqadi, Myriam, 152
Busays, Burhan, 52, 80, 81

Carothers, Thomas, 2, 13
censorship, 20
 Iraq, 5
 Lebanon, 44–5, 140n, 166, 167
 Tunisia, 34, 49, 58–9, 60–2
Chadwick, A., 14–15
Chahed, Youssef
 and arrest of Karoui, Nabil, 147, 148
 and Busays, Burhan, 80
 and corruption, 79, 80, 132
 and media, 88, 145, 146, 149
Chouikha, Larbi, 76–7
chroniqueurs, 21, 56–7, 79, 80, 81–2, 83–5, 88, 118–19, 120, 123, 124, 126, 133, 149, 151, 152, 181

clientelism, 16, 30, 36, 99–100, 180
 definition, 8–9
 Latin America, 10–11
 Lebanon, 21, 27–8, 103
 see also media instrumentalisation
Communism, 10, 43, 141
conflicts: horizontal and vertical, 16, 17, 18, 21, 23, 98, 101, 104, 110, 170
corruption, 37, 78–9, 97, 181
 Eastern Europe, 10, 16, 25
 Lebanon, 27, 56, 64, 65, 97, 100, 102, 103–10, 141, 142, 143, 155, 156, 159–60, 161, 166, 175, 177, 185
 Qatar, 6
 Tunisia, 14, 29, 30, 67, 69, 70, 71, 75, 78–9, 83, 85, 89, 113, 127, 129, 132, 148, 149
Cottle, S., 113, 128
Czech Republic, 38

Daraj (website), 33, 162, 174, 187
Davis, Aeron, 11–12
democracy
 deficits of, 2
 Egypt, 6, 8, 20
 and elections, 135
 and freedom of speech, 112
 and hybrid regimes, 13–14
 Lebanon, 14, 26, 30–1
 and media corruption, 10
 and media instrumentalisation, 11, 24–5
 and pluralism, 2, 5
 and political communication, 12

democracy (*cont.*)
  and terrorism, 119–20
  Tunisia, 2, 13n2, 14, 19, 26, 28–9, 30, 71, 89, 120, 127
Democracy Index, 13n2
disinformation, 7, 9, 94; *see also* fake news
Diyab, Hasan, 173

Eastern Europe
  corruption, 10, 16, 25
  media instrumentalisation, 10, 24–5, 38
Egypt, 6, 8, 20
elections
  and advertising, 137
  and democracy, 135
  elites and, 136, 154
  Lebanon, 134, 135–43
  and media instrumentalisation, 135
  Tunisia, 22, 134–5, 143–53, 154, 181
elites
  and corruption, 103
  and elections, 136, 154
  journalists' struggle against, 10, 98
  Lebanon, 1, 2–3, 158, 161
  and media capture, 186
  and media instrumentalisation, 16, 17, 23, 25, 93
  and media reform, 76
  political, 140
  and political control, 13, 46
  and political parallelism, 92, 109, 110, 111
  Tunisia, 1–3, 29–30

Erdoğan, Recep Tayyip, 11
Essebsi, Beji Caid
  and Busays, Burhan, 80
  and counter-terrorism, 113, 129–30, 133
  media reaction to, 124, 127–8
  and national reconciliation, 121, 122
  and political reintegration, 30
  and Tunisian presidency, 41, 116

Facebook, 7, 33, 131, 148, 150, 152, 163, 165, 166, 168, 169, 187
fake news, 9, 37, 77, 78, 153; *see also* disinformation
Fakhriya (Tunisian journalist), 78
al-Fihri, Samy, 145–6
Freedom House, 13n2
freedom of speech/expression, 179
  Lebanon, 44–5, 62–5, 93
  Tunisia, 44, 45, 59–62, 112–33, 117, 183
  United States, 112

el-Ghannouchi, Rachid, 30, 116, 129
al-Gharbi, Ilyas, 122
al-Ghuyariri, Ghazi, 122
grey zone: definition, 2

Habiba (Tunisian TV journalist), 51
Haddad, Jumana, 140–1
Haddad, Scarlett, 94
Hafez, Kai, 4n1
Hallin, D. C., 54, 92
Hamadah, 'Ali, 94

al-Hamami, 'Imad, 120
al-Hamruni, Muhammad, 117, 121
al-Hariri, Nadir, 143
Hariri, Rafiq, 56, 156
Hariri, Saad, 94, 95, 96, 143, 156, 157, 162
Hawi, Zaynab, 107
Hibou, Beatrice, 115, 126
Hisham (Tunisian legal scholar), 75
Hizbullah, 6
  attack on reporter, 171
  and censorship, 64, 65
  and elections, 136, 138, 142, 164
  journalists and, 95, 96, 101
  media support for, 32, 33, 39
  opposition to, 52, 53, 162
  and protest, 165
  and Syria, 28, 32, 105, 107, 108
Humayda, Marwan, 139
hybridity
  institutionalised, 44
  media, 14–16
  political, 12–14; and media instrumentalisation, 24–43

Ibrahim, 'Aliya, 162
identity politics, 6, 11
Ihab (Tunisian journalism teacher), 69, 73
International Media Support, 87
  Internet
  and change, 5, 6
  Internet-based media, 87
  Lebanon, 33, 51
  Tunisia, 87
  see also social media

Iran, 6, 28, 40
Iraq, 5, 120
Islamic State (IS), 104–5
Isma'il (Lebanese journalist), 51
Israel, 28
el-Issawi, F., 8
'Itani, Ziyad, 104

Jalal (Lebanese journalist), 159–60, 175
Jamil (Lebanese journalist), 98, 102
al-Jazeera (TV channel), 5–6, 80, 106
journalism
  citizen, 6
  civic advocacy, 174
  disruptive, 170–7
  free, 45–6
  interventionist, 69–72, 94–8
  investigative, 86
  and neutrality, 73
  role of, 7–8, 12, 185, 187
  standards, 4n1, 50–1, 54
  see also newspapers
journalists
  autonomy of, 21, 73–5
  community of, 46–8
  constraints on, 45–6
  control of, 57–9
  and elites, 10, 98
  grievances, 102–4
  and intelligence agencies, 101–2
  investigative, 159–60
  manipulation of, 3
  and media instrumentalisation, 16–18, 83, 148–9, 153, 179–83

journalists (*cont.*)
  as parliamentary candiates, 139–41
  and politics, 17, 22, 51–4, 56, 67, 74–5, 80–1, 88, 93, 97, 99, 108–10, 128, 131–2, 144–5, 152–3, 157–78, 181
  rights of, 43
  role of, 7–8, 12, 16, 68–75, 77, 98–110, 188
  and social activism, 91–2
  and terrorism, 117–29, 130–1
  unions, 175, 176, 183; *see also* Tunisia: National Syndicate of Tunisian Journalists
  violence against, 171–2, 175, 181
  working conditions of, 54–7, 82–3, 88
  see also chroniqueurs; Reporters Without Borders
Junayyih, 'Umar, 148

al-Ka'ki, 'Awni, 175
Kamal (Lebanese journalist), 45, 50
Karim (Lebanese journalist), 52–3
Karoui, Ghazi, 146
Karoui, Nabil, 1–2
  and media instrumentalisation, 77
  and Nisma (TV channel), 41–2
  and Tunisian presidential election (2019), 2, 14, 22, 36, 80, 134–5, 145, 146–8
Katya (Tunisian journalist), 59, 144–5
Khaldun (Tunisian journalist), 59
Khashoggi, Jamal, 64, 89
al-Khatt (non-profit foundation), 86

Kraidy, Marwan, 156
Kulayb, Sami, 3–4, 167–9
Kuwait, 5, 95–6

Lamin (Tunisian journalist), 59, 82
al-Latif, Kamil, 40
Lebanon
  censorship, 44–5, 166, 167
  'Citizens in a State', 141
  civil rights, 22
  clientelism, 21, 27–8, 103
  corruption, 27, 56, 64, 65, 97, 100, 102, 103–10, 141, 142, 143, 155, 156, 159–60, 161, 166, 175, 177, 185
  democracy, 13n2, 14, 26, 30–1
  elections, 22, 134, 135–43, 154, 181; Lebanese Association for Democratic Elections, 137
  elites, 1, 2–3, 26–7
  external intervention, 28
  Free Patriotic Movement, 94, 95, 138
  freedom of speech/expression, 44–5, 62–5, 93
  Future Movement, 94, 138
  human rights, 53
  hybrid politics, 26–8, 30–1
  intelligence agencies, 101
  journalism, 2, 31–3, 47, 48–9, 186
  Kulluna Watani coalition, 137–8, 142
  Lebanese Forces, 32, 95, 140, 158, 165
  MARCH Lebanon (NGO), 140n1
  media capture, 17, 134, 135–43, 180, 181

media instrumentalisation, 17, 38–40, 43, 180
media pluralism, 3, 5–6, 46, 125–6, 185
media regulation, 136–7
Megaphone (news website), 91, 161–2, 174, 187
Naharnet (news outlet), 96
newspapers: *al-Akhbar*, 33, 53, 91, 107, 160–1, 170, 175–6; *al-Mustaqbal*, 39; *al-Nahar*, 32–3, 64, 94; *Orient-Le-Jour, L,'* 94, 159; *al-Safir*, 32, 33
political parallelism, 21, 31–2, 58, 74, 92–8, 110
protests: (2005), 156; (2015), 108–10; (2019–20), 155–78
radio, 32, 33
religious communities, 26, 27
sectarianism, 32
and Syrian war, 32, 104–6
taxation, 1
TV channels: hierarchies, 57, 58; al-Jadid, 32, 108, 109, 138, 160, 183; LBCI, 32, 91, 94, 108, 109, 138, 141, 158, 160, 166, 183; MTV, 39, 106, 108, 109, 158,170, 183; al-Manar, 32, 39, 47, 64, 95, 96, 107, 138, 157, 183; al-Mayadin, 4, 32, 47, 167–8; al-Mustaqbal, 32, 39, 54–5, 138, 141143; NBN, 157, 183; OTV, 32, 39, 138, 157–8, 183; private, 136–7; Tele Liban, 136
websites, 33; Yasour.org, 162

women's rights, 53–4, 55
see also Beirut; Tripoli; Tyre
Libya, 40
Luma (Tunisian journalist), 60–2, 78–9
Lustick, Ian, 26
Lynch, Marc, 6, 185

Mabruk, Marwan, 79
McNair, B., 46
Maharat Foundation, 53–4, 62–3
Makhluf, Sayf al-Din, 124–5
Makki, Haytham, 88
Mancini, P., 16, 54, 92
al-Manif, Amna, 123
Marwan (Tunisian journalist), 55, 58
Marzuq, Muhsin, 122
al-Marzuqi, al-Munsif, 67
al-Masdi, Mufdi, 148, 149
Mashnuq, Nuhad, 139
Matirawi, Muhammad Amin, 148–9
Mayisa (Lebanese journalist), 159
Maymun (Tunisian journalist), 74
media
  and change, 5–6
  corruption of, 10
  digital, 6–7, 12, 91, 161–2
  free and manipulated, 3–4
  pluralism, 3, 5–6, 46, 125–6, 185
  role of, 4–5
  state-owned, 33
  see also Internet; newspapers; radio; social media; TV
media capture, 8, 24, 66, 172
  definition, 9
  impact of, 16, 185–6

media capture (*cont.*)
  Lebanon, 17, 134, 135–43, 180, 181
  Russia, 37
  Tunisia, 125–6, 134–5, 143–53, 180, 181
media hybridity, 14–16
media instrumentalisation, 8–12, 14
  chroniqueurs and, 179–83
  and clientelism, 96–7
  and corruption, 79
  definition, 8–9
  digital, 174
  Eastern Europe, 10, 38
  and elections, 135
  elites and, 16, 17, 23, 25, 93
  hybrid politics and, 24–43
  journalists' response to, 16–18, 93, 152–4
  Karoui, Nabil and, 77
  Latin America, 10–11
  Lebanon, 17, 38–40, 43
  manifestations of, 36–7
  political implications of, 184–5
  Russia, 10, 37
  Sub-Saharan Africa, 11
  Tunisia, 17, 40–3, 59, 180
  see also clientelism
media studies, 98
Melki, Jad, 57
Mellor, N., 7
Monde, Le (French newspaper), 30
Muʿizz (Lebanese journalist), 140
Mudawwar, Lana, 164–5
Muhammad (Tunisian journalist), 60–1
Muqallid, Diana, 162, 164
Murad (Tunisian journalist), 34, 44, 50–1, 59, 70, 80–1, 82
Murdoch, Rupert, 9
Murr, Elias, 39
Murr, Gabriel, 39
Murtada, Husayn, 95
al-Muru, ʿAbd al-Fattah, 149
Muruwwa, Kamil, 31
Musa (Tunisian editor), 45, 55, 88, 145
Myanmar, 11

NGOs, 53–4, 60, 68, 71, 87, 140n1
Naccache, George, 31
Nadim (Tunisian radio host), 71–2, 78
Najim (Tunisian journalist), 58, 73, 146–7
Nasim (Lebanese journalist), 47, 55–6, 64, 96, 137, 140
Nasima (Tunisian journalist), 68–70, 152–3
Nasrallah, Hasan, 138, 156, 157, 162
Nawfal (Tunisian journalist), 65–6
newspapers
  digital, 161–2
  Eastern Europe, 38
  Russia, 37
  see also under Lebanon; Tunisia
Nidal (Lebanese journalist), 24

Open Society Foundation, 87
Oreedo (telecommunication company), 59

Panama Papers, 85–6
Peters, C., 12
Pintak, L., 7–8
pluralism
   and autocratic rule, 13
   and democracy, 2, 5
   media, 3, 5–6, 46, 125–6, 185
polarisation, 4, 181
   chroniqueurs and, 83, 84
   and clientelism, 103
   and disinformation, 9
   and distrust, 148–51
   elites and, 111
   media and, 7, 32, 40
   and political unrest, 25
   politicians and, 110, 182
   religious, 108
   sectarian, 100–1, 109–10, 115
   and Syrian war, 106
   and terrorism, 121, 124, 125
political communication, 11–12
political instrumentalisation, 10–11, 20, 21, 40, 43, 56, 57, 92
political parallelism, 21, 31–2, 58, 74, 99–100, 103, 110
   elites and, 92, 109, 110, 111
   instrumentalised, 92, 93, 161
   Lebanon, 177–8
populism, 1, 6, 9

Qandil, Nasir, 139
al-Qarquri, Ilyas, 149
Qasir, Samir, 44, 93
Qatar, 5–6, 40
Qays (Tunisian journalist), 60–1
al-Qusuri, Maya, 124, 151

radio *see under* Lebanon; Tunisia
Rafiq (Tunisian journalist), 47–8, 49, 59
Raghib (Lebanese journalist), 106–8, 109
Rahma (Lebanese journalist), 174
reporters *see* journalists
Reporters Without Borders, 41, 65, 86
al-Riahi, Salim, 145, 146
Roudakova, Natalia, 10, 37
Rugh, William, 5
Rula (Lebanese journalist), 64, 176
Russia, 10, 37

al-Sabʿa, Basil, 139
Saʿd (Tunisian journalist), 60
Sadiq (Tunisian journalist), 71
Sadiq, Dima, 165–7, 168, 169, 174, 178, 183
Saghiyah, Khalid, 91–2, 111, 161–2
Sahar (Lebanese journalist), 142–3
Sahhar, ʿUqab, 139
Saʿid, al-Safi, 127
Saied, Kais
   election campaign, 1–2, 19, 29, 149–50, 151–2, 182
   and national security, 130, 131
   power seizure (2021), 20
   and private media, 151–2
   TV debate with Karoui, Nabil, 2, 36
Sami (Tunisian journalist), 87
Samir (Lebanese journalist), 64, 137
Samir Kassir Foundation, 53–4

Saudi Arabia
    and death of Jamal Khashoggi, 89
    and Lebanon, 28, 32, 40, 99
    satellite TV, 6
Sayf al-Din, Maryam, 171
al-Sayyid, Jamil, 164
Schedler, A., 25
Schudson, M., 46
Shafiq (Lebanese journalist), 96
Shawqi (Tunisian TV journalist), 52, 81
social media, 6–7, 33, 156, 160, 163–70, 187; *see also* Facebook; Twitter; WhatsApp; YouTube
Sunni Muslims, 27, 28, 39, 47, 95, 99, 101, 104, 105, 107, 108
Syria
    Jabhat al-Nusra (militia), 104, 105
    and Lebanon, 28, 32, 104–8
    uprising (2011), 91

Taha (Lebanese radio host), 63
Tamir (Tunisian journalist), 68–70, 72–3
    TV, satellite, 5–6, 20; *see also under* Lebanon; Tunisia
terrorism
    Tunisia, 113–23, 126, 128, 132–3; counter-terrorism law, 123–5, 129
    United States, 112
Transparency International, 79
Tripoli, 155, 173
Trump, Donald, 9, 95
Tunisia
    Authority for Access to Information, 130
    Babnet, 146

censorship, 34, 49, 58–9, 60–2
Cité de la culture, 85
civil rights, 22
corruption, 14, 29, 30, 67, 69, 70, 71, 75, 78–9, 83, 85, 89, 113, 127, 129, 132, 148, 149
    'Day of Rage' (2018), 130
    and democracy, 2, 13n2, 19, 26, 28–9, 30, 71, 89, 120, 127
    elections, 22, 134–5, 143–53, 154, 181, 182; *Sakin Kartaj* (election programme), 148, 149
elites, 1–3, 29–30
freedom of speech/expression, 44, 45, 59–62, 112–33, 183
High Independent Authority of Audiovisual Communication (HAICA), 22, 42, 77, 78, 125–6, 130, 134, 136, 144–5, 148, 150, 152, 180, 183
human rights, 123, 124
hybrid politics, 26, 28–31
Inkyfada (news website), 59, 85, 187
Institute of Press and Information Sciences (IPSI), 51
Islamism, 30, 77, 88, 113, 115–16, 117, 118, 119, 122, 125, 126; *see also* al-Nahda party
journalism, 33–6, 49–50, 186
journalists, 47–8, 55, 68–90;
    National Syndicate of Tunisian Journalists (SNJT), 21, 42–3, 62, 79, 86, 88–9, 131, 132, 133, 152, 175, 183
Karama coalition, 88, 183
Khalil Tunis (TV show), 42

Kulna Tunis (citizenship movement), 123
legacies of the past, 48, 49–51
media capture, 125–6, 134–5, 143–53, 180, 181
media instrumentalisation, 17, 40–3, 59, 180
media reform, 76, 183
al-Nahda party, 41, 77, 88, 116, 117, 118, 129, 145, 183
Nawaat (news website), 59, 71, 87, 132, 187
newspapers: *al-Damir*, 35, 117, 118, 121; *al-Maghrib*, 35, 120, 121, 124, 126; *Presse, La*, 35, 49; *al-Sabah*, 118, 121, 122–3, 124; *al-Sahafa*, 35, 49, 118, 121, 122–3, 124; *al-Shuruq*, 35, 118, 121
Nida Tunis party, 30, 41, 80, 118
political commentary, 85
Qalb Tunis party, 183
radio, 34, 35, 36, 52, 71–2; Mosaique, 88; Shams FM, 52, 85
talk shows, 122, 123, 124–5, 147, 148
Tahya Tunis party, 41
TV channels: Channel 9, 35, 80, 82, 146, 148, 149, 150; hierarchies, 57–8; al-Hiwar al-Tunisi, 35, 52, 58, 59, 80, 82, 85, 86, 115, 118, 119, 120, 123, 124–5, 131–2, 134, 145–6, 147, 149, 150, 151, 152; Nisma, 2, 22, 35, 41–2, 52, 58, 59, 77–8, 80, 82, 132, 134, 145, 147, 148, 150; al-Wataniyya, 35–6, 131, 144; Zaytuna TV, 149
terrorist attacks (2015), 113, 114, 115–23, 126, 128, 132–3; counter-terrorism law, 123–5, 129
Troika coalition, 150
Truth and Dignity Commission, 123
Tunis Afrique Presse (TAP), 61, 131, 132
Zakariya (journalists' syndicate), 51
Turkey, 6, 11, 42
Tuwayni, Ghassan, 31, 93
Tuwayni, Jubran, 44
Twitter, 7, 12, 33, 163, 164–5, 166, 169, 174, 187
Tyre, 162

'Umar (Lebanese journalist), 47, 63
United Arab Emirates, 97
United States, 46–7, 112
Usama (Tunisian journalist), 86
'Usman (Tunisian journalist), 68–9, 72–3, 152

violence
  against journalists, 171–2, 175, 181
  political, 128, 152
  see also terrorism
Voltmer, K., 14, 115, 135

al-Wafi, Samir, 79–80, 149
Wahhab, Wiam, 139
Waisbord, Silvio, 45, 174
Wartini, Nawfal, 124
WhatsApp, 33, 163, 169
Wolf, Anne, 116

women
  as journalists, 94, 109, 140, 142, 144, 151, 152–3, 159, 162, 164–7, 171, 174
  as politicians, 140–1, 142, 143
  rights of, 53–4
World Press Freedom Index, 49, 59

Yaqubian, Paula, 141, 142, 143
YouTube, 7, 162
Yusuf (Lebanese journalist), 53–4, 97

Zabib, Muhammad, 158–9, 171–2
al-Zabidi, 'Abd al-Karim, 145
al-Zaghlami, Muhsin, 123, 124
Zahr al-Din, Lina, 168
Zahran, Salim, 95, 101
Zayid, Sheikh, 97
Zayn (Lebanese TV journalist), 64–5
Zayna (Lebanese journalist), 137
Zelizer, Barbie, 46–7
Zielonka, J., 16, 24, 25, 28

EU representative:
Easy Access System Europe
Mustamäe tee 50, 10621 Tallinn, Estonia
Gpsr.requests@easproject.com